PRAISE FOR THE
THE LAST TRAIN FROM DJIBOUTI

"Skillfully using a train ride as a metaphor, Otis L. Lee, Jr.'s The *Last Train From Djibouti* is a remarkable journey through the experiences of two African-American women, who, each for their own reasons, return to Africa, the "motherland," and are alternately shocked, inspired, disappointed, and moved—and who return to the United States with a profoundly enlarged view of themselves as African-Americans who have come to recognize that America, for all its faults, is their true home. With useful reflections about the complex history of Africa, the lasting effects of colonialism, and the struggles of African-Americans to find their rightful place in the world, Otis L. Lee Jr. wisely enlarges the readers understanding of the two women's experiences. Along the way, he appeals to a rich assembly of historians, philosophers, and poets. *The Last Train from Djibouti* is a book, and an odyssey, you will not forget."

—***Larry Bechtel***, author of *The Tinsmith's Apprentice* and sculptor

"*Last Train from Djibouti* is really compelling. The core issue—African Americans' attempt to reconnect with a homeland where they never lived—is complex and deeply interesting. Otis L. Lee, Jr. draws the characters carefully and, as a reader, I'm hooked."

—***Stefan Bechtel***, best-selling author of *Through A Glass, Darkly*, *Mr. Hornaday's War*, and ten other books which have been translated into a dozen languages

The Last Train from Djibouti:
Africa Beckons Me, but America Is My Home

by Otis L. Lee, Jr

© Copyright 2019 Otis L. Lee, Jr

ISBN 978-1-63393-834-2
LCCN: 2019903935

All rights reserved. No part of this publication may be reproduced, stored in a retrieval system, or transmitted in any form or by any means—electronic, mechanical, photocopy, recording, or any other—except for brief quotations in printed reviews, without the prior written permission of the author.

Review copy: this is an advanced printing,
subject to corrections and revisions.

Published by

210 60th Street
Virginia Beach, VA 23451
800–435–4811
www.koehlerbooks.com

Other Publications by Otis L. Lee, Jr.:

From South Boston to Cambridge:
The Making of One Philadelphia Lawyer
A Memoir

Contributing author:

"*Estate Planning for Small Business,*" to the 1980 edition of the US Department of Commerce, "*The Local Economic Development Corporation Legal and Financial Guidelines.*"

THE LAST TRAIN FROM DJIBOUTI

AFRICA BECKONS ME, BUT AMERICA IS MY HOME

OTIS L. LEE, JR.

VIRGINIA BEACH
CAPE CHARLES

This book is dedicated to my wife, Dr. Michelle Palmer Lee, who planted the seed many years ago with her manuscript, upon which a portion of this book is based. Without her contribution, unflinching support and encouragement over the years this book would not have been written.

The Unrequited Return

TABLE OF CONTENTS

Foreword XII

Introduction 1

Chapter 1. A Blessing from the Quakers 5

Chapter 2. Two Points in the Circle 12

Chapter 3. The Awakening 17

Chapter 4. A Mournful Interlude. 31

Chapter 5. A Love Forlorn 46

Chapter 6. Au Revoir. 50

Chapter 7. Alone but Not at Home 56

Chapter 8. When in Rome, Do as the Romans Do 63

Chapter 9. Bound For the Promised Land. 69

Chapter 10. A Room with a View 81

Chapter 11. Oh, What a Beautiful Morning 84

Chapter 12. Harriett's Choice. 99

Chapter 13. *Chuo Elimu*, Swahili for
"A College Education" 107

Chapter 14. Nothing New under the Sun 113

Chapter 15. A Rude Awakening 120

Chapter 16. The Black American's Burden 130

Chapter 17. A Wildlife Adventure 146

Chapter 18. The Omakuma. 155

Chapter 19. Orem's Theory 164

Chapter 20. The Smock and the Duffel Bag 179

Chapter 21. *Neema Kwa Maharge,* Swahili
for "A Favor for Beans" 189

Chapter 22. A Return to a Legacy 194

Chapter 23. The Encore 205

Chapter 24. A Leopard for Mother 216

Chapter 25. Caught in Obete's Web 220

Chapter 26. The Return 231

Chapter 27. En Route to Safety 237

Chapter 28. A Final Sigh 242

Chapter 29. Denouement: The Last Train from Djibouti 246

Acknowledgments 268

Notes 270

Bibliography 283

Index 290

FOREWORD

Reflecting on both the journey of the people in this book and that of Americans of African descent in general, I am both inspired and humbled. As a professor of African-American literature and culture, I am continually enlightened and encouraged by the journey of African-Americans from the colonial and antebellum eras to the present. By people whose lives represent the difficulties and the triumphs of life they have endured—from the slave narratives of Frederick Douglass and Harriett Jacobs to the plays of August Wilson; from the poems of Phillis Wheatley to the spoken word poetry of today; and the music of jazz, blues and R&B.

This book is a quasi-fictionalized account of two women, both Americans of African descent, who travel to Africa in the 1970s. Harriett Karuhije, the elder of the two, is a woman of impressive accomplishments in the field of nursing education who is seeking to build a nursing program at the University of Botswana, while Michelle Palmer Lee is seeking an educational experience and cultural reconnection. Their experiences in Africa are formative ones that shape their lives in unexpected ways. And, although they discover much about Africa that enlightens them on their educational journeys as African-American women, they also discover, as Mr. Lee says in conclusion, that "Africa beckons me but America is my home."

Years ago, when I first had the pleasure of meeting Mr. Lee, he handed me a manuscript of his memoir, saying, "This is a one-shot deal." The memoir represented a significant slice of his life story and his family's story going back to the 1800s on both his mother and father's sides, and as such it would probably be the only book he would write. I am so glad that book wasn't "a one-shot deal" so that we had another opportunity to work together on this book, which takes us into a different place in African-American cultural life. The experiences of these two women were "an unrequited return" to Africa. The experiences of Ms. Lee and Ms. Karuhije and Mr. Lee's references to African-American and African scholarly and literary works give the reader much to contemplate. The depth and complexity of African-American cultural identity, the American cultural indoctrination of African-Americans, and the impact of both colonialism and postcolonial Africa on the liberation of countries and individuals are some of the primary themes one will encounter in this book. Furthermore, the train ride the narrator recounts in this story is a metaphor for the separation of African-Americans from Africa and the journeys the narrator and two women take to explore reconnection to the Motherland.

It has been, as always, an honor and a pleasure to work on a book with Mr. Lee, a man who has much to say and who has enriched my life with his stories, elegant prose and presence. I am both inspired and humbled by this story and Mr. Lee's rendering of it.

Justin Wert
Albemarle County, Virginia

INTRODUCTION

The place of Africa in the minds of African-Americans has been fraught with ambiguity, conflict, opaqueness and disinformation since the first slaves were captured over 400 years ago. Unless one has traveled there as a tourist, researcher, entrepreneur, employee, emigrant or repatriate, to see some of the continent for themselves, and to experience its rich and diverse culture, it is impossible to remove the conflicts and opaqueness. The portrayals of Africa as propagated by a political system antithetical to its existence, for the most part, is responsible for the uninformed mindset of some African-Americans. For the American of African descent to accept and have a love for Africa is to have a love and acceptance of him or herself because Africa and its progeny, whether accepted or not, is interred in the genealogy of Americans of African descent.

The place and perplexity of Africa in the minds of African-Americans has been memorialized in poems by many prominent American poets of African descent, including Claude McKay, Efe Benjamin, Phyllis Wheatley, Countee Cullen, Langston Hughes and others. Their poems strike at the pain of loss, the ambivalence of repatriation and the quandary of living in America with its unrelenting incongruent treatment of people of color. Being an American of African descent in all of this begs the question, "What does America mean to me?"

Juxtaposing Africa and America and finding meaning in one or both is the subtext of numerous poems and the unending quest of great African-American writers throughout the decades. This question is best answered, I think, by going to Africa and seeing for yourself and making your own observations and attaining a perspective worthy of real introspection. Finding the truth, as best you can, and separating fact from fiction and illusion from reality is the only way I have found to make an honest assessment of your true place in this world, and more precisely, in the African diaspora. Freeing oneself from the bonds of "mental slavery," as Bob Marley has sung, is a mission worth achieving. It is the food of liberation. Sorting out conflicting emotions can be a balm to the anguished mind. The issue of returning to Africa has been around since the nineteenth century, ostensibly promoted as benevolent repatriation but in reality, supportive of slavery.

Africans are not without culpability for their role in the ambivalence of African-Americans towards Africa. The fount of this ambivalence emanates from a legacy of poor governance, poor sanitation, health care and ruthless corruption in some parts of the continent. Instances of these failings are promoted aggressively by the Western media in support of its own surreptitiously baneful objectives. For those who study history, slavery must include the role of African and Arabian societies who captured Africans and used them in their armies and in domestic jobs as well as to extend their lineages.† African tribes sold other Africans to Europeans in exchange for baubles and beads. Arabs captured Africans and Ethiopes especially in East Africa in the eighteenth and nineteenth centuries and held them as slaves long before most Europeans profited from the transatlantic slave trade and European colonialism. Slavery by Africans and Arabs in this region has been defined as either "open or closed"‡; that is to say, open slavery allowed Africans that were captured and converted into slaves by these populations to integrate into the households of their masters or were otherwise able to integrate into the societies in which they were apart. Closed slavery did not allow such integration. The slaves were prevented from doing so and were ostracized.§

Arabs and European slave traders crossed paths in the business of enslavement of Africans. The institutions of slavery and colonialism engendered the notion of inferiority which otherwise would not have existed. Incorporating these phenomena into your perspective is essential to an honest appraisal.

The questions that Michelle and Harriett sought answers to, however, are not rooted in slave history so much, but in American history—the treatment of Americans of African descent in America and the severance from them of their indigenous African culture. Such a loss left these two women searching for salvation through endogenesis informed by experiencing Africa to the extent that they could.

This book is a story about the sojourn of two women in Africa in search of growth, contribution and the discovery that illusions can become real to the uninformed. These women sought to own their history. The source of illusions, though comfortable, can sometimes be painfully difficult to dispel, but at the same time can be a reservoir of profound internal growth.

Here are the questions that the journeys of these two women attempt to answer. We will revisit them at the end of their journeys to assess the answers.

What are the parallels in the stories of these two women?
Did identity affirmation turn into reaffirmation?
Did purpose turn into achievement?
Did heritage turn into identity?
Was the myth equal to reality?
Was ignorance converted into enlightenment?

What I have presented herein are two case histories, i.e. two personal experiences that enable a broader discussion of the implication and themes that eruct from these experiences related to the view of Africa by these two African-Americans and their perspectives about their relationship to America surveyed from Africa. The characters in this story are real. And the events that they experienced are real; however, I have creatively interspersed fictionalized elements to create a story rather than a chronology of events.

CHAPTER ONE

A BLESSING FROM THE QUAKERS

I once daydreamed of taking the Addis to Djibouti train in East Africa after reading about it some years ago. And I wondered just how different a train ride in Africa would be from my ride in the US. The Addis to Djibouti train was constructed between 1893 and 1897 to run from the Port of Djibouti to Addis Ababa, the capital of Ethiopia, covering close to 800 kilometers. The train was opened for service in 1929 by His Highness, the Lion of Juda, Emperor Haile Selassie.[1] This train would have been coal and steam powered, with bench seats instead of individual seats, and of iron and steel construction, with its rivets clearly visible along the broad sides of the iron and steel plates that enclosed the cars. There were small, square windows encased with steel frames on each side of the passenger car. Its steel broadsides were painted in gray and red and at other times a dark green that reflected an empty "plain geography." Steam flowed from its exhaust pipes powered by coal, and its passenger cars looked more like cabooses than classic passenger cars. Late nineteenth-century third-world construction was its vintage.

Djibouti is in East Africa at the crossroads of the Gulf of Aden, the Red Sea and the Indian Ocean with easy access to the Arabian Sea. In my imagination, I gaze upon the sandy fields, barren plains, rice fields and green savannahs of the hinterlands as the train meanders toward its terminus. The train crosses lakes adjacent to the Awash National Park in Ethiopia en route to Dire Dawa halfway between Djibouti and Addis. There, I see the wildlife, birds, sea creatures of all species, all from one of those rickety, worn-down train seats through hazy train windows. Asphalt and skyscrapers, tenements and slums are distant reflections as I pass through cities. Sure, even the least of the amenities of the Amtrak Train would probably surpass the offerings of the Addis–Djibouti train. But this trip is in Africa—in the lands of my ancestry.

I heard about this train in my travels and reading. A decade or more ago, I traveled to three countries in Africa and spent almost a month there. So, I think about those days as I travel north toward New York, reading quietly and becoming engrossed in Michelle's story.

I often take the train north along the I-95 corridor: to Washington, DC, Baltimore, Philadelphia, New York City and Boston. When I ride the train north from my hometown of Charlottesville, Virginia, the smell of diesel engines, motor oil and electric fumes from electric wires burning sting my nostrils, but over the years I have adjusted to them and expect them. These offensive odors are the most poignant, familiar reminders of the journey north.

The clickety clack of the train wheels turning and the clang and clatter of iron grinding against iron along with the loud burst of the train whistle, not once but three maybe four times, signals to those who know the translation what the engineer's intentions are. The herky-jerky swaying from east to west, the stop and go, pull and push from north to south make for unsettling movements. Jolts of varying degrees make assembling your study papers and books a magic trick until the train gets underway. Passengers walking up and down the aisles holding on to the passenger seats and overhead luggage racks to steady themselves is a common sight. Stability is rare except when in your seat. Passengers struggling with their luggage, often too big for the overhanging luggage racks, are ever present. Occasionally, I help these beleaguered travelers hoist their bags up, especially women, but often I resist the temptation and just observe this snippet of the human struggle.

I remember for a fleeting moment, as I look at the undercarriage before boarding the train, that while traveling in Russia several years ago, one of our travel companions, an elderly white gentleman whom we had befriended, fell underneath the front tires of our tour bus after one too many vodkas. Fortunately, for him, the bus did not move. The giant cast-iron wheels that form part of the iron-and-steel undercarriage dare you to fall underneath them. My fear of being run over by something of this magnitude is sobering.

I put memory and fear aside to enjoy a ride on my favorite mode of transportation. On this occasion, I am traveling with my wife, Michelle, to New York City—a trip of about five hours. Finally, the conductor makes his rounds, walking steadily forward through the coach in his worn gray coat and pants, official cap insignia fastened above the visor, wearing black, ankle-high boots. He booms out to all of us, in a voice of command, "Have your tickets out. This is the train to New York. If you are not ticketed for this train, now is the time to leave." Everyone is momentarily brought to attention. We all know that he is in charge. To reassure ourselves, we glance at our tickets. *Charlottesville to New York*, the ticket reads. So we are okay and ready to go.

As the train moves slowly along the tracks, heading north, my mind relaxes. The hustle and bustle is over, everyone is settled in, and my attention begins to focus on my wife's papers. She has typed them, so reading them will not be difficult. This is my reading for the next several hours. As I read through some of her papers and take notes, her experience of going to Uganda and that of her mentor, Harriett, in Botswana and what caused them to go to these countries grows more and more interesting. I sometimes pause and ask her to tell me her story as we ride along. Her memory is less than exact because these events occurred forty-three years ago, but she recalls enough specifics for me to grasp not only the overall picture but also the essence of two women's travails from chimera to reality, from fantasy to actuality, concerning a continent steeped in meaning for her and her "race."

Slowly but steadily, we make our way to the outskirts of town. The ride gets easy, and cares drift away. A train ride can soothe the conscious mind and lull you into contemplation like a lovely classical piano piece. Observations and daydreams occupy the otherwise cluttered space in my mind. This is what makes the train my preferred mode of travel.

Michelle's story began in the fall of 1970. She was a dreamer. "If I dreamed of something, I *really* wanted it would come true." Her awakening began in the fall of 1970 when Swarthmore College[2]— an elite college in Swarthmore, Pennsylvania—opened its doors to a young, hardworking African-American student from Chester, Pennsylvania. Swarthmore was cofounded principally by Joseph Wharton of Philadelphia, Pennsylvania, and Lucretia Coffin Mott of Nantucket, Massachusetts. Joseph Wharton was a Quaker, and a capitalist who also founded the Wharton School of Business at the University of Pennsylvania. Lucretia Coffin Mott was also a Quaker, abolitionist, suffragist and civil rights advocate.

Michelle's dream was to attend Swarthmore, but she was uncertain of her chances of gaining admission and was just as uncertain about how to pay for her expenses if she was admitted. Her mother, Mary, though supportive, thought in her heart of hearts that Michelle would not be admitted. All of that angst would soon be overcome.

Michelle was working in a local downtown music store in Chester when the letter arrived from the admissions office of Swarthmore College, admitting her to the freshman class, along with the award of a full academic scholarship, including a monthly stipend for spending money. When she opened the letter, she exclaimed, jumping up and down, "I got in! I got in! I can't believe it, I got in!" waving the paper in her hand. Her mother was the only family member present in the home at that time. Her sister, Shelley, was away attending nursing school in New York City.

Michelle looked at her mother with an expressive glance. Her mother returned the expression of satisfaction because Mary knew the history of Michelle's work and struggle to achieve. The two of them squeezed each other tightly for a few moments until the energy of the frisson drained away. She was very happy. *I made it*, she thought. She exhaled the anxiety that had accumulated in her body as she waited for this uncertain moment to arrive. An inner peace pervaded her being as she thought about how her world would be changed forever. All of the hard work had paid off, after all. She was the only female from a group of students interviewed from her high school by the college to be admitted that year. And she was first in her family to be admitted to a four-year college of that rank.

The gravity of her admission to such an elite college weighed heavily upon her shoulders. This was an opportunity of a lifetime. An opportunity to prove she had the stuff to make it academically, that she was for "real" when it came to the seriousness of her academic life. She had always loved school. Now she could bask in the radiance of an unlimited future. Michelle was driven to do well. She was scrupulous in her dealings and above all she wanted to validate the trust that had been demonstrated by the college in awarding her admission and a scholarship. She was a Horatio Alger paradigm. Her life up to this point was encapsulated in a small box of typical Americana: movies on TV; family TV programs; side trips from her modest home in Chester; trips to New York for visits with her great-aunt and for summer stays; trips to Detroit to spend time with her maternal grandfather, whom she so adored; and trips to Philadelphia for shopping and holiday celebrations. Her attention to politics was nonexistent. One could say she was apolitical. She worked after school in a music store to earn extra money.

At that time in her life, like so many of her peers in her community, she had not traveled outside of the United States. Her horizons were not completely parochial, but her vision *was* obscured by a societal burqa[1]*: a web of social strictures that made opaque the wider world of experiences available to her beyond the locale of her upbringing and the means of her mother. The mundane could now become the sublime with the hijab[2]* removed from her head; there were no limits. The heights to which she could climb would be solely determined by her work ethic and her values. She had been given a chance.

The reality of her academic preparation to compete at Swarthmore soon became evident. Though she had worked hard, the public schools she attended were not as competitive as some private schools. Michelle found herself competing with students who had graduated from some of the most prestigious private schools in America, such as Phillips Exeter Academy, the Trinity School, St. Paul's, the Lawrenceville School, Horace Mann and many others.

"It was very, very tough. My secondary public education paled greatly when compared to the students from private schools, upper middle-class homes and from abroad. But I kept my major and worked as hard as I could," she says with a sense of concession to this daunting reality.

"I was young and gifted but also very naive and apolitical," she continues. The competitive gap was wide and unrelenting. Her advisor at Swarthmore discouraged her from pursuing a major in biology because it was his opinion that she was ill equipped to compete for that major. She was advised to try English as an alternative. "I did not listen to that guy," she recalls. "He hurt my feelings. I returned to

---

1 * Also known as a chadri, a burqa is a type of clothing worn by Muslim women that covers the face and body in public places.
2 * A customary covering made for the neck and head and a portion of the chest worn by Muslim women after reaching puberty while in the presence of adult men.

my dorm room, collapsed on my bed and cried. The put-down hit a sensitive nerve in the delicate texture of my ego, but it made me even more determined to prove him wrong," and she did.

Notwithstanding the benefits granted by Swarthmore to Michelle, the presumption of mediocrity and patronizing condescension regarding some American students of African descent was ingrained in some elites at this branch of the white American academy. Her challenge was to prove the doubters wrong. These kinds of odds place undue burdens on the subjects of this ideology. It may produce a better product or an undervalued product, or perhaps a scarred and resentful product. In this case the former resulted, though she remained ever mindful of the struggle she had to wage to overcome negative presumptions.

CHAPTER TWO

TWO POINTS IN THE CIRCLE

*That Justice is a blind goddess
Is a thing to which we black are wise:
Her bandage hides two festering sores
That once perhaps were eyes.*
　　—Langston Hughes

Harriett Karuhije, an American woman of African descent, sub-Saharan in complexion, sat in the gallery of a courtroom on the second floor of the circuit court for Montgomery County, in Rockville, Maryland, on a bright summer morning in July 2013. Harriett had long since retired from a long and distinguished academic career. She was of thin build, some would even say frail as she has aged, but with an ebullient personality defying her age and health, a genteel woman, polished and cultured. She wore nothing particularly special this day: black slacks with a black leather belt of braided crinoline twisted into a pattern of overlapping threads, and a plain white cotton blouse with a collar covered by a black, button-down sweater. Her shoes were worn, black, flat leather slip-ons with leather soles. And her gray hair she styled in a short Afro cut—a style she adopted many years before and retained. Was she dressed casually for a funeral? No! Quite the contrary; freedom was her pursuit that day.

The ornate redbrick courthouse located in the center of this small Southern town, once occupied by two brigades of Confederate troops in 1863, was a curious place for this eventful, heartbreaking day in Harriett's life.

Beside her sat Michelle, another African-American woman, twenty-three years younger than Harriett. Michelle was of medium height, about 5'5" or so with a full but slight frame and an attractive face—a handsome face, one could say—and with gray hair sprinkled richly in with brown and black strands that she styled in a French twist. This woman was fair skinned, with a light-tan complexion. For this occasion, she also wore nothing special: dark-blue slacks, a floral blouse and leather-soled brown loafers. By this time, she too was an academic. She and Harriett's families were very close going back to the 1960s and '70s in Chester where Michelle's mother and Harriett had grown up and lived. It could be surmised that Michelle was in some respects a protégé of Harriett's, both having pursued careers in health care.

Michelle was there to provide support and to testify as a witness for Harriett in the court's proceedings that day. These two women shared a lot, and both had come to the same judgment about living in Africa, the motherland, though the arterial pathways to their destination diverged in space and time. Love of the motherland and of the people was not an issue. Their purposes for going to Africa differed, yet they eventually arrived at the same conclusions.

The key man who played a crucial role in all of this was "Mr. Eric," Michelle had called him, using an old Southern handle to show respect. Eric's role was indispensable in both of their lives, but at different times, and at pivotal junctions in their maturing lives. He was, at one point, Harriett's husband and at another Michelle's savior.

Eric Adyeri Karuhije was Ugandan. An African male of sub-Saharan color, brown skinned with beautiful teeth—a handsome man, short and slim with a receding hairline, a beautiful smile, a youthful countenance and a gentleman. Eric was a mathematician, an academic, a man with facial features as sharp as edges chiseled from a slab of granite. His physiognomy conveyed character, moderation and a coolness that was reassuring. The type of man any woman looking for a certain composite of Africanization could fall in love with.

"Karuhije vs. Karuhije," the crier called, exerting his presumed judicial authority, little of which really existed, raising his voice loud enough to be heard above the whispers of those seated in the gallery. An air of nervousness, expectation and anticipation precipitated the constant chatter.

All eyes in the courtroom immediately focused upon a short, bespectacled gray haired white man with the shadow of a midriff bulge who sat behind a raised mahogany bench. No one knew what to expect or what impact this man of little physical stature but significant judicial power would exercise over their lives.

He wore a brown paisley necktie, a faded yellow dress shirt underneath a brown suit jacket. His clothes appeared to have been purchased "off the rack." This man was a family division master in divorce, not a judge as many supposed. Circuit courts, in order to save judicial resources, use masters, in lieu of judges, to hear rudimentary divorce cases. Contested divorce cases involving property disputes, child support, child custody, spousal support and alimony, etc., often go before a sitting judge.

The courtroom was stark. The people assembled, with cause to be there, provided what little adornments there were. The height of the master's raised bench enabled him to look over the court from his perch. A large window behind the master's bench provided a view of the cityscape in the distance. The witness box was to his left, and the counsel table was a few feet in front of his bench. He rarely looked into the gallery but focused his attention to his left toward the witnesses or directly in front of him to any attorneys who were present representing their clients.

Harriett sat two rows back from the front of the gallery. Michelle sat left of Harriett and I sat on Michelle's left. Before Harriett's case was called, I leaned over to Michelle and whispered in her left ear, "Tell Harriett to listen to the other cases as they are called, so she'll know what to expect." But Harriett was not paying attention. Instead, she was in awe of the event itself and amazed that she was even there. Harriett had been used to being in a classroom, standing before a lectern lecturing on her philosophy of nursing education not a courtroom being lectured to by a judge and cross-examined by a lawyer. Michelle on the other hand had many prior experiences with the law. She had worked in a law office and had seen and participated in several court hearings.

I accompanied Michelle to the hearing to lend support to her and Harriett. I knew them both. I knew Michelle more intimately than Harriett knew her, and Michelle knew Harriett way better than I did. Having a background in the law, I knew exactly what to expect as we sat there waiting for Harriett's case to be called. But then I began to wonder, *How did these folks end up in this courtroom for this case?* I knew why we were there and the purpose to be served, but the irony of it all, I thought, was perplexing. Harriett's dreams had been idealized and fantasized yet not realized. Why?

After the hearing I sat down with Harriett in her well-appointed apartment with artifacts and memorabilia reflecting the life of a woman well-traveled, a cosmopolite. Her apartment building, formerly known as the Irene, was located in Chevy Chase, Maryland, just north of the District of Columbia. It was owned by one of the Washington area's richest men, Abe Pollin.[3] Her building was sophisticated, genteel in its mooring, befitting a person of her ilk. An oval driveway led to the front of this beige-colored 500-unit multistory building. A doorman used to have a station to the left of the yellow-gold revolving doors, but now there was a marble-topped front desk there. The accoutrements in the lobby and in her apartment reflected similar taste. The entranceway and the vestibule of her apartment building were emblematic of the Salvatore Ferragamo–style she still favored.

I asked her about the events that resulted in her being in the divorce court in Montgomery County. I was not trying to pry, I was just interested and curious. She heaved a sigh of insouciance and stared away pensively as if contemplating not only how, but whether to respond. I could tell that she was hesitant to discuss aspects of her story. Much of what I wanted to talk about dredged up hurts and scars that had lain dormant in the recesses of her mind for many years and that she wanted to remain buried. Her countenance went from worry, to nonchalance, to an expression that said, "What the hell! I'm proud of my story. Let me tell it." And with that, she began to tell me of the escapades that led to her day in court. As she talked, I listened attentively and took copious notes in my trusty old Moleskine.

In contrast to Harriett's oral history, some time ago in the mid-nineties, Michelle wrote about her experiences as a young college exchange student in Uganda, a country almost the size of Illinois on the east coast of Africa. Her writing was structured as a manuscript but easily could have been a journal had she thought of writing it contemporaneously as the daily events occurred. But I suspect she was too busy soaking it all up. She wrote this material decades later, drawing upon memories seared into her consciousness by the sheer impact upon her life of the observations and events that occurred while she was there. She thought of publishing it, then put it away and moved on to other pursuits: raising her family, working and completing her graduate education. The document lay dormant until I reread it many years later and said to myself, *Hey, this is an interesting story! It offers remarkable insights into the experiences of an African-American woman experiencing Africa for the first time.* Over the years, I had weighed the place of Africa in my consciousness as well. Perhaps some of the themes in Michelle's manuscript had application to another African-American woman we both knew that could be combined into one fascinating story.

CHAPTER THREE

THE AWAKENING

Michelle says, "I dreamed of the opportunity to see the world . . . to see Africa, ever since high school. I participated in the International Relations Club. Our group sponsored the visit of an African student to our high school. I admired his stature and countenance. His English was perfect with an engrossing accent. And he shared information about his village and family in western Africa."

This was her first encounter with an African man, a real live person. Michelle described the African man as short, between 5'5" and 5'8" with a beaming, infectious smile, coarse, black hair closely cropped, and with the whitest teeth she had ever seen. Perhaps it was his smile that accentuated his teeth. He was clearly a happy man, glad to be in the United States, because to be chosen for such a special experience, he had to be either from an upper-class African family or a tribe politically connected, or he was especially smart. But maybe he was enrolled in a student exchange program sponsored by the American Field Service, AFS, which since 1915 has been sponsoring foreign students in the United States. Or perhaps he had been sponsored by some other student exchange program, of which there are many—all seeking, in one way or another, to expose US students as well as foreign students to the culture of other nations.

His clothing was ordinary. He fell into the dressing dilemma un-Westernized foreigners often fall into. They frequently have problems coordinating their choices of patterns, solids, stripes, plaids and colors in their clothing selections. The young man wore horizontal stripes against plaid pants. For all she knew this young African could have been from West Africa or East Africa, Ghana or Djibouti; from Addis Ababa, the capitol of Ethiopia or Dire Dawa, the second-largest city in eastern Ethiopia, home to Haramaya University and Dira Dawa University; or from somewhere along the route of the Addis-Djibouti train line.

After observing this young African, Michelle says, her imagination was stimulated, and the desire to travel was ignited. "Do Africans really look and act like this?" she wondered. She had seen images of Africans on American and European TV shows such as *Tarzan* that depicted Africans as heathens, uncivilized, wearing grass skirts, bones through their noses and with freakish headbands on their heads, usually dancing or congregating around some unfamiliar ritual. This young man was far from that caricature.

This young high school African student was the first, but would not be the last, nor for that matter the most consequential African male to have an impact upon Michelle. Eric Karuhije would be the most influential African man to have an impact on her life.

Michelle first met Eric before she entered Swarthmore College in 1970. Harriett introduced Eric to Michelle and her family just before Harriett and Eric married in 1971. Harriett's family and Michelle's family were close. Michelle's mother, Mary, was Harriett's best friend. They grew up together, and as young women they hung out together. Harriett pursued formal higher education, but Mary chose to begin her working career after high school. Harriett told Mary several years before that she did not want to marry an African-American man, only an African man. At Columbia Teachers College at Columbia University where Harriett studied and worked, the white women went crazy over the African men who were students there. However, Harriett told Mary after her marriage to Eric that she had not given much thought to the fact that African men take more than one wife—that she had in fact been uninformed about this element of African culture.

Michelle remembers when she first met Eric. She explains, "My mother gave Harriett a wedding shower at Harriett's home in Chester, at 1209 West Seventh Street near State Route 13. The neighborhood was a mix of row houses and single-family detached homes."

Fully grown deerberry and maple-leaved viburnum trees lined some parts of the neighborhood. The small square front yards that characterized the neighborhood ran perpendicular to the sidewalks. The cement walkways, now many years mature, ran alongside the front yards of detached and semidetached houses. Harriett's home was a detached redbrick single-family three-bedroom house with a living room, dining room and kitchen on the first floor and a deep backyard.

"As I approached the front door to her home, Harriett greeted me with her usual Harriett style of ebullience, a voice inflection like no other. Harriett always spoke to her friends in an up, bouncy inflection with an air of conviction. I walked into the living room and immediately encountered my mother, Great-Aunt Bea and Harriett's mother, Isabelle, along with several ladies that were there to celebrate with Harriett.

"Isabelle was short, brown skinned, and wore her gray hair up and neatly styled. Isabelle was from the old school, and an admirer of oriental rugs. Isabelle introduced me to the people gathered in the room. Harriett made sure her mother got all the names right because some of the people there were only known to Harriett and Mary.

"The living room was airy, bright and lively. Gifts and crumpled wrapping paper were scattered about on a table reserved for the gifts that sat opposite the front door, evidencing that the party had already started. A green sofa about eight feet long ran along the wall nearest to the front door on the left. Alongside it was a beige love seat flanked on each side by two Queen Ann–period wing chairs.

"The women attending the affair were dressed casually, a combination of slacks, jeans, jumpers and plain, unembroidered blouses. The chatter was about marriage, babies and conjugality. Harriett's mother liked the finer things of life. Isabelle sought a place in the middle-class black community in Chester and she achieved that goal. My Great-Aunt Bea, my mother's maternal aunt, was full figured, a gracious brown-skinned woman with short black hair curled tightly against her head and parted to the side. Great-Aunt Bea was a lover of hats; she collected them and wore many styles. On this occasion, she also helped serve the refreshments, some of which she made herself. Great-Aunt Bea had known Harriett from early adolescence.

"After the introductions, Harriett paused for a moment and switched her gaze to this short, medium-build brown-skinned African man with nice features." Mary said later, "He did not have a broad nose or thick lips. He was a Sidney Poitier type guy with keen features. He spoke with a heavy British accent. He was personable, a fine young man. I couldn't even pronounce his name."

Michelle continues, "Eric was dressed conservatively in a white long-sleeve shirt with the sleeves half rolled up just below the elbow and indistinctive khaki trousers. His shoes were nondescript. His rich brown skin was a striking contrast to the white shirt and cotton pants.

"'Michelle, this is Eric Karuhije. He is a graduate student at Columbia where I teach and he is from Uganda,' Harriett said. Mary and Great-Aunt Bea met him earlier before I arrived. Everyone was intrigued by Harriett's choice in a man. He was *African*. Feeling his way slowly, Eric smiled but said little; he let his smile do the talking. After all, his smile was intoxicating. Harriett was tall and he was short; oddly enough, they looked like each other.

"'How are you, Michelle? It's nice to meet you. I am enjoying being in your country,' he said sincerely. We exchanged niceties, and small talk ensued. Harriett and my mother huddled near the kitchen to talk girl talk, leaving Eric and me one-on-one for a few moments in the living room even though we were surrounded by a host of other folks. Eric seemed to relax a bit now that the introduction was over."

And he said to Michelle, "Harriett has mentioned you to me before. She tells me you will be going to Swarthmore this fall."

"Yes, I'm looking forward to going," Michelle answered.

"Swarthmore is a very good school I hear," he responded.

"Yeah, it is one of the best. I want to study biology and then go on to medical school," Michelle said.

"Oh that's good! That's very good!" he said, acknowledging Michelle's aspiration. His British twang was clearly noticeable. "In my country, we have a need for many more well-trained doctors." Before Michelle could formulate a response, and before the moment became awkward, Mary and Harriett returned to the living room. Harriett said, "I am going to take Eric out to dinner in Delaware when we leave here. Would you guys like to go?"

"No," Mary said. "Enjoy yourselves. Maybe we will get together next week or when you are next in town. We are going to eat in tonight. I've got a long day tomorrow." Mary worked in the juvenile justice department in the Court of Common Pleas for Delaware County in southeastern Pennsylvania.

Michelle in 1971, on Swarthmore's campus.

In the following days and weeks, Harriett brought Eric around, and slowly the stiffness of their initial introduction waned. Being in Eric's presence, Michelle got a sense of who this man was, and she would later find striking coincidences that the two of them shared. The relationship between the families was of such a nature that a spirit of camaraderie developed. Michelle felt as though she knew enough about Mr. Eric that she could count on him, that she could trust him, even though most of the time she was a skeptical believer. She looked up to him. He was a professor of mathematics at Makerere University in Uganda studying in the United States. Eric had applied to the PhD program at Columbia and had been accepted. But she had no way of knowing under what circumstances that reliance would be tested.

Harriett and Eric married in September 1971 in Philadelphia, Pennsylvania. Oscar Wilde said, "Marriage is the triumph of imagination over intelligence." Perhaps had there been more intelligence and less imagination or a healthy balance of the two, the marital fortunes of the Karuhijes would never have been in doubt.

Michelle went about her routine as a freshman in college: getting used to the library, getting to know other classmates, chit-chatting with other students about how they liked or disliked the place. What did they think about how the white students treated them? How were they getting along with their classwork? What did they think about their professors? Who was easy and who was hard? Some of the African-American students had attended private schools just like some of the white students and had had expansive travel and cultural experiences. She made friends during that time with people who would remain her friends decades later.

But, occasionally, "I heard many stories from other students who had gone to or read about Africa. They were proudly wearing their African treasures of colorful galas, dashikis, beads, bangles, and earrings and of course the Afro headdress or cornrows. It was ironic, but I heard more about Africa from the African-American students than from the few Africans that attended our school." To her, the African students were aloof, detached and in some instances dismissive of their African-American counterparts.

In her naiveté, Michelle was unaware that African societies reflect, to an extent and in many instances, the social stratifications of both their native culture and that of their colonizers, the British, French, Italians, Portuguese, Spanish, Belgians, and Germans. A blended cultural landscape of class and caste exist. Kwame Nkrumah in his book *Class Struggle in Africa 1970* explains how elites were established in pre and postcolonial periods and the emergence of the African bourgeoisie—what Nkrumah calls the "indigenous bourgeoisie."[4]

Eric and Harriett in 1971, the year they were married.

Some African-Americans observe that in Africa some Africans feel that they are above it all, especially the elites, because they were not enslaved. Many would differ with them on this issue, but Michelle observes, "The African students acted differently than the African-American students. They were not actively involved in many black activities on campus, and I do not recall having any lengthy conversation with them about their native countries. They never gave any group presentation about themselves or their homeland. There was always a friendly exchange but nothing else. Maybe it was me. I could not seem to engage beyond light conversation. The few African students that attended our school were male students. I was a little uncomfortable striking up a relationship because of their gender. I did not want them to misinterpret my interest in them. If any of the students were female, I am sure the relationship would have been different."

Michelle recalls that at Swarthmore during this time, "Africa was a place everyone wanted to connect with, to touch and to feel. Miss Harriett shared her stories with me, and her stories brought me closer to understanding more about the continent. She said her husband's family lived in the Rwenzori mountains area of Uganda, a region close to Rwanda, and Burundi, a French-speaking country. Eric had three sisters and two brothers. Eric was next to the oldest. The family members spoke French and Swahili but no English, and Eric's mother was not interested in learning English. So, Harriett said she was at a real disadvantage."

When Harriett arrived in Uganda for the first time, all his kinsmen were there to greet her. A grand feast was prepared. They concocted a special ceremonious brew of animal blood and other ingredients she did not want to know about. She took the required sip of the potion. In those few moments before she swallowed the potion, she thought for a moment that she had returned to a postlapsarian period where animal sacrifices and tributes were common. She took the required sip, closed her mouth, blinked slightly longer than usual and forced the concoction down her throat, trying not to taste the brew as it made its way down to her stomach. She prevented it from being expelled by swallowing hard to keep it down. She was close to vomiting, but her determination to be "one of them" overcame her innate impulse to disgorge the mixture. Those of the family that gathered around then rapturously shouted, calling her affectionately, "the lost one, the stolen one."

Michelle continues her story. "The first semester continued its course, and I was making the freshman transition. Then one day, we received information about exchange programs to the Caribbean and to Africa. I had dreamt about the opportunity to see the world ... to see Africa. The announcement identified Africa as a possible exchange."

It was as though the gods had planted African seedlings in Michelle's backyard to be grown into flowering tall fruit trees that, when ripened, would yield fructuous cultural benefits, like nuts and berries ready for the experience of tasting.

"So, I began dreaming," she said, "and I saw myself going to Africa, kissing, holding, feeling and squeezing the silty dark soil between my fingers, reconnecting with my ancestors, whose genes held the secrets to my past, my present and my future. Reconnecting with the souls of generations whose footprints were imbedded in the sand along the shores of the eastern Atlantic Ocean shoreline where many had walked en-route to slavery and suffered through the trials of colonization and dehumanization. Through my kiss, I touched them and lived with them, and I stretched out my arms, as I whirled around and looked to the ocean and cried with the fullness of my glee, 'Here I am! here I am! I have returned!'"

Michelle had this dream—an allegorical construction, one could say, created by her imagination, of what it would be like for her and others to reunify with her lost culture, and to receive the ancestral patrimony of her forefathers to which she laid claim.

Michelle's dream was not unique. Generations of African-Americans and white Americans also dreamed of this fanciful but fantastical repatriation. As John Hope Franklin noted, "As early as 1714 a 'native American' broached the subject of sending blacks back to Africa." Then in 1777 Thomas Jefferson headed a Virginia legislative committee that brought forth a plan for the emancipation and deportation of free as well as enslaved blacks. In 1815 Paul Cuffee, one of the richest, if not the richest, American of African descent at that time, at his own expense transported thirty-eight blacks to Africa.[5] His overture illustrated that many free African-Americans and freed slaves supported the idea of emigrating to Africa. Some blacks were in favor of the Colonization Society project and many were opposed. Between 1821 and 1822, James Monroe, the fifth president of the United States, subsidized the United States Navy to help support the establishment of a colony for blacks in Liberia; hence the capital of Liberia is named Monrovia in his honor.[6]

The way Michelle puts it is, "I was awakened from this intoxication by a reality that chilled the warmth of my imagination and disquieted my longing. I really didn't think I had a chance to go. I was only a freshman and just starting out.

"At the Black Cultural Center, the atmosphere was revolutionary, lively and festive. Red-green-and-black flags emblazoned on black-Power signs and black Panther posters were everywhere, along with pictures of Angela Davis, the black Power countercultural militant from California sporting her famous big Afro, and in the background there was the music of Gil Scott Heron, singing, 'The revolution will not be televised.' The sixties had been a period when black people reveled in their blackness. They were drunk from the nectar of their African-ness. This was the post-sixties, a period still brimming with the hum of an Afro-centric hangover. There was incessant rhetoric about Africa, the chatter of romantic ideas about the motherland, the pride of being of African descent, to the extent we knew we were."

In retrospect these exuberances were superficial, a substitute for substance.

"In the midst of all this clamor, I kept saying to myself, 'You don't have a chance of going with all these advocates and upperclassmen possibly competing for the chance to go as well.' So I did what I could. I started wearing an Afro. That was all I could do at the moment to show I felt as they did and that I was a part of the movement. It was in vogue. I wore a 'curly fro' in the Angela Davis style. My hair was of such a grade that the only way I could imitate the Afro style was by curling my Afro cut. I learned many years later that I would never have been considered 'African' because my skin color was not dark enough.

"This was the kind of stuff we, the African-American students, were interested in. We thought we were emulating them, their culture and our culture. But we weren't. We were romanticizing a vision of what we thought Africa and Africans were like."

Africa was indeed a place everyone wanted to connect with, to touch, to feel and to embrace. Harriett had recently married Eric, but no children were born of the marriage. And though romantic intensity characterized the early years of the relationship, the relationship became attenuated by long periods of estrangement. Harriett did not tell Michelle or her mother, Mary, until years later that Eric's family, specifically his mother, did not want her son to marry an African-American woman. Instead, the mother wanted and expected that her son would marry a girl from the local village or some other native-born Ugandan woman. An African woman who had already been selected.[7]

Harriett's stories enchanted Michelle as well as her mother. And even though Harriett was older, she too had imbibed deeply the elixir of the African nostrum. After all, not since the days of Marcus Garvey in 1914[8] had there been such a furor about "visiting" Africa, which Michelle wanted to do, and "embracing" Africa as a place to live, which Harriett sought to accomplish. The sixties were a renaissance, an African reawakening, if you will. And Michelle's excitement about things African as well as Harriett's passion for Africa was a residue from that era. It is amazing that what Garvey started in 1914 resonated in the 1960s and was now reflected in the psyches of youth and in some black adults fifty-six years later.

Harriett's exploits drew Michelle even closer to Harriett. Michelle began to see herself, except for the marriage part, reflected in Harriett's pioneering spirit and cultural relevance. Their friendship served to heighten and to personalize her desire to go to Africa. She said to herself in effect, "I can do this. I want to do this. I want to have this experience beyond the hoopla of the day." But why did she feel so compelled to have this experience? Was Michelle seeking to free herself from the scourge of perennial victimhood, to overcome the dearth of closeness and the cultural dislocation so often surmised by her fellow African-Americans? Or was it simply the overwhelming desire to see the world, to see Africa, not to live there but to explore, to move beyond the provincialisms of Chester?

Michelle has told me that when she was young, her mother and a close family friend, Samuel Williams, affectionately called

"Daddy Kake," took her and her sister for Sunday drives in his car to surrounding communities to show them that the world was bigger and greater than Chester. He was of average height, a dark-skinned, slightly rotund man with short, neatly brushed black hair and a jovial attitude. Ruefully she says, "Daddy Kake filled the male void in our family. He was a friend to my mother and a surrogate father to my sister and me."

There are many types of voids to be filled in human experience. A familial void is one type. A cultural absence is another. There is an old adage that says, "You can't miss what you never had." But is that true? Logically the statement makes sense but yearning for what one thinks it would be like to have or to have had what is absent can cause sadness, depression and a lack of fulfillment. All people want to satisfy their desire to experience their dreams, to fill the void, if any exists in their lives. It is a rare individual that has no bare spots to fill.

The desire to satisfy that unrequited need, that unsatisfied dream or that fixed appetency makes us grow and develop and try new things in search, perhaps, of delusive satisfaction. But when and if one is lucky and obtains that which is perceived to have been lost or absent, and that "thing" turns out not to be what it was touted to be—has that longing, that yearning for that lost culture and all that it is supposed to supply, been an illusion of absence? Conversely, is one's present reality more important and all that is essentially needed to be fulfilled without the other, absent ancestral culture? Chasing an absent culture, in this case with the intent of assimilating that culture and integrating it into one's present reality, can be fraught with complications, possibly disappointment and opposition.

Filling in blank spaces is not easy. Especially when those blanks have existed for generations. One's ability to fill them in is problematic and full of uncertainties. But perhaps just the experience of trying to fill them in is worthwhile, successful or not. The experience has intrinsic value.

Michelle was falling in love with what she thought she had been deprived of. Her enthusiasm to see the world and to see Africa overcame her skittishness. *Esse quam videri*: She wanted "to be" rather than "to seem." Yes, she had the guts to take the leap. So she signed her name on the prospective list. Michelle recalls, "I noticed that the list had only one other name on it, but I was sure that this was the second or third page of the list."

In the order of things, a meeting was scheduled about the African Exchange Program in Parrish Hall on the second floor. The room was well equipped. The walls were painted in a flat, off-white color that was easy on the eyes. A bulletin board was on the left side of the door. The bulletin board was filled with thumb-tacked announcements of one kind of opportunity or another, whatever your interest. A modern green chalkboard housed in an alloyed aluminum frame was present in the front of the room. Audio-visual equipment was on the right side of the chalkboard. Overhead lighting illuminated the space, and theater seating was the style. The room had the patina of a casual lecture hall. Here, one could listen, learn, and relax.

"I opened the door and held my breath. The room was empty. I figured the boastful upperclassmen would stroll in soon, close to the meeting hour. They would walk in slowly, not showing their excitement, being nonchalant about the whole matter," she recalls. "Anticipating that the room would be full of students, I arrived early to sit up front, a habit of mine born out of a desire not to be left out or considered to be uninterested. This practice was also a competitive habit intuitively adopted over the years. I wanted to write down every detail.

"Mr. Clement Cottingham, the director of the program, was a stout, dark-skinned African-American man who wore glasses and always wore a suit whenever I saw him," Michelle remembers. "He was highly intelligent. He had to be to work at Swarthmore. He was well mannered, and well spoken, meaning he spoke with facility and his conversation flowed smoothly without hesitation. But above all else he was a nice man, a caring man, sensitive to the needs of the African-American students attending Swarthmore.

"When Mr. Cottingham entered the room, he took a seat at the head table. One other student followed. Mr. Cottingham called the meeting to order and asserted that everyone was now present who had signed up." Michelle recalls, "I was flabbergasted. Was it just me and one other student who had signed up?! I couldn't believe it. I thought, *Where are all the 'gung-ho' types who met in the Black Cultural Center and spouted out and rapped about all that 'back to Africa' stuff? The ones wearing the African garb, waving the red-black-and-green flag, the display of the raised fists of black unity, African motherhood, Garvey's Pan-Africanism, the back-to-your-roots rhetoric. Was it just rhetoric, much to say about nothing?* A pseudo-attempt to feign being relevant, the zeitgeist of the moment. They were not willing to make the sacrifice necessary to make Africa real in their lives.

"From that time forward, I began to look at people not for what they said but for what they did. My mother always told me, 'Actions speak louder than words.' I felt I had been betrayed, tricked, misled, hoodwinked, taken advantage of. Yet I was not discouraged; in fact, I was emboldened because *I* was willing to be real, to make the sacrifice and take on the challenge; to take the risk and have the experience. These other folks were pretenders.

"*Why me?* I asked myself. *The less endowed, the less knowledgeable, the less studious.* Because I wanted to see Africa for myself and not through the eyes and voices of other people—to kiss the ground and feel the spirit of the motherland."

CHAPTER FOUR

A MOURNFUL INTERLUDE

Michelle continues her story: "The trip was scheduled to begin in July 1971 and continue until March of next year. The trip was cancelled due to bureaucratic complications of some sort. But the director was very optimistic that next year would be our year. I was disappointed. I had done a lot of planning, and now, no success—at least not yet. I looked forward to next year when I would be a sophomore and more ready to take on Africa."

As it turned out, it was better for Michelle that the trip was cancelled because some of her family members died during the time she would have been in Africa.

The quiet before the storm was not so quiet; it was filled with spasms of anguish. Michelle recalls painfully that her maternal grandfather, James W. Palmer, a proud black man from Detroit who worked for Chrysler Motors, died several months before the end of her freshmen year in 1971. His would not be the only death she experienced that year. Her maternal grandmother's oldest sister, her great-aunt Bea, as she was called, also died that year. And yet, despite all that had happened, death was not finished with her.

Michelle says, "During Great-Aunt Bea's funeral, my maternal grandmother's youngest sister, Aunt Margaret, whom we affectionately called Great-Aunt Honey, looked down upon the face of her dead sister Bea, lying in her gray metallic casket, her body dressed in an off-white suit and surrounded by white, linen-covered cushions underneath white embroidered sheets, lifted up her hands and shouted, 'Hallelujah Jesus!' and collapsed to the floor. The clap of her body hitting the floor shattered the silence that pervaded an otherwise somber service like the bang of a cannon. She died of a massive heart attack right there at that moment." Her grandfather and her two maternal aunts were now dead.

"My grandfather died of cancer," Michelle says. "I took my first plane ride not to Africa but to Detroit for my granddad's funeral. Granddad had left our hometown many years before to make a new life for himself in Detroit working in the car industry. As I listened to the many comments from his friends at the funeral and afterwards, I realized I did not know a lot about him. He was originally from Florida and we were told his family once owned property where Disney World is now located in Orlando. We have pictures of him and his parents. But we don't know much about them except for their names. Two of my fond memories of him are that he enjoyed drinking ginger ale. He introduced me to Vernors ginger ale, and I have loved it ever since. It was new to me, but to him and his fellow Detroiters it was an old favorite.

"He also was quite a singer. He belonged to a singing group and he sang in his church choir, a baritone, I would suppose, based upon the sound of his voice. I also am fond of singing, so perhaps there is an inherited connection.

"I looked around in his apartment and touched his things. They all meant something to him, but I did not know what that something was. I loved my granddad dearly and he loved us. I felt ashamed. Ashamed that I did not know him better. Ashamed that I had not sat and talked with him about his family, his childhood and his dreams.

I was about to travel eight thousand miles to Africa in search of my ancestral roots, to find what I thought was my severed past, and yet in this present moment I knew nothing about a man who was my immediate past, my immediate ancestor. What a paradox!

"My Great-Aunt Bea had a round face, was full figured, stout, with light-brown skin. She always wore her hair curled tightly, parted to one side, and neatly balanced on both sides with the top. The sides of her hair rested just above the ear lobes. Facially she resembled my sister, Shelley," Michelle recalls. "Great-Aunt Bea lived alone in Chester not far from our home. Her residence was quaint: an attached home, a dwelling with a masonry veneer of red brick on a quiet street. From what I remember, Great-Aunt Bea rented this house from a local church group known in the community for its charitable work with housing and education. Though Great-Aunt Bea had more room than she needed as a single woman living alone, she lived a Spartan life, with no frills, modest furnishings conveniently placed, plain accessories and unadorned trappings. Not long after Great-Aunt Bea moved from her single-family home to an apartment in the city, her demise began. On an otherwise clear and sunny day, she was stung by a bee in her left eye while hanging out clothes in her backyard. She went to the hospital for treatment and never came out alive."

Michelle recounts, "If I had been in Africa, I would not have been able to look in Great-Aunt Bea's eyes as she lay in peace in her hospital bed. As she lay there her countenance reflected the ethereal serenity of her final hours. If l had been in Africa, I would have missed her final hours.

"However, her unexpected death prevented me from sharing with her the voices, smells, the sights and sounds and scenic beauty of Africa; as well as my excitement, souvenirs, poignant experiences and observations of the people. It would only be through my dreams and spirit that I would be able to share these things with her—probably a much better medium, and better representation of my truer feelings, than I could ever describe to her.

"The doctors carelessly stated at her bedside that Bea would die. It bothered us greatly that they would say such a thing in Great-Aunt Bea's presence, but perhaps they knew she could not hear them, or at least that is what they assumed. I knew in my heart that she did hear them! Although she could not speak with her voice, she spoke with her eyes. Her eyes and visage were with and of God. Her countenance bespoke of her peace with the Holy Spirit. Had she passed on, even though she lay there with her eyes open yet devoid of motion?

"At the funeral, I kissed her cold, unresponsive face. There was no return, not even a dent in the skin where I placed my lips. Perfect stillness. I thanked her sincerely for all that she had done to make our lives better and joyful. I had always been appreciative of what she did for our family, and I am sure I thanked her while she was alive. But my heart pinged with an urgency to thank her again, for I knew this would be the last time. My thanks fell on deaf ears this time, but I felt better for doing it.

"When my sister, Shelley, and I were much younger, Great-Aunt Bea took us on many church trips in New York City to New Jersey and Pennsylvania, places I had never seen before, initiating for perhaps the first time a view of places outside of Chester that ignited my imagination. Great-Aunt Bea loved to cook and enjoyed good food. In our family, she was the gastronome. It was she who always came to our house, bogged down with shopping bags in both arms, carrying bountiful gifts of food and clothing. She was the one who, at every Christmas, baked large batches of Christmas cookies—molasses, chocolate chip, oatmeal, coconut, peanut butter, and sprinkled sugar cookies—and stored them in large potato chip and pretzel tins. She brought bags of fruit and all kinds of candies plus the old-fashioned Christmas candy, the mixed straws, art and ribbon candy. Her mincemeat pies were my favorite. All my friends loved to come to our house for Christmas and see our living room tables overloaded with her goodies. We filled our bellies with all her goodies until we were stuffed."

Michelle reflects, "I promised myself that when I went to Africa, I would share Great-Aunt Bea's story and her spirit with those who would listen and embrace it and press her claim to her African heritage.

"At a time like this, I was saddened by my ignorance of not knowing who Bea really was. This woman who enjoyed foods of all kind. This jovial, stout woman with the neatly curled black hair. Who was this woman who gladdened my heart and filled my stomach with her good cooking and who brought our family closer together? Who was the person divorced from the cookies and cream? What was the nature of her true self as much as I, a young niece a generation removed, could discover? The fact that I had been around her numerous times and ate her cookies and laughed at her jokes revealed little in the way of true knowledge about her. I should have known her better, but I didn't. She grew up during the roaring twenties, so I am sure she had jaw-dropping stories to share. I was about to travel to another continent to study in the motherland, yet I didn't even know my great-aunt's story, a story easily accessible.

"Honey, as my mother called her, the younger of my maternal grandmother's two sisters, was 'the fairest of them all.' Great-Aunt Honey lived with her husband, James, in New York City in the Bronx. We grew up calling him Uncle James. Honey was heavyset. She had the same face she had when she was much younger. A brown-skinned woman with thinning black hair, she wore a wig, something that she deliberated about over many months before deciding to wear it. Honey was an honest person true to her Christian beliefs, and she wanted above all else to be true to herself and her faith. She eschewed artificial embellishments. I think that she thought as a Christian one should be themselves and accept what God had given you. But in the end vanity overcame the religious conundrum she resolved.

"Uncle James was a private investigator. Darker skinned than Honey, he was a balding man of medium build with a distinguished persona. Uncle James was a dapper man, always looking good in his suits, bow ties and stingy brim or flat fedora hats." Michelle remembers that he wore black-rimmed glasses and resembled the cartoon character Mr. Peabody created by Jay Ward in the early sixties, with his glasses on and without the hat—in form but not in manner. Perhaps he was a precursor of the gumshoe depicted in black America's 1971 hit movie *Shaft*.[9] black private investigators were rare back then, usually drawn from police or military backgrounds. People in this business did well for themselves even though they operated undercover most of the time.

Michelle reminisces, "Great-Aunt Honey and Uncle James invited Shelley and me to stay in their home every summer when school was out during our elementary and teenage years. Daddy Kake drove us up. My mother always accompanied us. It was a chance for us to get out of Chester. Great-Aunt Honey and Uncle James lived in a stunning three-story attached redbrick home that had a small front yard and two full baths. Our home in Chester was a two-bedroom house with one bath with only a tub and sink and no shower. Their home was the biggest home that any of our family members owned. Honey and Uncle James were solidly middle class. In the living room, they had a ceiling-to-floor mirrored-glass wall with a beautiful davenport placed in front of it. The steps leading to the bedrooms were carpeted in royal cranberry red that reflected beautifully in the mirrored wall. We were required to take off our shoes before walking up those stairs.

"When Uncle James went from the second floor to the third floor, he would mimic Teddy Roosevelt in his mythic command to his troops, the Rough Riders, as they assaulted San Juan Hill during the Spanish-American War, and yell out, 'Charge!' as he ran up the final flight of stairs to the bedrooms. Each time he did this my sister and I would laugh heartily until our sides hurt. We thought it was so funny. Uncle James was also a big fan of the New York Mets' professional baseball team. The headboard to his bed had a shelf built within it with enough space to place a radio. I can see him now lying in his bed listening and cheering as the Mets game was being called. Between 1962 and 1968 the Mets had a losing record, but that did not stop Uncle James from supporting his beloved Mets. The legendary Casey Stengel was their manager from 1962 to 1965. The Mets won the World Series in 1969.

"Great-Aunt Honey and Uncle James bought us school clothes for the next school year and we always went to Macy's. 'Now, girls,' she would say, 'pick out what you want. You can have two dresses apiece and be sure to get underwear and socks and let me know if you see a pair shoes you like.' It was like Christmas shopping in a large New York City department store. The experience was magical. They not only bought us clothes, but they also took us on trips around the city to see the many sights: the Empire State Building, Central Park, Broadway, the Bronx Zoo and Coney Island. We visited often enough that we had a girlfriend several houses down from us whom we got to know and with whom we played.

"My great-aunts were always there supporting us. They attended as many school affairs as they could. Great-Aunt Honey even visited me at Swarthmore when I was a freshman living on the fourth floor of a building with no elevators. The stairs were steep. Even I had trouble climbing them day after day. I told her she did not have to climb the stairs to see my room. But there was no way to turn her around. She climbed them and she was completely out of breath when she reached my room. Perhaps a better use of her energy would have been to see a doctor for advice on her apparent heart condition. Had I known about such things then, I would have strongly urged her to seek help. But she climbed those steps despite her condition just for me.

"After the death of these family members," Michelle recalls, "I was quite sorrowful and depressed for many weeks. At that time, Africa was the farthest thing from my mind. After all, I had lost three principal members of my family in less than a year and a half, members whose deaths foreclosed the opportunity to learn more about them firsthand. Who knew better about their lives than they did? A lost opportunity. There I was, looking forward so anxiously toward traveling to the motherland to discover roots long lost, my distant roots, yet I was ignorant about the present. Things were upside down, not right side up as they should have been.

"Because I have such an overpowering love for my family and for my brethren in Africa, my heart is overcome with emotion and causes tears to fill my eyes when I reflect upon what I know of my family's history and the history of African people. What can you do with history other than read it and learn from it?"

Michelle continues, "I am told that we were one of the first black families in Chester with businesses and notability. I should have asked what happened to the families and their businesses. I should have pulled out the photo albums and had them identify who these people are and were. What made them special if in fact they were? What kind of businesses did they operate and from whence did the type of business originate? What else did they do for a living, and did they have any peculiar behaviors, traits, or predilections that set them apart from other family members? Answering these questions would be like finding out about my genetic code, the history of my family diseases. Then, I would know where I got this habit or that trait from, and perhaps why I act the way I do. Instead, I bumble around groping in the darkness of ignorance with far more questions than answers; searching for confirmations wherever I can find them, if any exist at all, talking about rumors about this family member or that member without really knowing anything concrete. So here I sit, with photo album after photo album in hand, the dried glue of years past, of people who lived and died, and nobody knows their names or what import they were to the family. They are ghosts from the past.

"The paucity of information about my immediate relatives stood in stark relief to my yearning and heartfelt desire to learn more about my African ancestors. I asked myself, *Is it more important to learn about the past than it is the present?* Which time period mattered more? Which had more relevance to the cultural wellness of an individual, especially a person like me, prejudiced by a dearth of knowledge about my past and my present? How does one go about measuring the significance of time, people and place in the family culture of an individual? Is the cultural gulf less a void if the past is unknown but the present is known? Or is the past more important to the cultural wellness of an individual than the present? I surmised that to be complete, I needed to know not only where I came from but who I presently belonged to. It is best if the continuum of family heredity and ancestral heritage is unbroken, but that ideal condition is not the reality of most African-Americans, our cultural heritage was deliberately made inaccessible.

"I realized that going to Africa was not going to answer these questions for me. But this journey would be a start along a difficult pilgrimage toward self-discovery, a trek to find the proverbial 'source of the Nile,' to explore the continent where my family roots began. Move over David Livingstone and Henry Stanley,"[3*] she declares. "Here I come, naïveté and all.

"I needed to learn about the African continent, as I had learned about the United States since my elementary school days. I was indoctrinated with American history, reading and being tested on events and history written to support and continue certain political ideologies and objectives. Many of these 'learned facts' were dispelled by the truth about our American history, meaning the true American history of all of our peoples, the Native Americans, blacks and Hispanics—the true melting pot of all of our cultures—which make up America. I wanted to learn about our history before America. I wanted to learn about Africa not from television and movies. I wanted to see it for myself, make my own assessments as I had assessed America. Learning about both worlds would truly give me an informed identity as an African-American."

Michelle was aware that her nascent inquiry had not revealed any tribe or country from which her ancestors sprang, but going to Uganda was a start, a prominent beginning. Her purpose for going

---

3 * A Welsh explorer who was famous for his exploration of central Africa and his search for missionary and explorer David Livingstone.

to Africa was to study and have a cultural experience, not solely to discover her roots. Going to Africa to embark upon a discovery of self and history was equivalent to going to Africa to discover the cradle of sub-Saharan African culture and civilization, all of which have disparate derivations, such as in Ghana, Mali, Egypt, Sudan, and Senegal or in the forty-five other countries that comprise the sub-Saharan portion of the continent—a continent of 1.1 billion people and 11,668,599 square miles;[10] a continent with a land mass of 30.7 million square kilometers, where between 1,500 and 2,000 languages are spoken in six different linguistic sectors.[11]

An undertaking of such a search would require overcoming the "inarticulate major premise"[4]* that the culture and civilization of "Negroes" from West Africa was developed by the Hamites, ancient peoples of northern and eastern Africa such as the Egyptians, deriving from Caucasoids of European extraction and from white Africans known as the Berbers.[12] Michelle's quest would be complicated and made more difficult by the multitude of variances in language, tribe, culture and ethnicities.

There are many sites from which sub-Saharan African culture and hence African-American ancestry began. This is the problem to be solved, the anvil shackled around the ankle, the millstone around the neck of the African-American explorer—the wayfarer in search of who he or she is and where he or she came from; the nonimmigrant who had his ancestry wrested from him in a heinous act of barbarity. And so it is that the act of finding an ancestral threshold, a cultural genesis, is akin to catching in the palm of your hand the Great Purple Hairstreak, a butterfly with velvet black wings and assorted blues or purples arrayed across each wing, without knowing anything about its cocoon. This one is perched on the leaf of a green dewy tulip tree. The searcher must recognize the "flight of the butterfly," the staccato and elusive nature that underlies the dispersion that characterizes it.

---

4 * In an unrelated context, Justice Holmes enunciated "the inarticulate major premise" in his dissenting opinion. See Lochner v. New York, U.S. Supreme Court 1905

∴

Michelle recalls that her room on the fourth floor in Parrish Hall, the symbolic building of Swarthmore, was built in the Pennsylvania German tradition of stone and logs. There was a dormer,[13] a period feature of the architecture in the era when this grand old building was rebuilt in 1881.

"The ceiling," she says, "slanted toward my only vertical window, underneath a slanted roof in the rear of the room. A twin bed along with a built-in closet sat on the left side of the room. Above the bed were posters of some of my favorite people, places, and my favorite sayings. My room had plenty of light. On the right side of the room was my bookcase, dresser, my desk and a chair, a small refrigerator, and a toaster oven. In the center of the room in the back, where the slanted ceiling abutted the window, was a black leather swivel rocker my Uncle James had given me. I placed the rocker in front of the window to enjoy the view of the campus and to aid me when moments of introspection overtook me, of which there were many.

"On a spring morning in April of 1972, I awoke in my room from a sound sleep to the beams of sunlight shining brightly through my window. Once awakened, the sounds of fellow students walking and talking in the hallways and getting ready for classes ensured that I would stay awake. After readying myself for my first class, I went downstairs to check my mail, and in the box was a letter giving notice to me that I was one of two students at Swarthmore selected for the African exchange program at Kampala, Uganda. I was terribly excited, beyond words. I began making my lists of things to do: getting a passport, immunization shots, and getting an international driver's license. My childhood friends couldn't believe I was going so far from home. I was so brave to do such a thing, they thought. But for me, it would be pure excitement."

Michelle says, "Uganda would be my home for the next year and be my greatest adventure. I couldn't wait. I began reading about Uganda, the pearl of East Africa. On the surface, my family was excited about my new pending adventure. Nana, my maternal grandmother, who lost both her sisters the previous year, was not excited at all about me going. In fact, she even disliked my Afro, said it would 'ruin my hair,' and now I was going to Africa? Are you kidding!

"My grandmother had suffered a stroke at age fifty and lived in a nursing home. She lived for her family and bragged continuously about her granddaughters, what we were doing and where we were going. But she did not brag about my African trip. She felt my family was already at home in America. Why the need to go? She couldn't understand this quest of mine to go to the motherland. After all, she had been born in America, and my mother was born in America. America was our home.

"Nana's only perspective of Africa came from television shows of her era that depicted Africa as all jungle with apes and monkeys swinging from the trees. She had been totally brainwashed by television over the years, as so many are today. The image of a white man reigning over ignorant wild African savages was the propaganda espoused by the power structure to perpetuate a white supremacist ideology. Tarzan movies and television shows of like themes formed the image of Africa and for many was their sole source of information about the land of their ancestors. My Nana in her perceptions represented what I was seeking to destroy, the misperception about Africa. She held these beliefs even though Harriett and her new husband, Eric, from time to time made it a point to educate her about Africa. The ineradicable nature of her beliefs made it impossible to persuade her otherwise."

• • •

During this time, Harriett and her new husband, Eric, went to Uganda to visit Eric's family. Ugandans were proud of the fact that they had never been enslaved by Europeans and that they spoke and kept their language, Swahili.[14] Harriett was besotted with all things African, and her excitement resulted in a renewed commitment to expand upon her initial experiences. Harriett shared her adventures with Michelle. Her stories enchanted Michelle and brought both her and her mother closer to understanding more about the continent. Mary said, however, "that she was sad because her best friend was leaving her and going to Africa."

Harriett told me that for the first time, after this introduction, thoughts came into her mind about living and working in Africa. She had an African husband. Why not? Was it not expected that when Eric's studies were completed at Columbia that they would return to his beloved Uganda? All of this became a real possibility now, and she became amenable to opportunities that went in that direction.

Before she met Eric, she had studied for her bachelor's degree in nursing at Episcopal Hospital at Temple University in Philadelphia, Pennsylvania. During that time, she met Dr. Martin Luther King, Jr., when he studied at Crozier Theological Seminary[15] in Chester, Pennsylvania, and she was friends with Mary, who knew a female student who had dated Dr. King.

Mary, Michelle's mother, had fond and vivid memories of that period. She said that the student, Annette Williams, was one of her good friends at the time. Annette told her that Dr. King had asked her to marry, but Annette declined because she did not think she could live the life of a minister's wife. She also recalled meeting Dr. King's parents when they came up to visit their son at his graduation party. Mary further related, "We were all going clubbing—Dr. King, Annette, me, and one of Dr. King's friends, whose last name was McCall." She remembered with a laugh that her Great-Aunt Bea had remarked, "What's going on with these young ministers?"

Harriett remembered that when Dr. Martin Luther King, Jr., was assassinated in April of 1968, she was awakened about Africa.

In the 1970s, Harriett had been a graduate student at Teachers College at Columbia University studying education. Her major interest had always been curriculum development and instruction for nursing education programs. While at Columbia University she received her master's degree in nursing education from Teacher's

College. And upon receiving that degree she pursued and attained a doctorate in that field at Columbia.

Her dreams had been fulfilled. And the anti-war movement was alive and well at Columbia. Henry Kissinger, the national security advisor to President Nixon during this time, was invited to speak and she attended. She says she was caught up in the movement and even took a course in "The African Experience" while at Columbia.

• • •

The letter Michelle received officially advising her of her selection to be in the exchange program and informing her of which country she would be going to and what university she would be attending caused her to mentally review all her assets. Reality took hold and her security became an important issue to her and to her immediate family now that she knew she was about to travel to another continent by herself. Michelle calmed her nerves when she remembered, *Oh yes! that's right, Mr. Eric, teaches at Makerere University in Kampala, Uganda. Wow! That's great; that's where I will be. I will know someone in Uganda. What a blessing!"*

"God always looks out for me," she quietly mumbled to herself after the initial excitement passed. Harriett gave assurances that Eric would be there to look out for her. This not only assuaged Michelle's anxiousness about her pending circumstance but also went a long way toward making her family feel better about her trip.

Michelle was not the only student from Swarthmore College participating in this exchange program. A fellow student named Randy Connell, a tall, light-brown-skinned man with an Afro-style haircut was also going. "Randy was well raised, a nice guy," Michelle remembers. A student from the University of Pennsylvania named Vixena Brown was also planning to go—a short and stout brown-skinned female with a short-cut Afro and an outgoing personality.

Upon learning that Randy had been successful, Michelle reached out.

"Hey, Randy, I read that you are going over to Africa with me," she said jokingly.

"Yeah, you're right, but I thought it was the other way around. You're going with me," he responded. They both laughed happily, celebrating an achievement that they were both proud of, yet they knew the trip could be life changing or at least full of discovery and unforetold adventure.

Michelle, after thinking a moment, said to Randy, "You know, one of us should get in touch with the student from Penn who is going."

In a few days, Randy got word to Michelle that he had contacted Vixena, and all three met together to plan their trip during the end of the school year. Michelle and Vixena decided to travel together. "We had one week to get to Kampala, so we scheduled a one-week trip through Rome. Randy would make his way alone, making a stopover in Paris." For the women, especially Michelle, the steady creep of their security needs prompted her to make decisions that satisfied that concern.

They would all meet at Makerere University.

CHAPTER FIVE

A LOVE FORLORN

Michelle remembers wistfully, "I was ready, in my mind, to leave for Africa. But what about my heart? My girlfriend, who was from New York, and I often met at our mailboxes. One day she told me about a friend she knew at Columbia University in New York City who was a great guy but who was lonely. Her sincerity in describing his plight struck a chord in my heart. I understood about loneliness because I too felt that way often. Because at Swarthmore, though I had friends, there was no one special. And the minority community was small. We all did not get along swimmingly all the time.

"Since my girlfriend and I met at our mailboxes, the idea of me writing to him was a natural suggestion. She thought that was a great idea. So I got his name and address from her and asked her about his courses and his interests.

"She smiled and said, 'He took Latin, and G is his name for short.'"

"So I'll write him in Latin," Michelle responded gleefully, knowing that to correspond in Latin was a limited occurrence. It was an unusual beginning. Other than French, Latin was the language of love. Their correspondence in Latin would make their relationship more special.

"G was tall, brown skinned with black hair. He was not a pretty boy. Pretty boys never held any special sway with me. We started our relationship as pen pals, writing letters to each other. Not just any letters but Latin letters, *litteras amore*. My friend, the matchmaker, thought that was a cool idea. So, I sat down at my desk and wrote him. The first letter was a crazy, humorous, lighthearted letter to someone I did not know but who I knew was lonely. At least I could send some sunshine to another lonely soul. Without ceremony or qualm, I mailed the letter to G."

As she speaks, I imagine that two lonely people seeking refuge in one another romanticizes and deepens the fondness from absence.

Michelle says, "I had my imagination and amorous expectations but at that time no real sense of what he looked like or how I would relate to him in person. But all that would change. It was like an English love story of the heart-sore lover forlornly corresponding by mail, waiting to see her expectation realized. Two weeks later he responded. He was surprised and excited to get my letter. He kept his response general. We did not know each other, so that was fine. He had a great sense of humor. What had me screaming about his response was that he wrote back in Latin too!

"I answered his letter in Latin and we became Latin pen pals for almost six months until we decided we had to meet. I invited him to a college arts festival weekend. I was nervous. We had only written to each other. We had never spoken on the phone or exchanged any pictures. So, I did not know what he looked like and vice versa. Our mutual friend was the important key. We made arrangements for him to bunk out with some of our male classmates. We stocked my refrigerator with food and juices. The campus was decorated for the arts festival. My modern dance group was performing that weekend for the festival, so I was busy rehearsing and getting extremely nervous about the whole thing. But the weekend was planned, and I made sure he had plenty of stuff to do. His train arrived Friday night around 8:30 p.m.

"The night arrived," Michelle says. "My girlfriend and I were walking down the main campus to the train station. It was dark and I was glad because I was a nervous wreck. I began thinking to myself, *Why didn't we stay pen pals? We don't need to meet! Everything is great the way it is.*

"My girlfriend could tell I was nervous, and she said, 'Don't worry. It will be fine. He's a nice guy. We have everything planned. He'll have a great time. Don't worry.'

"We saw the commuter train arrive and depart. We gave him instructions to walk across the walkway to the campus and we would meet him at the underpass tunnel. By the time we got to the tunnel we could hear footsteps, one set of footsteps coming toward us. The echo from the footsteps made the moment unbearable to me. My girlfriend grabbed my hand and said, 'You'll be alright,' and then she hollered, 'G, is that you?'

"As soon as she asked, a tall figure appeared. His full name was Garrett Johnson. I could see him talking to her. I had moved back and was not in view of the light from the tunnel, so he couldn't see me. I was in total darkness. My girlfriend called my name and said, 'Hey, girl, where are you?'

"I walked into the light and said, 'Here I am.'

"He looked at me and said, 'You must be Michelle.'

"I said, 'Yes, I'm Michelle, but my friends call me Mike.'

"We had a great time! The weekend went so fast. The arts festival, our modem dance program, the coffee shop night where students performed with song and guitars, it was a blast! On Sunday, I walked him to the train station. We said our goodbyes. I said, 'I will write to you.' And he grabbed me by the arm and said, 'You better. I'm counting on it.' He kissed me. He jumped on the train and I waved goodbye. I literally ran all the way back to my room and screamed with joy."

Michelle pauses for a moment but then resumes. "Our letters continued and we began talking on the phone. We fell in love. He invited me to meet his family. He lived with his mother and sister in his grandfather's home, a cozy old home nicely appointed on a quiet street. His parents were divorced. His grandfather and sister were wonderful and very warm to me. His mother was not. I had done nothing except develop a romantic interest in her son. At dinner, when G left the room, his mother gave me the third degree. She did not think I was good enough to be with her son and pretty much said that to me. My background did not meet her standards. She was cordial but distant. While G was giving me a tour of his neighborhood, we stopped at his old high school. I shared with him my thoughts about his mother. He told me not to worry. He loved me.

"G was happy for my opportunity abroad, but he disliked us being so far away. Our distant relationship was working, but it was not ideal. It was hard, and sometimes our letters and phone calls were not enough. But we were making it work. He knew I had to go, and he did not discourage me."

CHAPTER SIX

AU REVOIR

Spring turned into summer and the day of Michelle's departure was upon her. Michelle tells me that on the morning of her departure, her house was a beehive of activity. Everyone was in a dither.

"My mother pretended not to be nervous, but I knew she was. She was shaping a part of her left eyebrow with a razor and hurriedly shaved off half of it. She was anxious and exasperated. She used an eyebrow pencil to make up the difference. We had to drive from our home in Chester to Kennedy International Airport in New York City in two hours, a distance of at least 111 miles, without making any stops, no traffic backups or car breakdowns. But even before getting to the airport I had to pick up my visa from a gentleman who worked at the Ugandan embassy, which meant that we had no time to lose. We needed more time, none of which we planned for. We were in a panic to make our timetable. I tried to remain calm, but I was getting nervous myself. I kept thinking about the itinerary: New York to Rome, Italy to Nairobi, Kenya to Kampala, Uganda. Wow! What a trip. What a deal!

"My luggage was packed. I squeezed an assortment of sundries, including malaria pills, aspirin, two cans of Raid, and Lysol, into two

American Tourister suitcases, one green and the other blue, and into a big yellow canvas duffel bag. I was ready. My mom would send me a trunk with additional items once I forwarded my address and telephone number. Obviously, I thought these things would be needed not knowing what I would encounter once I arrived in Uganda.

"Daddy Kake drove us to New York in his late-model green Pontiac. My mother, my sister and her boyfriend, Floyd, who was in the Navy at the time, home on leave, went with me to catch the flight. We arrived in New York City early that afternoon. My flight was scheduled to leave around 6 p.m., so there was enough time to make the essential stop at the Manhattan home of the embassy worker who had my visa. The embassy official lived in a nondescript apartment building in Manhattan. When we arrived at his apartment, he greeted us warmly and invited us all in to have a seat. We told him immediately why we were there, and to some extent he had been expecting me. This African fellow was of average height, wore glasses, and his hair was black and short with evidence of balding. But to my chagrin and the disquiet of my family, he couldn't find my visa:

"'I misplaced it,' he said sheepishly. I visually searched the room without moving from my seat.

"'Well, I am sure you will find it soon,' I said, trying not to disclose my utter annoyance with this fellow. 'Can we help you look for it?'

"'I am sure it is right around here somewhere,' he said. 'My wife will be here soon, and she will find it. She knows where everything is in this house,' he reaffirmed confidently.

"He kept looking and making small talk, but we began getting visibly nervous.

"'My flight leaves in a few hours and rush hour is approaching. Do you know when your wife will be coming?' I asked, this time with more anxiousness in my tone.

"'Soon, soon, she will be here. She will be here,' he repeated. He sensed that his ineptitude was becoming manifest. His foreign accent did him no good the longer this episode continued. When we first heard his voice, we were all impressed by it. It made the reality of traveling abroad more exotic. But now it made him look incompetent. The first hour passed and we were now in the 4 o'clock hour. The second hour was ebbing away. Rush hour was imminent, and his wife still had not returned. We had no choice but to wait until his wife came home to help him find the visa, he was incapable of finding."

Michelle continues, "When his wife finally did arrive well into the second hour, he explained the situation to her. 'Lololi,' he said, in a tone of frustration and embarrassment, 'these folks are here to pick up a visa for Uganda. Do you know where it is?' She thought for a moment and immediately went to where the document was located on top of the hutch in the dining room. This relatively short, dark-skinned African woman with black hair much longer than his but still in a rounded Afro style was a take-charge kind of person. It was apparent that she ruled the roost in that household. He was very apologetic, and we accepted his apologies. We immediately said our perfunctory thanks and left, mumbling all the while to each other how stupid the whole situation had been and how much time was lost.

"Rush hour was now in full swing and traffic was literally at a standstill. Unfamiliar with the highways, byways and shortcuts of the city, we crawled our way to the international airport just in time for me to miss my flight. G was waiting at the gate wondering what had happened to me.

"Vixena, the student from Penn with whom I had expected to travel with, made the scheduled flight and was on her way. I, however, was stuck with confusion and anxiety and the arduous task of making alternative flight arrangements. Vixena and I had discussed possible hotels for us to stay in, but no agreement had been reached, so I did not know where she would stay when she arrived in Rome. I couldn't think about that now.

"There were no other flights to Rome until the next day. My sister was living at my deceased great-aunt's home in the Bronx attending

Bronx Community College studying nursing, and my great-uncle was pleased to accommodate us. We had a final bon voyage party at his house. Unfortunately, my mother had to return home and could not stay over. I kissed her, hugged her for a whole year's worth, pulling her ever so closely, and said goodbye."

Mary had only a few misgivings about her daughter's trip. But these misgivings were allayed by her relationship with Harriett and knowing Eric gave both she and Harriett assurances that would not otherwise have been there. I asked Mary decades later what her thoughts were about this experience her daughter undertook as a young college student. With an untroubled sense of calm, she said, "I thought the experience would open doors and that Michelle would be able to meet different people, broaden her scope."

She went on to say, "Michelle was growing up and had her own ideas. She had a thinking mind and instinct to judge people. I had no fear about African people. I trusted that Michelle's instincts would help her avoid the bad people." Later, though, she said, "Michelle was going to a foreign country. Her life would be at stake; she could be killed or disappear." She stared straight into my eyes and I saw signs of tears. She went on, "I had less fear about Africa than about the wild animals there. She was a biology major." Mary's exposure to foreign travel was nil. It would not be until many years later that she would cross the Atlantic. Reflecting further, Mary said, "I always taught my girls that if that inner voice told you not to go or do something, don't you go; if you go, you would be in trouble." Mary had gotten this admonition from her mother, her Aunt Margaret, and Aunt Beatrice.

In earlier years Mary had been enthralled with *National Geographic Magazine*. Her imagination took her places she physically had not gone. She wanted for her daughter what she had not be able to experience for herself. She said she had not been brainwashed by the Tarzan movies of her era, nor had she given any thought to going back to Africa, though she was well aware of the continent and its importance in the black American experience. She was not oblivious to the current or past thinking of the Back-to-Africa movement. None of this was new to her.

Born in 1927, though she had knowledge of the events of her day with Garvey and others of like mind, Mary knew she was not going back to Africa. In fact, she said, "I never thought about it, maybe because of where I was born, in the North." She had no thought about reconnecting with her African ancestors. She recalled that her late husband, Ace—a worldly-wise man from the South of medium height and balding, richly brown skinned, who spoke with an earthy grit—once told her, "You don't know nothing about the white folks," though she said she knew about racism and prejudice. Being from the North did not shield her from these twin evils. Mary said, "My focus in those days was on raising my daughters, not on the broader picture, because of the schools I had gone to." Perhaps the school she was referring to was not a school that educated black people about their own history but an "uneducated school" of the type talked about in Dr. Carter G. Woodson's *Mis-education of the Negro.*

As Mary went on to recall the day Michelle left for Africa, her mood visibly changed, and she grew plaintive. A sadness pervaded her countenance as she said, "I was sad that my child was leaving, and I thought about the Pan Am plane she would be flying on the next day."

I asked Mary about her feelings about Harriett, her best friend, going to Africa. She said she had no fears about Harriett's safety. Folks in the street from Chester would ask Mary, "How's Harriett doing?" because Mary was the only source of information about Harriett in Chester at that time.

We concluded our talk when Mary said, "The first time she [Michelle] called it sounded like the call came from a telephone pole." She said she wondered what Michelle was doing and how she was getting along. Mary said, "Michelle wrote letters about the culture, and these letters never came close to filling the void." But what they did do was heighten her imagination, one that had already been ignited by those *National Geographic* magazines.

The next day, Michelle and her sister and her sister's boyfriend drove to the airport. G met them there. Her flight flew out of JFK International Airport, a sprawling facility located in Queens, New York. JFK is one of two international airports in New York City. The airport is filled with all of the modernisms one would expect from a first world international airport in one of the world's most sophisticated cities.

Michelle remembers, "I tried to pack everything into those final moments. My emotions were running wild. My heart was aching. The flight departure was announced, and passengers were boarding. I hugged and kissed my sister and her boyfriend goodbye. I said my final goodbye to G and we embraced for a long time. I told him I would write his name on the African shore and send him a picture.

"I turned and looked at them as I wistfully walked down the boarding ramp, and it came to mind that I was not going to see these people, the people I cared most about in the world, for a whole year. What if I never came back? What then? I began to panic. At this moment I had to reconcile my personal desire to have this experience with the pain of separation and the accompanying sorrow. All of this pulled at my heartstrings. Was all of this really worth it, the risk?

"I swiftly concluded that it was, relying on my past internal debates about this subject. I fought back my tears, but the tears did not retreat. I pretended to smile, but it was tough. I walked down the ramp and boarded the plane alone in my spirit but with hope in my heart, for I knew these people loved me and I loved them. I was alone in my thoughts but optimistic because I knew a fantastic opportunity awaited me, a new world, a new culture, even though timidity characterized my state of mind. I knew it would only be through a chary and sagacious mindset that I would survive."

CHAPTER SEVEN

ALONE BUT NOT AT HOME

Michelle harkens back to her flight to Uganda. She says, "My first transatlantic airplane trip on a Boeing Pan Am 747 was breathtaking and it was grand. Movies, soft pillows, reasonably good airline food, friendly stewardesses, and prayer got me through. My first stop was Rome, the Eternal City. My flight was eight hours and forty minutes. We landed at Leonardo da Vinci Airport, Italy's first and Europe's sixth-largest airport." This highly cosmopolitan complex has over 130 shops located throughout its many service areas.

Michelle says, "When we arrived in Rome, I exchanged some dollars for liras. The exchange rate was good approximately $1 to 625 lire. I thought I was rich, but that feeling was short lived. I soon learned that the prices the Italians charged in lira essentially equaled what I would pay in dollars for the same thing; it just took more lire. I asked about the most reasonable hotels, particularly the Hotel Diplomatic because that was one hotel I remembered on the list Vixena and I had reviewed before we embarked. I asked the cab driver to take me to the Hotel Diplomatic."

The only difference between the driving in New York City and the driving in Rome was that the drivers in Rome spoke Italian. The driving was wild and speedy. The airport was sixteen miles from the city of Rome. When she arrived at the Hotel Diplomatic, Michelle discovered a small, well-furnished boutique facility. This was an English-speaking hotel, meaning that there was always someone at the front desk that spoke English. After registering, she took the "lift," which was designed like an imposing birdcage, up to her room, unlocked the door and struggled to get her heavy bags into the room. There was no bellman to assist her with her luggage. Every guest was on their own.

Her window, which was on the opposite wall from the entrance door, overlooked a busy street below. She walked to her window, opened the louvered wood shutters and marveled at how beautiful everything was. Pretty white lace curtains hanging from the cornice blew gently from the breeze. The cityscape was green with trees, speckled with tall buildings, and motor bikes scuttled by. She says, "It was beautiful, just like in an old Doris Day movie. white pigeons flew up into the blue sky."

Back then, as now, Michelle was an avid movie fan. She probably had seen all of Doris Day's movies and remembered this scene or something like it especially. "It was picture perfect. I looked down at the street, turned around and looked at my room. Everything was so nice and pretty. I ran and fell on the bed and cried. I had traveled far from my mom and home. Now I was in Rome all by myself. What was I thinking! What was I going to do?"

Having once exhaled upon arriving, she exhaled again after entering her room and finding it pleasing to her taste. She especially liked the bathroom. She described it as "a gorgeous bathroom of white Roman Italian tile on the floor. There was a very ample pedestal sink and counter space, all white porcelain. I also had a big bathroom window." She was exhausted both mentally and physically because of the jet lag. The fleeting moment of tearfulness faded. She took a nap, and when she awoke she unpacked the clothes she expected to wear while in Italy.

Being the curious sort, her tour of the area started with a tour of the hotel. She walked slowly this time through the lobby. It was small and cozy and furnished with oversized furniture. The restaurant was in a square-shaped garden courtyard that seemed especially suitable for that time of the year. Flower urns painted white, Grecian flowerpots with hanging vines of all types and varieties dangling over their sides. Greco-Roman statuettes from three to five feet tall were placed in each corner of the garden, and a grayish-white Eolande waterfall figurine, that of a small girl whose frame was molded into a small, elegant pillar, stood prominently in the middle of the garden. A sense of elegance and peace suffused the garden as drops of water flowed from the waterfall figurine.

Michelle turned her attention to getting postcards to send to family back home. The concierge directed her to a tobacco shop a few blocks away, well within a safe walking distance. By default, her mind shifted into safety mode; her sense of vulnerability took control. And why not? A single woman alone in a foreign city, anything could happen.

Michelle describes her experience visiting the Vatican: "The next day I took the bus to the Vatican. It was an unbelievable sight. It appeared to resemble the contours of a sundial, perhaps representing the eternal light that beams from the spirit of God upon all peoples of the world, providing hope, life and refuge. Saint Peter's Square, with the statues of saints in a semicircular form embracing the large piazza, was awe inspiring, as was the Basilica of Saint Peter itself. I felt I was dreaming: was I really there, standing there?

"I took several pictures and proceeded to the church. As I entered, I felt I had walked into heaven and experienced a religious moment. I automatically bowed and said a prayer of thanksgiving. I had plenty to thank God for: the safe flight, my hotel accommodations, and being there in His presence in such a beautiful cathedral, not to mention the life I was fortunate to have, the family that loved and nurtured me, and the gift of education I was receiving. I wanted to sit up front in the pews.

"As I walked toward that area, a priest confronted me and advised that I could not proceed any farther because of the length of the dress I was wearing. Unbeknownst to me, this advisement would be a harbinger of things to come. Unwisely I had worn a miniskirt. He felt it was inappropriate for the church. As he spoke, I saw how unthinking I had been—of course this was improper dress! I pleaded with the priest, telling him that I had traveled far, all the way from America to see the church, and that I did not intend to offend. He understood and allowed me to pass.

"In retrospect, I am sure that this was not an uncommon experience for the custodians of the basilica. Luckily, I had a light jacket, which I wrapped around my waist. I covered up my exposed thighs as best I could. After a joyful prayer, I stood in front of the Pieta, a Renaissance statue sculpted by Michelangelo of the Virgin Mary holding the dead body of Jesus Christ. A maudlin mood overtook me as I looked at the sculpture. I was overcome for many reasons: the pressure, the reality and my faith all converged. I thought not only about the sacred story but also about myself; I longed for my mother's arms to surround me. After all, there's nothing like the reassurance of a mother's touch. I looked up at the ceilings, the stained glass and the statues, and I felt that maybe man was indeed attempting to reach high enough to touch God if that were possible. Like in the tower of Babel, man was desperately trying to reach God in the firmaments. And I too was trying to build my 'City of God,' but I was daunted and perplexed by the divergent emotions twirling within me, and so I was scattered, emotionally unable to speak to myself in one language.

"The cathedral transformed me. Although St. Peter's was full of tourists and local worshippers, I felt it was just me and God. I felt the solemnity of the moment there, all alone and without one plea.

As the well-known Baptist hymn recites: 'Just as I am, without one plea, but that thy blood was shed for me and that thou bidd'st me come to thee O lamb of God I come, I come . . .' I spoke to God that day. I prayed for safety in my travels as I continued my adventure alone and that my decisions and my thinking would be prudent, assuring my safety.

"Several hours had gone by, and I had not moved from my pew. After seeing the Sistine Chapel, I wanted to fall on my knees and shout, 'Hallelujah' just as my great-aunt Honey had screamed before succumbing to death at the funeral of her sister, my great-aunt Bea. She had seen what I was seeing: God."

As a child raised by a single mother, Michelle sought refuge in religion. It offered her solace for the familial and emotional losses she sustained as she made her way through life singularly, save for the love of her mother and sister. Her losses were lessened by the love of a dedicated mother, the love and caring attention of her sister and two great-aunts, and the presence of a sincere male family friend.

The bleak and sometimes desolated plain on which life's struggles are played out requires the refuge of religion for some people. In Michelle's case, the absence of a father in her life did not necessarily make her stronger as Nietzsche would attest. But, as Marx would propound, "Religion is the sigh of oppressed people," a means to assuage or to put a salve on the open wounds from life's arrows. Except for a few, aren't we all refugees to a certain extent, coping with the immutable challenges of life and the certainty of death, seeking some sanctuary or understanding? Michelle's life required that she work hard, be provident, circumspect and have faith. She is the incarnation of the female Horatio Alger, working to pull herself up by her bootstraps.

After the serenity of the religious experience at the Vatican, Michelle returned to her hotel room. She purchased some niceties and went for a walk window shopping. As she shifted her focus from herself to the clothes she was admiring in the window, she recalls, "I noticed that people were not only smiling at me, but they were staring at me. I looked at my reflection in a store window: a young black woman, Afro, T-shirt, jeans, wire-framed glasses, nothing usual, a typical American." She says, "I began feeling as if someone was touching me. I looked down and several children ages seven to about nine had surrounded me and had their hands touching me on my back, stomach and breasts. It felt like something was crawling all over me. Their gentle fingers, though soft, were foreign and unfamiliar." She explains that the slight but noticeable pressure these tiny fingers exerted against her body shocked her physically, and she was stunned emotionally that something like this could be happening to her. She adds, "It was so unexpected. I shrieked, 'Get off me! Get off me! Get away, get away, and get out of here!' I shooed them away like the pests they were. After my screams, the children scattered like small birds frightened by the approach of danger. Reflexively I ran as fast as I could back to the security of the hotel and to my room.

"I lay on the bed for a while and bemoaned the incident. After regaining my composure, I thought about what had just happened. I said to myself, *we are living in the twentieth century, aren't we?* Had these people never seen a black person before? Is Europe so white that it cannot fathom color, so ethnocentric that it cannot accept other cultures or think for a moment that other cultures, races and ethnicities exist? The answers must be 'yes' and 'maybe.'"

Perhaps in reality these kids were not good examples of European exposure to people of color. And what the kids did was simply explore something that was new to them at their young ages. But touching Michelle without her permission was not acceptable under any circumstances, to her or anyone else.

Michelle's experience in Rome during the summer of 1972 recalls the experience I had while visiting Russia several years ago. Some Russian people stared at me as though I were an oddity they had never seen before. The experience is unforgettable. It is unbelievable. But should it be? There are many localities in the white world and in

North Asia that have never had contact, absolutely none, or limited interactions at best with people of sub-Saharan color. It is hard to imagine, but it is a fact. In the age of technology, the world we live in at first glance appears to be so small, yet vast spatial differences exist even today. Black presence in some white societies or in some Asian societies is not *ordinaire*, regular. We are present in the Americas because of actions and misdeeds taken centuries ago. If some of these enclaves never met black people or could rid themselves of those that are present, I believe they would; our purpose has been served.

CHAPTER EIGHT

WHEN IN ROME, DO AS THE ROMANS DO

O ur train steadily makes its way toward New York. Because of the silver façade of the coach, one could call this train the "silver streak." The conductor continues, "The dining car will close when we reach the Washington DC station. The bathrooms will not operate when the train is in the Washington DC terminal." Pause. "Three minutes to Washington DC. Three minutes."

The train changes its engine from a diesel engine to an electric engine at the Washington DC terminal because the train lines north of DC are electrified. This allows the trains to move much faster along the track and has additional safety benefits. We will be stopped in Washington DC for about thirty minutes while the engines are changed, and new passengers board the train.

After the engine changes, Michelle returns to her story:

"*Enough with the crying and self-pity already*, I said to myself. *This is an adventure; this is an adventure.* I kept repeating those words to reassure myself and pump up my courage. I began hearing my mother's words: 'Just be safe, careful, use your head and continue to think for yourself.'"

Michelle describes how she summoned up her "verve" and her will to move forward.

"I decided to ask the hotel desk clerk if another black American female student by the name of Vixena Brown was staying at the hotel. It was a slim chance that she would be, but I figured I would ask anyway. The desk clerk surprisingly said yes. I couldn't believe it. *Hey, great!* I said to myself. I was both comforted and reassured that I had made the right hotel choice. We were in the same hotel. I hadn't seen her since my arrival. She was out, the man said. But he would ring me when she returned. When Vixena and I finally got together, we shared our experiences. I suggested we share the same hotel room to save money. She had twin beds in her room as opposed to the one full bed in mine. But to my surprise she said no. 'I might meet someone while I am here,' she said.

"I asked, 'Who are you going to meet in Rome? You don't know anyone.'

"She winked and said, 'You never know.'

"Vixena was clearly more worldly than me, and this was probably not her first trip abroad. Her signal that she was out for 'whatever' was disconcerting because that was the last thing I was thinking about. Vixena and I enjoyed our time together, sightseeing and eating ice cream cones. We met some interesting people. At our hotel, we met a black American couple from Englewood, California, who were on their honeymoon, and we saw them again at the Trevi Fountain. We also met a white American woman who was a teacher. She had wonderful brown-and-white Collie dogs. She said that she enjoyed the city and her stay there but stated that her neighbors were suspicious of her because she was young, single and living alone. She said that she tutored some of her students in her apartment, which gave the neighbors more to gossip about.

"Toward the end of the week, we met some black American guys who were driving in a van touring Europe as far as they could go—by road. It appeared that Vixena had met them earlier because she was very friendly with one of the guys. But she acted as if she had just met them. They asked us to join them on their road trip, and Vixena was aching to go. She was flirtatious and took more risk than I was willing to take. I had not suspected that she was that way until I asked her about sharing her room. From then on, I was 'on notice.'"

Michelle elaborates, "So it was not a shock that she was promoting an encounter with one of the guys. She grabbed his hands and said, 'Let me talk to her' as if she would have some persuasive power over me. She rubbed his back and then pulled me to the side. She was a poli-sci [political science] major and was used to serving up nonsense and crapola. She was of the view that we could tour some places around Europe with these guys and return to Rome in time for our flight to Africa. It would only be two days. She said, 'Hey, these are some good guys and they are Georgetown graduates,' as if that gave them instant credibility, but it did not. At least not with me.

"The thought that this woman had the gall to think that she could persuade me to do something that was against my best interest and my basic nature rankled me. After all, her values were not my values. Who she slept with was her business, not mine. Character not charisma was more important to me; plus, I didn't even know these guys. My mother's advice swelled in my mind. 'Just be safe, careful, use your head and continue to think for yourself.' They could rape us and leave us stranded someplace. How would we get help and get back to where we were supposed to be? Then what? Perhaps I was being too cautious, but my sense of vulnerability was my state of mind.

"I did not want her to go for her own safety. But if she decided to go, that was her decision. Vixena was furious with me.

"She stated, 'I have a boyfriend at home too. But we are not home! Right? And isn't this part of the adventure of being in Europe and traveling? You meet new people. This is Rome and you do as the Romans do.'

"*What does that mean?* I said to myself. *Is this what the Romans do? Go off with people they don't know? I think not.*

"Vixena continued in this way. 'Do you really think your precious G is going to wait until you return home? That he is not going to date and have other relationships? You must be living in Disneyland,' she wailed. Her last comment about G really hurt me. The truth of her assertion was not unreasonable; nevertheless, I still was not going with them. I had only known Vixena for less than a year, and I owed her no further explanation. If she wanted to go, she could go. Her judgement was on the line, not mine.

"Upon reflection she realized that she had struck the wrong chord with her comment about G. In her zeal to sell the outing, she had gone too far and tried to smooth things over to no avail. She was persistent. She did not give up. She urged again, 'C'mon, girl, go with us, at least for dinner tonight, since it is the guys' last night in town.' She wanted to be with her 'Billy.' I held fast again. I said no. And then I said goodbye, *ciao*. In retrospect, how far could we have traveled if today was their last day in Rome? It made little sense.

"I could not understand her priorities. I did not travel across the Atlantic to a wonderful place like Rome with so many sites to see to—instead of touring these sites—spend time with some guys from the States. Spending time with some guys from the States was not a unique experience; you could do that at home, at any time. Sure, if G was there, it would have been a fantastic trip. Sharing these new places with someone you love is the grandest thing. Rome is a romantic place and the sights and sounds are overwhelming. But G was not there, and I was not interested in some quick fling as a substitute."

Michelle returned to the hotel and had dinner with the honeymooners, who were leaving the next day. Afterward, she went to her room and readied herself for bed. She called Vixena's room, but she did not answer. Before the encounter with the guys, they had made plans to see the Roman ruins and the Colosseum the next day. She decided that if she didn't hear from Vixena, she would go by herself. She reminded herself that everybody was doing their own thing. She forced herself to face the reality of adulthood, the reality of travel—that you are on your own when traveling, and to make of it what you will.

She didn't see Vixena until the following evening. Vixena said she was exhausted from her evening out with the guys. They had found another single woman at a club and had a great foursome. They were going out that evening since the guys would be leaving soon. For some reason, Vixena decided not to travel with them. Vixena never mentioned anything about missing the tours they had scheduled that day and neither did Michelle. That was fine with Michelle.

Michelle says, "As soon as you take a firm stand and do what is best for you, putting yourself first before them and their screwy plans, they get an attitude. What I felt was missing was honesty. She appeared to be onstage and playing a part with me. I let her play that part, whatever role she was playing. It was her life, not mine. From that point on, I could tell something had changed in our relationship. Vixena was still nice and we had a great time, but something was missing. People are funny. If they can manipulate you and get you to do what they want, they are happy."

Was this a harbinger of things to come, a metaphor for the experience Michelle was about to have? A small incident that might mirror a greater realization about truth and falsity, reality and fantasy and self-determination? Outside coercion and atmospherics must yield to self-interest, and self-interest must pierce the veil of illusion. To get to Africa was the objective, but what did it all mean in the broader context of her personal reality? In her life beyond this experience and her ability to separate a yearning from a need?

Of all the places and attractions she visited in Rome during this stopover, she most enjoyed the Trevi Fountain with the god Oceanus, the god of water surrounding the earth in the niche, and, of course, the Spanish Steps, *Scalina Spagna*, overlooking the Eternal City, where people of all ages gathered to sit and reflect, or to be with a loved one or to just pass the day observing people, her favorite pastime. She thought of how fortunate she was to have this opportunity, realizing more keenly that this was indeed an opportunity of a lifetime. Even though she traveled alone, she realized much in return. She was way ahead of the risk-reward balance. God's handiwork was visible in so many places there. She hoped she would be able to visit there again sometime in the future. Twenty years later, her fortunes allowed her to revisit Rome, and nothing had changed. Its scenic beauty and the majesty of its edifices were still as she remembered them.

Michelle's sojourn to Uganda, for a young black woman with little exposure to the wider world and with high security needs, would be "a profile in courage," undaunted by trepidation, an act of bravery wrapped in a shroud of timidity.

CHAPTER NINE

BOUND FOR THE PROMISED LAND

Harriett had not accompanied Michelle to Europe en route to Uganda during the summer of 1972. Harriett, at this time between 1970 and 1972, was in graduate school at Columbia University in New York City working on her master's degree in education. She had been on the faculty at Widener University in Chester, Pennsylvania, since 1968. To pursue her master's degree, Harriett asked for and was given a leave of absence for this purpose—the first of two leaves of absence. After she completed the master's program at Columbia, she returned to Widener to resume her teaching career until 1975.

Eric, whom she married in 1971, was back in Uganda teaching at Makerere University in his beloved mathematics department. Eric did not stay in the United States during the time that Harriett resumed her teaching career at Widener between 1972 and 1975, preferring to return to Uganda because he had been in the United States for over seven years, working to obtain his bachelor of science in mathematics from Franklin and Marshall University in Lancaster, Pennsylvania. When Eric was studying at Franklin and Marshall, he stayed with a white Pennsylvania Dutch couple. After he left Franklin and Marshall, the couple stayed in touch with him and with Harriett for a long time. During this time, the couple bought them food and money to help support them.

Uganda paid for Eric's education in the United States. He was loyal to his country and respected the sacrifices his country, a poor country, had made for him. He owed them.

Harriett fell in love with Eric and he with her between the time she first began teaching at Widener and during her study at Columbia to obtain her master's degree. Harriett and Eric had classes together when they were at Columbia, both pursuing their master's degrees—his in mathematics and hers in education.

When Eric and Harriett agreed to marry, they reached a compromise, as married folks do, that they would alternate every five years between Uganda and the United States because Eric did not want to live permanently in the United States. A host of concerns, not the least of which involved his love for his native country, gave Eric a reason for pause: coping with the onslaught of Americana, with its vacuous pop culture, fads and trends, and sinews of high culture reserved for a select few, that promoted a Eurocentric culture to the exclusion of all others, and for a multitude of other reasons.[16] During the course of their marriage, Harriett bought a home on West Seventeenth Street in Chester, Pennsylvania. Eric came to visit as often as he could. Eric had an office in that house, and Harriett remembered seeing him in his pajamas working in his office there.

Harriett and Eric often discussed how their students acted in the classes they taught. Harriett told Eric how energetic her African students had been, how seriously they took their work. "They do everything you ask of them to do," she said, compared to some of her American students who "complained about everything but wanted the A." Eric, after receiving his master's degree, taught as an adjunct professor at Hunter College, a sister college in the City University of the New York system, a collegiate university. Eric responded that he was so strict and his students so industrious that they had to ask him if they could cough. Eric said his students had a seriousness of purpose. Between the two of them, Eric was the martinet.

An excerpt from a translated poem by Léopold Sédar Senghor entitled "A New York"[17] captures the essence of Eric's New York experience:

> New York! At first your beauty confused me, and your great long-legged golden girls.
> I was so timid at first under your blue metallic eyes, your frosty smile
> So timid. And the disquiet in the depth of your skyscrapers streets
>
> Lifting up owl eyes in the sun's eclipse.
> Your sulfurous light and the livid shafts (their heads dumbfounding the sky)
> Skyscrapers defying cyclones on their muscles of steel and their weathered stone skins.
> But a fortnight on the bald sidewalks of Manhattan.
> —At the end of the third week, the fever takes you with the pounce of a jaguar.
> A fortnight with no well or pasture, all of the birds of the air
> Fall suddenly dead below the high ashes of the terraces.
> No child's laughter blossoms, his hand in my fresh hand. No mother's breast.
> Legs and nylon. Legs and breasts with no sweat and no smell.
> No tender word for mouths are lipless.
> Hard cash buys artificial hearts. No book where wisdom is read.

The painter's palette flowers with crystals of coral.
Insomniac nights O nights of Manhattan, tormented
by fatuous fires while the Klaxons cry through the
empty hours.
And dark waters bear away hygienic gloves like the
bodies of children on a river in flood.

The use of culture for political purposes is not new. "Art for art's sake" has not, even in recent times, been a primary facet of African-American cultural critiques. Consider the prominent sociologist, William Edward Burghardt Du Bois, an American of African descent who was foremost a sociologist, a historian, Pan-Africanist and prolific writer. It was W. E. B. Du Bois who said, "All art is propaganda."[18] Alain Locke, a former preeminent professor of philosophy at Howard University, also postulated that propaganda was a tool to enshrine black inferiority and argued for a wider goal for black art to dispel this notion. And finally, the noted Columbia University professor Edward W. Said, an Israeli Arab and an American citizen, postulated in his book *Culture and Imperialism* that art, literature and other products of high culture are reflections of imperialist culture to the detriment of non-Europeans.[19] So with Du Bois and Locke of the 1920s and Said of the 1990s, we have a concurrence of opinion. Though separated by over seventy years, their views about the use of culture are similar. As we have seen before in other aspects of African-American modern history, ideas propagated early on continue to reverberate, to resonate, if you will, throughout the spectrum of African-American life.

In order to maintain his African cultural fidelity, Eric chose not to become ensnared in or captured by these cultural debates, even though he understood them very well. Eric doubted that, when he died, Harriett would bury him in his native land. He wanted his bones to "bleach in the soil of Uganda." Years later in a meditatively doleful conversation with me, Harriett said that Eric was prescient because she might not have honored his wishes and buried him in Uganda had he predeceased her. She spoke of several reasons why in hindsight his wish might not have been honored: the death of her mother, the estrangement of his family from her, and the political upheaval that went on in Ugandan politics. But to Eric this issue was *élan vital*, an important concern. To be buried in his homeland was as important as having been born there; it was no passing fancy. Years later, on a trip to Ghana, Michelle and I were shown a burial site where a husband and wife who were African-Americans of Ghanaian descent had their remains interred in a cemetery in Ghana.

Harriett's visit to Uganda soon after they married not only acquainted her with Eric's family, but also afforded her the opportunity to see what work, if any, she could get in Uganda to further her professional aspirations. She concluded that she could find suitable work there. So, Harriett knew that, after finishing her doctorate, a life in Africa with her husband was feasible, but not guaranteed.

During her visit to Uganda, Harriett met with local nurses and nurses high up in the Ugandan bureaucracy. After all, she was a nurse from a prestigious American university. She determined that obtaining a job would not be an issue, except for one insurmountable problem: to live and work permanently in Uganda would require that she give up her United States citizenship, which she was not prepared to do. She certainly wanted to stay in Africa, but the price was too high. She had just been admitted to the PhD program at Columbia.

Three thousand air miles to the north, Michelle was about to end her stay in Rome.

After what amounted to a fantastic stay in Rome, it was time for Michelle to depart. Her experience in the Eternal City would last a lifetime. This time, she arrived at the airport on time for her flight.

Michelle recalls, "Vixena and I would be on the same flight, so that meant that I would not be traveling alone. The sights and sounds of the gate area were unforgettable. Most of the passengers were Africans. Their smiles and comradery were infectious. It put everyone in a joyous mood. Singing broke out as well as hugs and laughter. The various African dialects exposed in the common chatter permeated the area like a glue that adhered to everyone.

"I could not distinguish one dialect from the other. They all sounded exotic to me. *Are we there yet?* I asked myself. We had not even left the airport, but it felt as though we were already there. We were bound for Africa, the motherland, the promised land for all of those who sought its bounty."

I visualize this scene and feel the spirit of reunion, the coming together of kindred souls—native Africans and the lost ones, "the stolen ones" from America, as Harriett had been labeled. Back to the womb they were going, especially those that had been expelled prematurely. Time stands still in those moments. Mother Africa extends her open arms, beckoning us to come, waiting for us to embrace her steadfastness. She is there, as she has been from the beginning of time.

Michelle continues, "My flight to Uganda was by way of Nairobi, Kenya. From there I flew on East African Airlines[5*] to Entebbe Airport in Kampala, Uganda, my destination. Though I did not know it at the time, Nairobi would figure greatly in my future activities. As the plane approached the Jomo Kenyatta Airport in Nairobi, I saw Africa for the first time to know what I was looking at. The land was green, brown and blue. The land was enormous and enveloping. As the plane came closer to land, the trees and the ground came more sharply into view, and the reality that I had arrived in Africa was epochal, yet it seemed apocryphal at the same time. In short, I could not believe I was there, but I was. I was giddy. I pinched myself to make sure this was my reality, and I smiled, not knowing what to make of it all.

[5*] An airline established in 1946 run by a consortium of three countries, Tanzania, Kenya and Uganda.

"When we landed at Jomo Kenyatta International Airport[6*] in Embakasi, a suburb of Nairobi, the sky was blue with only thin white stratus clouds immediately visible. Beyond them, as I gazed at the clear sky, were cumulus clouds with rounded sun-like shapes. This was an African airport, not a European or American airport. As I walked to the terminal I inhaled deeply. My excitement distorted my sense of smell and I imagined the faint smell of a rain forest tinctured by a whiffle of urban refuse."

Inside the airport, a small facility comparatively, the usual stations for checking in and baggage claim were all there, but she noticed that the smell of the place was different. Instead of no smell or the smell of perfumes, this airport had a tropical smell, a smell dissimilar to any that she had smelled before. Perhaps her senses were keener with the expectation of seeing new flora and fauna. Not knowing what the smell was, she guessed perhaps the smell was that of a rain forest, of pine cones and damp leaves mixed with the smell of the fragrant yellow leopard orchid, a flower native to some East African countries. As a biology major and in her preparation for the trip, she read about some of the native plants and trees of East Africa.

Michelle remembers, "We hugged our companions and said our goodbyes. Each of us wishing the other safe travels, and some even wished Vixena and me a 'happy year' in Uganda. I thought to myself, as if realizing for the first time, *I am going to be over here in 'this land' for a whole year*. I knew it intellectually, but now I realized it spatially.

"After a short layover, Vixena and I boarded our flight to Entebbe Airport in Kampala. This was a short flight of one hour and five minutes. Our plane was of lesser stock, a regional jet. I immediately noticed the uniforms of the stewards and stewardesses. They were dressed in khaki-colored blouses, skirts and trousers with caps trimmed in a leopard-skin motif. I thought at the time that this was very 'African,' a safari look emphasizing that this was Africa.

[6*] An airport opened in 1958 when Kenya was still under English colonial rule.

You are in Africa now, Michelle, I told myself. Upon our arrival at Entebbe Airport, an airport of less size than the one in Nairobi, the atmospherics changed."

Entebbe Airport was made famous on July 4, 1976. It was on that date that the Israeli government, under the leadership of Yitzhak Rabin, the Israeli prime minister, dispatched 200 Israeli special forces along with aircraft to rescue more than 248 passengers, not including a twelve-member French crew taken hostage by the Popular Front for the Liberation of Palestine and the German Revolutionary Cells, an offshoot of the German radical left-wing group Baader-Meinhof. The Baader-Meinhof gang, also known as the Red Army, was considered a terrorist group by Germany and caused that country much consternation and trouble for over three decades prior to and during this time. Idi Amin was the leader of Uganda when the rescue mission took place. It is alleged that Amin was complicit in the hostage taking, but this allegation, though possibly true, conflicts with other facts.

The Israeli commando raid was top secret and viewed as an invasion of a sovereign country by most of the world. But since Amin was viewed as such a detestable despot and Uganda did not have the military forces to repel such an invasion, the world sanctioned the rescue mission, which was successful. In a recent article published in the *Washington Post*,[7*] this event is revisited. A commemoration of the event included the current president of Uganda, Museveni, and the current Israeli prime minister, Benjamin Natanyahu. The *Post* article makes prominent mention of the fact that Mr. Natanyahu's brother, a leader of the commandos, was killed during the raid.

Upon arrival Michelle discovered that "things were now less friendly and more official." The slack that had been present in her relations with other African travelers was now tautened by a sternness of sorts. When she exited the plane, she had to stand in a long line that moved slowly as each person's luggage and passport was checked and approved. This was her first real introduction to

---

7 * Ruth English, July 5, 2016.

African culture and the way business was done in Uganda. Things moved slowly and patience was required by all unaccustomed to such a dawdling pace. Many books have been written about the difference between how Western countries and non-Western countries view the importance of time.

When her time came to be processed, she handed over her luggage to the immigration agent. The agent was dressed in a greenish brown military-style uniform made up of pants, a belt and a shirt with epaulets on it. His belt was black and shiny, as were his shoes, though a bit scuffed up. His skin color was dark. Much darker than Michelle's. Clearly Michelle's skin color was not sub-Saharan. She wondered what the official might be looking for in her luggage as he rummaged through her possessions, disarranging her neatly folded clothes and neatly placed sundries.

When he put his hands on her very personal items, she was appalled: "No, No! What are you doing? Get your hands off my things! Don't touch that; those are my personal things!" She looked him straight in the eyes and stood her ground against the foreign invasion into her personal belongings, but the reality was that *she* was viewed as the foreign invader, an intruder from America. The agent's countenance inferred his displeasure and implied, "How dare you come to this country and tell us what to do and how to act!" She says she was scared and intimidated by his apparent authority, the harshness of his tone and his austere approach. She was starkly reminded that she was no longer in Kenya at the Nairobi airport where procedures were more genteel.

After this inauspicious encounter, the officious agent waved her through. For the life of her, she just could not fathom the need for such an intrusion into her privacy. She was new at this "world-traveling thing" and was unaccustomed to the customs and security requirements of different countries, especially those in the African continent. A dose of reality upon arrival. *What was the need for all of this?* she wondered. *Did he think I was smuggling dope into the country?* Such a hubbub over nothing, as far as she was concerned.

The Entebbe Airport is near the town of Entebbe, a town in central Uganda with a population of less than 80,000. The airport is not far from the coast of Lake Victoria, Africa's largest lake by area and one of Africa's great lakes, a basin of which is in Uganda. Uganda forms a part of the East African Rift. "The Great Lakes region" is formed by Kenya, Rwanda, Tanzania, the Democratic Republic of Congo, Uganda and Burundi.[20] As she would soon learn, the airport was thirty miles from Kampala where Makerere University was located—her home for the next year.

Kampala, the capital city, "the Hill of the Impala," a slender antelope, is a bustling metropolis of seven hills. It is the largest city in Uganda with a population of 1.7 million people. The single largest ethnic group is the Baganda, a Bantu ethnic group from the central part of Uganda also known as Buganda, the largest subnational tribal kingdom in the country—essentially an administrative division within the country.[21]

Makerere University was established in 1922 as a technical co-educational school. It soon evolved into a school offering a variety of academic courses in a multitude of disciplines, including agriculture, medical services, engineering, arts and humanities, the social sciences, language and cultural studies and a school of law. It is Uganda's largest university and one of Africa's most prestigious universities. Makerere is also the alma mater of some of Africa's noted leaders, including Apollo Milton Obote, a political leader of Uganda who led the country to independence and the second president of Uganda until he was deposed by Idi Amin in 1971, and also of Julius Nyerere, a former president of Tanzania, among several others. The university currently has ten schools and colleges serving 3,000 postgraduates and 35,000 undergraduates. The university awards both undergraduate and graduate degrees.

Michelle got to the university by way of an eight-passenger yellow-blue-and-white jitney with luggage in hand. The vehicle was a cross between a van and a small school bus with an assortment of painted twirls and swirls in other colors and with a luggage rack on its top. Upon arrival, Michelle explained that she and Vixena discovered that all of the administrative offices were closed because they had arrived on the weekend. They had been assigned to stay in African Hall, one of three dormitories for women on campus, the others being Mary Stuart Hall[8*] and Complex Hall. But because of the weekend, African Hall was not open. A male student stepped forward to help them. He was an accommodating fellow. A man of modest height, with hair cut close but not bald, dark skinned and with glistening white teeth.

He said, "Ladies, do you need help? Can I help you? I am a student here. What are you looking for? Where do you want to go?" His accent was very British.

"Yes, yes, we just arrived from the United States," they both said almost in unison. "We are to study here for a year," Michelle said as Vixena stood beside her, seeking understanding, implicitly pleading for help, and thinking about what to do next. Staying at a hotel for the weekend did not seem realistic. This was not, after all, New York City, although there were hotels in the city that would probably have accommodated them. *These folks should have expected us*, she thought critically.

"We cannot get into our dormitory," she explained.

"Which dormitory is it?" he asked.

Michelle looked at her papers to confirm her information, and Vixena looked at her own papers. "African Hall."

"Well, that building is over there." He identified an august building across the campus from where they were standing. "But it is closed because of the weekend." Back then, African Hall was a brick multistory women's dormitory surrounded by a six-foot decorative wrought iron fence within which were built several adjoining buildings.

---

8 * The residence hall was named for Mary Stuart, wife of Bishop Stuart, who worked to enhance women's education in Uganda in the 1950s.

His assertion did not tell them anything new. She and Vixena already knew that African Hall was closed! However, as an alternative, the helpful student took Michelle and Vixena to Mary Stuart Hall. But when they arrived, the guard refused to open a large imposing wrought iron gate, preventing their entry onto the grounds of Mary Stuart Hall.

Michelle recalls, "The security guard nonchalantly told us to go home and come back tomorrow. He was much taller than our friendly upper-class student. The security guard was thin and slender, his English tortured, his hair unkempt, and his untutored officiousness overbearing. You could tell he was from the working class. He had a bony face with high cheekbones. His hair, however, was similar in grade to that of our upperclassman friend. The skin color of the guard was also like that of our friend: deep, dark, rich and black.

"By his manner and his approach, we could tell that he took pride in his position, in his job. It meant something to him. We told him, with the help of the male student, that we had come a long way, from another part of the world, and that we could not go back home. The male student argued with the guard, or at least it seemed that way, and made him realize how impractical his demand was, and reluctantly the guard opened the gate. Soon thereafter, we were given our keys and we went to our rooms."

Exhaustion was an understatement. It had been quite a day so far, and the day was not over. So, with help from a resourceful African male student and a big fuss with a security guard, Michelle and Vixena were allowed to stay temporarily in Mary Stuart Hall.

Michelle says "I thought to myself, my African journey is now in full swing. I will be here for a full year until 1973! What would be my next experience?"

CHAPTER TEN

A ROOM WITH A VIEW

I am a stone covered by ruins. I am an island hooded like a falcon by guano. I am a pyramid planted by a dynasty vanished from all memory a herd of elephants a mosquito bite a small city ... Face of man you will not budge you are caught in the ferocious coordinates of my wrinkles.

Aimé Césaire, "Solid"

Michelle remembers, "To get to our room in Mary Stuart Hall, Vixena and I had to climb a flight of circular concrete stairs inside the building and walk down the outside walkway to what looked like a motel wing." She describes a building with finished, gray, concrete stairs that were smooth and tight. The modest dormitory was a seven-story, rectangular, garden-style apartment building of cast-in-place exterior walls. A four-foot white, wrought-iron railing system supported by white, wrought-iron balusters extended the width of the building. Every six to eight feet, a slim cement pillar extended from the roof of the building to just above the ceiling of the ground floor. A similar wrought-iron decoration extended from the porch ceiling of each story down approximately two to three feet directly above the bottom railing system, resembling a Spanish-style façade.

Michelle recalls, "When I opened the door to my room and walked in, I was struck by the unadorned utility of the room. The size of the room was approximately seven by ten feet. On the left as you entered was an open closet with wide shelves and a metal rod below for hanging clothes. The bed was on the same side of the room as the closet with space beyond the head of the bed for a chair if I had an additional one. There was a built-in desk and a desk chair across from the bed against the opposite wall, and bookshelves, one of which held a fluorescent tube that illuminated the desk. There were no windows because this was an exterior room with only a small balcony at the back, separated by a sliding door covered with thin, rose-colored drapes.

"The balcony came with a small round table and a metal chair. It had been swept clean. From my balcony, I could see the African countryside, a bucolic pastoral scene of small white houses, thatched huts and an array of structures serving one purpose or another, all on brown-orange dirt. I took a moment to appreciate the view.

"After I settled in and took a deep breath, I realized that this room, not the one I had been assigned to in African Hall, would be my room for the duration of my one-year stay. I set about making the room suitable for my tastes. My heightened sense of cleanliness required that I clean my room as thoroughly as I could, in order to calm my anxieties about the condition of things and how they might have been used before I got there. I brought a can of Lysol with me and I used it to wipe down all of the furniture, including my bed and the mattress. Terrified of bugs, I used the can of Raid that I also brought with me to spray under the bed and into every crevice I could find. I imagined that in Africa the bugs would be bigger and more aggressive. Using the bed linens I brought with me, I made up my bed and placed some of my clothing on the closet shelves. My toiletries and cleaning supplies I placed on other shelves in the closet, and I set my suitcases on the floor at the bottom of the closet. My books and pencils, clock and notebooks I put on my desk.

"Finally, I decided at some point to get some African material to make a curtain to cover my clothes and toiletries. Later I would place a throw rug on the side of my bed and decided to get some posters and other artifacts to add flair to the room.

"The bathroom was at the end of the walkway. An interlocking door system secured the bathroom area with locking doors separating the bath area from the water closet. I made sure that I locked all the doors, especially the outside door, to prevent any intrusion. What alarmed me the most was the fact that passersby could see you entering as well as leaving your room. This was unsettling to say the least and required some getting used to."

After exploring all of the essential accommodations, Michelle says she ventured out to explore the other parts of the dormitory. The flight of stairs from her floor led down to the lobby area where the wooden mail slots were located. Big green plants were placed around the corners of the room. The lobby had a television, tables, couches and chairs. The dormitory was a nicely appointed building. She was not surprised but took note; after all, she reminded herself, this was one of Africa's leading universities. She was excited to be there and wanted to make the best of her experience. The dormitory contained a dining facility, and an adjoining section of the dormitory contained all interior rooms. That was where she preferred to be.

The security guard that initially resisted their entry into the dormitory turned out to be an important cog in the wheel of life in the dormitory. He controlled the entrance to the dorm and supervised the mail and the telephones for local as well as long-distance calls. He was, in essence, a de facto concierge. A man of stature. She acknowledged him with a smile to show respect, and he responded in kind. From that point on, they grew to have a mutual respect for each other.

CHAPTER ELEVEN

OH, WHAT A BEAUTIFUL MORNING

I must hide in the intimate depths of my veins
The Ancestor storm-dark skinned, shot with lightning and thunder
And my guardian animal, I must hide him
Lest I smash through the boom of scandal.
He is my faithful blood and demands fidelity
Protecting my naked pride against
Myself and all the insolence of lucky races

Léopold Sédar Senghor, "Totem"

Uganda, the "Land of the Ganda," is a landlocked country in East Africa about two times the size of Pennsylvania, bordered by South Sudan to the north, Kenya to the east, the Democratic Republic of the Congo on the west and Rwanda and Tanzania on the south. The former president of Tanzania was a graduate of Makerere University, as was the president of the DRC, Joseph Kabila. The country is known as the "pearl" of Africa, a name bestowed upon it by Winston Churchill because of its beauty and its topography *inter alia*, its beautiful lakes, mountains and verdant valleys as well as its moderate climate. The population of Uganda is approximately 40 million. When Michelle visited Uganda the population was approximately 10 million. And it has had one of the highest birth rates of any country in the world.

Between 1889 and 1897, the kabaka, the king, was Mwanga II Mukasa, a man with richly melanated skin and Arabic bearing. He was a striking man—tall, dark and handsome in appearance. His skin reflected his indigenous African phenotype. This son of Muteesa I of Buganda sought successfully during the time of his reign to balance the religious power struggle among the Islamists, Catholics and Christians. Mwanga II, however, was also the leader who tried to expel the Catholics and the Christians from his country. To his credit, Mwanga II adamantly refused to sign over his kingdom to the British.

Uganda fell under the British sphere of influence during the prelude to European colonization of Africa. On December 18, 1890, in stepped the deus ex machina in the form of Frederick John Dealtry Lugard to resolve a problem the British found somewhat intractable. Lugard was a British soldier who later would become the British colonial administrator for the kingdom of Buganda. He established his headquarters in Kampala on a picturesque belvedere now known as Old Kampala Hill. When Lugard arrived in Buganda he found a functional and well-organized tribal system of administration. Lugard was an advocate of local rule and tribal administration and thereby tried to build upon it. He was able to subdue the region by using his old but functional Maxim gun that could fire 500 rounds a minute.[22] He killed hundreds if not thousands before he pacified the region. By so doing, he stunted the growth of Islam in the defunct British colony.

The British had installed a traditional colonial structure during colonization, which failed for financial reasons. As a result, the country was organized as a British protectorate[23] in 1894. From that time until 1962, whereupon the country gained its independence, the country experienced a gradual political evolution. Following independence in 1962 until 1986, despotism characterized the governing process.

The country was ruled by an unsavory group of military strongmen and dictators parading as elected office holders that plundered its resources and killed tens of thousands of its people.[24]

The king of Buganda, Sir Edward Mutesa II, was Uganda's first president after independence. Milton Obote served as its first prime minister. Obote overthrew Mutesa II with the help of Colonel Idi Amin. This conspiratorial partnership was one of contrasts. Obote was a handsome man. His skin was as black as a raven whose ancestors nested over North Africa and migrated to East Africa. His tightly knotted hair, woven into a matted appearance and styled to the back and left, coupled with his English, bespoken pinstripe suits and white shirts, made for a sophisticated look and that of a distinguished man. His sartorial effects said much about how he viewed himself.

Amin, on the other hand, was a strappingly stygian and corpulent man. Amin was an imposing figure, and when fully uniformed with all of his many military decorations might have been the African atavistic version of Kaiser Wilhelm II of Germany, especially during World War I, with his flair for the ornate. Better yet, perhaps Amin saw himself as Charles II, the last crowned king of Scotland before Scotland became a part of the United Kingdom, known for his love of revelry and carnality, minus the cruelty. Obote and Amin illicitly collaborated to extract diamonds and other commodities from the Congo to be used as payment to Ugandan troops, but the adventure failed. Idi Amin overthrew Obote in 1971 and intended to rule as well as reign over Uganda, if one can call it that, until 1979.[25]

Harriett recalled that when she visited Uganda during the Christmas of 1972, Amin had just taken power. He found out that she was there and sent her an invitation to attend a ribbon-cutting for the opening of a new supermarket near where her husband's family lived. Eric was a jealous man. And he did not want his wife exposed to Amin. Eric felt that if Amin saw Harriett, it would be very difficult to deny Amin what he wanted. So Eric quickly arranged for Harriett to leave the country to avoid what might have been a consequential event.

During Amin's rule, several hundred thousand Ugandans perished. Perhaps more than any other African leader in modern times, Idi Amin was stereotyped and vilified in the Western media as the most vile, heinous, murderous and inhumane African dictator ever invented. Ironically, Amin had been trained by the British in its African British army when Britain occupied Uganda.

The Western media has not, with the same intensity, celebrated the good works of other African leaders such as Julius Nyerere of Tanzania, Ellen Johnson-Sirleaf of Liberia, or Samora Machel of Mozambique and many others. Why has there not been equal treatment of African leadership? An inauthentic but vivid portrayal of Idi Amin by the black American actor Forest Whitaker in *The Last King of Scotland* resulted in his receipt of the Academy Award. His portrayals lived up to the stereotype and reinforced the Western-Anglo narrative: that Africa is a savage continent of nations perpetually at war with each other and ruled by inhumane monsters. In August 2003, Amin died in exile in Jeddah, Saudi Arabia, at the age of seventy-eight.

There were approximately 80,000 Asian Indians living in Uganda during Idi Amin's rule. Amin, as one of his objectives, drove out the Asian Indians who owned many of the stores and shops and who had built for themselves a secure economic footing in the country to the detriment of the native Ugandans. After this campaign, their numbers were reduced to under 10,000, although many returned after Amin's rule was ended by Julius Nyerere during the Ugandan-Tanzania war.

After Amin's despotic rule ended, a varied assortment of commissions, political parties and generals ruled the country, resulting in Milton Obote's return to office in 1981. Obote was supplanted after a year-long war called the "war in the bush," a guerrilla war led by Yoweri Museveni. In this conflict, the loss of Ugandan life exceeded the losses during Amin's military dictatorship, all out of a shaitan-type Shakespearean drama.

This truculent period ended in 1986 after a brief interim government led by a military commander collapsed, and its current president, Yoweri Museveni, came to power.[26] Uganda, since its independence in October 1962, has taken a circuitous route to an illiberal democratic form of government.

Ugandans speak over thirty different languages. Chief among them is Swahili, which is also spoken in Tanzania and Kenya, neighboring countries to the east. The country is majority Christian with a small minority who are Islamic, the bulk of whom are Sunni. Traditional beliefs still hold sway and are resorted to when required. Uganda has experienced stable economic growth, and with financial assistance from the United States, one of its major trading partners and its leading donor, has had success reducing the HIV/AIDS spread in country. Many problems remain, however. Uganda is a poor country by any measure. Its many problems have been enhanced by a civil war between the Ugandan government and the governments of several adjacent countries and the Lord's Resistance Army, a terrorist group with an ill-defined and subversive objective.

Michelle explained that her first night was restful and uneventful. She slept soundly and rose early as is her custom and opened the drapes. She was taken aback by the beautiful morning that greeted her. She described the scene as an "African morning." The vista was sheer magic in its expanse. An orange-red clay-colored sky with a fulgent yellow sun rising over the horizon cast a silhouette from the background over the pastoral scene. Low-hanging clouds brought a mist or fog that obscured, for the moment, the otherwise clear view of the small white houses and thatched huts, the mountains and hills she had seen before. Tree tops barely visible in the evening shade were radiantly aligned in a symmetrical uniformity when observed from afar in the morning. And though she did not see any wild animals grazing on the fertile green grasses that stretched out before her, she imagined that they must be out there somewhere.

Shortly thereafter, Michelle tended to her morning needs,

dressed and prepared to go to breakfast. But by the time she had finished dressing, Vixena knocked on her door. They went to their first breakfast in Africa together. All had been forgiven. Surprisingly, the food offerings were essentially Western in nature: hard-boiled eggs, fruits and pastries. The most surprising food choice was baked beans. Michelle and Vixena associated baked beans with hot dogs or an evening meal, not a breakfast food. Toast was also an offering, but to make a piece she was required to use an antiquated contraption on which the slice of bread rotated over a heat source within the machine. A gadget out of the forties or an earlier period. She and Vixena were required to master the toast-making skill since this exercise was repeated almost every morning.

Michelle and Vixena began to take notice of their environment and the people in it—most notably Africans—more closely now that the rush of arriving and getting settled was behind them.

"One discovery that really shocked us was their hair. There we were, wearing the ultimate Afro declaring our return to our African roots and identity, and most African female students wore wigs and had their hair processed."

This observation calls to mind James Baldwin and Kwame Nkrumah's writings on the subject of imitation by Africans of their white colonizers and the imitation by African-American women of white American standards of beauty. Both authors say that Africans and African-Americans imitate the white standard in lifestyle and in cosmetics.[27] Another noted author, Nell Irwin Painter, discusses the evolution of white beauty as a social standard in her book, *The History of White People*, wherein she traces this evolution back to a period of white slavery in Asia in the seventeenth and eighteenth centuries.[28]

Michelle tells me, "A few of the students wore beautiful African cloth wrapped around their heads, but mostly the maintenance staff wore this." This observation again illustrates that African headwraps, or *geles* as they are referred to in Yoruba African culture, which are colorful headdresses, speak loudly about a woman's view of herself in the context of Africa and African nationalism. These wraps come in many beautiful colors and designs, but their history is long and strikingly meaningful.[29]

So what does "hair" and how it is worn symbolize, if anything? Does it tell us what we think about ourselves, our political views, self-image, self-esteem, our politics or even our mentality and mental stability? The style in which hair is worn is above all an exercise in vanity. Each hairstyle reveals how we want to be seen and what culture impacts our sense of self. Hair denotes all of these issues, attributes and qualities, or none at all. How we present ourselves speaks volumes about how we see ourselves, especially in relation to others. How we wear our hair is "speech," to use a legal analogy.

Michelle and her compatriot went to Africa to affirm their African roots and to be socialized by things "African," but in this observation, among many, and in this segment of African culture, they discovered that Africans were trying not to be like black Americans but to be like white Americans or Europeans—to imitate white beauty. What say you then about all this ancestral cultural specialism? Does it have value? Does it really matter? Yes, it does. It informs you about yourself, where you come from, and sheds light on the layers of character dimensions that make you who you are. It enables you to be stronger in the face of the barrage of negative white culture that dominates and suffuses all aspect of life in the West. And it allows you to intelligently appraise your relationship with others, your dealings with individuals of other cultures, and what the nature of that relationship with "your race" has been. And to see that you as an individual and as a race, a population, have a history, and that "your race" has value.

Michelle notes, "Some of the African females wore a lot of makeup, very light—in fact too light for their dark complexion, so it resulted in a clown-like mask."

It does not take a lot to see where all of this comes from, but these females were attending a college, trying to become educated and to someday fit into the wider global culture that awaited them. Michelle's perception that these African females used makeup unbecoming to their natural skin color and tone indicated that these African women felt the need to "whiten up"—or brighten up, as the case may be—their facial appearance. This reality is understandable, though disconcerting. We see this on American television all the time when darker-skinned female and male television personalities mask their rich dark color to appear lighter and hence more acceptable and less threatening to the majority white public.

I am of a split opinion to some extent on this issue. Ironically, in some white quarters the darker-complexioned black man is more attractive, possibly because of the stark contrast, than the hybrid. Ratings count more than personal identities. Bleaching creams, unbecoming makeup and hair relaxers all say the same thing.

Michelle recalls an incident involving a group of African women to whom she was talking in the cafeteria. She had settled herself down at a table where several African women were seated. She wanted to engage with these women to find out more about their culture and perspectives. Not long after their conversation began, another African woman whom she had befriended previously walked over and said, "Why are you talking to these women?" Michelle was dumbfounded. She said she was caught totally off guard and did not know how to respond. She said to herself, *What is this all about?* To her, all of the African women seemed the same. Michelle said that what she was doing—talking to these women—was perfectly normal and to be expected.

Michelle later met an Indian premedical student whose name was Ferry Rawj. "Rawj was older and wiser, and I enjoyed our relationship from the start." It was Rawj who explained why the African females were not warm and friendly toward outsiders or to each other. She said it was because of tribal differences. Michelle eventually spoke with the African woman who raised the issue and was told that the women at the table were from a different tribe and that the tribes did not intermingle. This was news to Michelle. She wondered, *Not even to talk to one another?*

Tribalism in Africa is alive and well. It has bedeviled progress that otherwise could have been made. Tribalism is to be distinguished from ethnicity, which is a broader concept of cultural similarity and cultural identity, reduced to the individual group within the ethnic enclave to which one belongs. So this, too, was a lesson to Michelle: stay in your own tribe.

As far as the dress of the African females was concerned, "Their dress was multicolored with either a wrapped African skirt or Western skirt with usually a non-matching blouse."

This too is not unexpected. As Michelle noted of the African student who came to her high school, and though not restricted to Africans solely, it seems that when Africans who have not been sufficiently Westernized try to imitate Western dress, they often wear discordant schemes.

Michelle elaborates further by saying, "After breakfast we walked through the lobby and I walked to a mirror on the wall. I looked at myself. I looked at my Afro, my colorful dangling earrings and my dashiki. Reflected in the mirror behind me was an African female student with a wig and powdered face. I asked myself, 'Will the real African woman please stand up?' I continued staring in the mirror at myself and at the African woman's reflection. I realized that neither of us should stand up. We were both at the same crossroads. There I was trying to look like what *I* thought the modern African educated woman would look like, and there reflected in the mirror *was* a modern African educated woman behind me. But she was not dressed like me. She wore Westernized clothes and false hair and makeup. Her appearance was a fake.

"But then what about me? What about my appearance? If she looked phony and ridiculous to me, how did I look to her? Probably phony and ridiculous. To me, my Afro represented the natural look, the non-processed look. In my opinion, it was the true way to wear hair in Africa. But the only people wearing Afros were the African-American students, not the African students. On the other hand, she was wearing a wig trying to get that processed straight-haired look. A look that we abandoned in our 'black is beautiful' campaign."

It would seem, then, that perhaps the Afro hairstyle is in large part an African-American invention—an affectation designed to be an ethnic symbol of a native African hairstyle. I too have never seen a native African male or female with an African-American version of the Afro hairstyle.

What a difference thirty-three years make![9]* It appears we have come full circle during this time, or has there been a convergence of circles as in a Venn diagram? The convergence, one could say, occurred when African-American women adopted en masse the wig, synthetic, processed, or the straightened-hair look observed by Michelle in Africa in 1972. This look has been prevalent in the West for a long time among American women of African descent, American males of African descent, and perhaps African women who have become Westernized. For example, Michelle's son dated a Nigerian woman in 2011, and though this woman was beautiful naturally, she wore a black wig with hair flowing down to her shoulders. Both Michelle and I questioned the reason for this otherwise beautiful African woman to wear her hair this way. Further inquiry revealed that this Nigerian woman spent considerable time in Italy and later migrated to the United States. Obviously, the impact of the culture of the "Occident" had made a strong impression on her.

The popularity of this processed look appears to have grown in the twenty-first century among women but not among men. In the twentieth century, many black men who were disposed to do so wore the processed look—conked hair. Hair and the quality of it as judged by white norms has always been a distinguishing line within the race.

---

9   * Borrowing phraseology from the lyrics of Stanley Adams and Maria Mendez Grever made popular by Dinah Washington in 1959 in the song "What a Difference a Day Makes."

There are many hairstyle exceptions to the white standard of beauty being worn by American women of African descent: ethnic hair styles made up of cornrows, braids, Havana twists, dreadlocks and others, or a combination of these styles. Not to belabor the point, but what Michelle observed was simply the acquiescence by African women and American women of African descent to the white woman paradigm of beauty.

The actor and comedian Chris Rock presented a documentary piece entitled "Good Hair" in 2009 on "black hair." The conclusion of which was that black hair is the most devalued and unappreciated human hair on the hair market and, to some, the most disrespected. Why is that? It is indeed passing strange and shameful, but understandable, that, as Baldwin has written, some in black society have lost respect for and appreciation of hair native to our "race" that is naturally beautiful and unadulterated by a superficial synthetic pretense born of the need and pressure to assimilate. American men of African descent share responsibility for this devaluation by their inability to accept as beautiful and attractive the natural hair native to African peoples. This deviation from what we would ideally want to see is because of their acceptance, embrace of, demand for, and attraction to the Caucasian long straight-hair look. Many of them have contributed mightily to this phenomenon and encouragement of its adoption by buying into the white prototype, unapologetically. Hair and how it is worn or styled as a part of one's physiognomy is just a segment of culture—a highly personal aspect.

Michelle's observation about the African woman's hair moved her toward untangling the riddle of her quest, a poignant discovery of contradiction brought on by the sheer force, unrelenting demands and exigencies of Western culture.

Perhaps I am being too hard on Americans of African descent. It is not outré, bizarre or unusual to expect people whose culture is subservient to the dominant European culture to emulate that culture when their culture has been bowled over. To chart a way through this paradox, which has existed for centuries in the world of the African and his progeny, reference must be made to Léopold Sédar Senghor, the cultural poet and the first president of Senegal, who postulated the concept of Negritude. Senghor was joined in this conception by Aimé Césaire, a Martinican, and Léon Damas, a French Guianese—all kindred spirits who lived and studied with Senghor while he was in Paris in 1931. Césaire, who became the mayor of the capital city in Martinique, is quoted as having said during a speech to introduce his friend, Senghor,

> For forty years, we have lived in Parallel . . . leaving each other, as life went, but nonetheless never truly separating. Was this surprising? After all, our adolescences were entirely blended. We read the same books, and often the same copy, shared the same dreams, loved the same poets. We were torn by the same anguish and, above all, were weighted down by the same problems . . . our youth was not banal . . . It was marked by the tormenting question, who am I? For us it was not a question of metaphysics but of a life to live, an ethic, to create communities to save. We tried to answer that question. In the end the answer was Negritude.[30]

In this concept he urged Africans wherever they were located to adopt the salutary aspects of white culture, to disdain the unsavory portions but to retain their African culture and mystique.[31] Some African leaders, especially Kwame Nkrumah, president of Ghana from 1957 to 1960, disavowed this notion and relegated it to the trash can, or, as some would prefer to say, the dustbin of African bourgeois irrationally, and called it "racist and non-revolutionary."[32]

Perhaps Nkrumah sought a more striking divorce from European imitation and advocated for a real manifestation of the

African personality. Nkrumah moved to the left as his vision of Pan-Africanism developed, but he embraced the tenets of Negritude as a political ideology to advance his advocacy of a divorce from European dominance of Africa. Nkrumah believed, and rightly so, that "the emancipation of the African continent is the emancipation of man." Senghor, Nkrumah, Kenyatta and Nyerere sought the same result—an independent Africa free of European colonialism and an economic policy that reflected the needs of the people. But Senghor, an apostle of Negritude because of his French acculturation, was more of an assimilationist. But the question is, "Where does this leave African-Americans?"

The answer is it leaves us with a history of the struggle of African peoples for their rights; knowledge about the emancipation of Africans and people of African descent that took place on the shores of the eastern Atlantic and on the shores of the western Atlantic; awareness that the African branch of the human species is endowed with great intellects who over time have developed political philosophies that have led black people out of bondage and away from the fictional baggage of inferiority. And finally it leaves black people with a concept and a definition of "who we are," as opposed to "who I am."

After this encounter, Michelle realized that she and her fellow African females were emulating a false object. Michelle says that *she* was "reaching to the past, to Africa, to enrich my sense of self, while my African counterparts were reaching to be acceptable in the Western world." Michelle realized that her dress did not reflect how real Africans dressed—that she was, in fact, emulating exaggerated, unauthentic African-American ideas about how Africans dressed. Michelle says, "To be a real African-American, we had to embrace Africa's past and what Africa is."

Michelle sums it up best: "I laughed out loud. My mom's words were speaking in my mind so clearly. 'It's not what's on your back that identifies who you are, but what's in your head and your heart.' Symbols. The Afro, the dashikis, the red-black-and-green flag, the raised black-gloved fists, they were all symbols. Symbols to say, 'We are here. We are here to learn who we really are. It may take us a while, but we are learning that we can be who we really are, still succeed, and not be clothed in pretentiousness but be natural.'

"I laughed again and thought about the brothers and sisters at home on campus. We needed that rhetoric, that façade to help us discover who we really were until we could finally present our true selves. But some folks were putting on a show, an act, and would continue to do so, too afraid to reveal who they really were. Or maybe they were just cowards and jealous of others who were bold and brave enough to be their true selves. I was not putting on a show. I believed in me and I believe in Africa within me. I looked at the African student's reflection in the mirror again. I hoped she was not putting on a show either and that she believed in the Africa in her."

• • •

While the train is stopped in Baltimore, existing passengers whose destination is New York remain on the train. Those passengers going through will jockey for new seats that become available before the new passengers board the train, in order to better their existing seat assignment. I have been taking this train trip for many years now. The desk office train staff in Charlottesville, specifically the guys at the ticket counter, know me. Aycock, a veteran trainman with a thick, brown, walrus-style mustache and matching hair brushed to the side, once got me a train reservation number when I did not have a ticket.

However, I ride the train so often that I started having a feud with one of the train conductors working this route. This fellow was a middle-aged white man with no distinguishable facial features except that he wore thin, wire-rimmed glasses. He seemed to relish the conflict. He would even smile when he thought he had done something that got under my skin. Perhaps he was bored and needed the novelty to keep him interested. He enjoyed the agitation. His police-like conductor uniform was navy blue with a suit jacket and matching vest with yellow-gold buttons but no epaulets on either shoulder. His hat was a wide-crowned Pershing with a matching yellow-gold metal badge attached to the front. He would make snide remarks and try to needle me every time we encountered each other. This dispute between the two of us lasted for quite a few months before he was either reassigned or I stopped riding the train for a while, whichever one came first. Familiarity has its benefits but also can bring conflict. Even a dream-like interlude such as a train ride can be sullied by unwanted and unexpected external forces, shattering even a temporal illusion.

Michelle and I have been talking for a while. She is tired now, and so am I, but I have many more questions to ask, and I know Michelle will have many of the answers. We have just under three hours of additional riding time ahead before we get to New York.

As Michelle rests, my attention turns to Harriett. My mind wanders, imagining what was going on in Harriett's life at the same time that Michelle was experiencing Africa for the first time. Harriett was adjusting to life as a married woman, married to an African, a patriotic Ugandan.

CHAPTER TWELVE

HARRIETT'S CHOICE

While all of this was happening to Michelle in Uganda, Harriett's career was continuing apace. Before Harriett completed her master's degree at Columbia, she applied for and was accepted into their doctoral program. Of course, she was elated, but the question became, *How can I finance it all?*

To continue to pay for tuition at Columbia as well as being able to support herself in New York City demanded that Harriett look for employment. Bereft of funds but not of will, Harriett thought, *I've got to find a job to earn some money. Between the rent and the tuition here in New York City, I cannot go on.* She said this to herself over and over again, as she plotted herself out of this situation. *Let me call the dean of the school of nursing at Widener*, she thought. *He's always been in my corner. I'm sure he will find a placement for me.*

Widener University[33] at that time had been the love of her academic career, the university she felt most indebted to. After all, Widener had given her leave to pursue her master's degree at Columbia University.

Widener again extended the right hand of fellowship, but this time there was no faculty position available at Widener for

Harriett. But through the interconnected workings of the academic community in Philadelphia and its suburbs, the dean of the school of nursing at Widener knew the dean of the Jefferson School of Nursing at Thomas Jefferson University, so a position was found for Harriett in Philadelphia at Thomas Jefferson.

In the approaching fall of 1972, Harriett was very much involved with her faculty duties at Thomas Jefferson University. However, Harriett disliked the way the nursing program was organized at Thomas Jefferson. The medical school was the de facto controlling force of the nursing school. This was not something that she accepted or embraced. It had always been her view that nursing education should stand alone and be independent, in order to offer those who pursued the nursing career an education not only in the nursing sciences, but also in the social sciences and the humanities to broaden the students' horizons, and to deepen their perspectives about how nursing is integrated into the treatment of the total person. She disliked the fact that the medical school—with its bent toward male faculty at that time, although females were represented—controlled the nursing curriculum and nursing school.

Harriett assumed her position on the nursing school faculty and taught for one year before returning to Columbia to resume her studies. Her finances had improved, and so had her resolve.

Musingly melancholic, Harriett said that she returned to Columbia in 1975, this time to work on her doctorate in education with a specialty in education and curriculum development. But pangs of anguish arose because upon completion of the doctoral program in 1978, she was invited to join the faculty at Columbia, for which she was very elated, but this opportunity required her to sever her ties to Widener, the university that had been so pivotal to her development and so magnanimous in their treatment of her.

Upon returning to Columbia, she earned the additional money that she needed to continue her education working as a nurse practitioner for students in the student health center clinic after classes and on weekends. The clinic was located at 120th Street and Amsterdam Avenue in New York City. Sometimes she would work from 3 to 5 p.m. after classes and from 7 to 10 p.m. on the weekends. It was a natural fit for a person in nursing and for a graduate in need of money—an accommodation made by Columbia University for one of its own. She was able to get this job because she was, after all, a registered nurse with a master's degree in education. The money from this work enabled her to meet her financial requirements.

In the clinic Harriett wore a white lab coat that hung just above the knee. Her dark skin and graying hair reflecting strikingly against the white fabric of the lab coat, she could easily have been mistaken as a physician. Harriett was hired specifically as a nurse practitioner, and she dealt with all manner of student maladies. Some illnesses required referral to a physician, but on many occasions she was able to recommend treatments that solved most of the problems the students were having. As the students entered the clinic office, a nursing assistant receptionist directed the students to an examination room to await Harriett's assistance. The room was not large, yet large enough for a doctor and, if need be, a nurse, to assist the student in the same room. The room, painted in an off-white color bland to the eye, contained a desk and examining table and two chairs: one for the patient to sit and give basic information about his or her illness and background, and one chair for a friend or family member to provide assurance to the affected student. In the clinic Harriett practiced her profession. No theory here, only the practical application of medicine.

Nurse practitioners are of a different breed. They are registered nurses with advanced training who can diagnose and treat illnesses. Nurse practitioners can prescribe medicines. Their focus is preventive, not remedial. This focus differentiates nurse practitioners from physicians. Harriett completed the doctoral program in 1978, earning an EdD in education with a specialty in curriculum development.

Harriett and Eric had what could be described as a whirlwind relationship: he over there and she here in the United States and at times, though sparingly, both in the United States. They had taken several classes together at Columbia during Harriett's master's degree studies. There was tension in those classes between the African-American male students and the African male students over the African-American women. Both groups sought the favors of the African-American women. "The white women in the classes went wild over the African male students," Harriett recalled, but not so much over the African-American male students.

Harriett confided that she could not ask Eric to give up his citizenship nor could he ask her to give up her citizenship. Eric and Harriett did not have in-depth discussions about his loyalty to Uganda or the consequences of giving up citizenship in their home countries. The citizenship issue did not have to rise to the level of abdication because US immigration rules, if carefully followed, provided for a less stringent or radical solution. Eric no doubt entered the United States on a F-1 student visa, which allowed him to stay in the country as long as his studies required. Then, subsequently marrying an American citizen as he did would strengthen his "adjustment of status" application to apply for and eventually obtain a green card or even permanent residence status. All of this would take time and required persistence to accomplish, but it was certainly doable.

So the issue of citizenship was not the obstacle; it was "allegiance." Allegiance by a citizen to his sovereign government—an allegiance Eric was unwilling to sever for any reason. The burden would be on Harriett to make the required sacrifices. She knew instinctively and from her relationship with him that his view of his mother country was sacrosanct. This issue was at the vortex, or one could say the heart, of whether their relationship could endure under these circumstances. Inevitably, Harriett knew that if she did not find a way to surmount, by way of compromise, this intrinsic sense of loyalty that Eric maintained for his country, the long-term success of the marriage would be problematic. Hence her willingness to go to Africa to live and to work there professionally mattered greatly in the scheme of things.

Residency and citizenship were not the only significant issues in this evolving "combination." Cultural issues regarding African marriages and what was expected of the woman in that marriage as well as familial issues involving children and the immediate family awaited resolution as the nascent marriage continued. In her rapture, Harriett failed to ruminate over these cultural issues, perhaps out of naiveté, timidity or procrastination or dwelling in her world of unreality. Whether she considered these issues early on or not, they found a place in the recesses of the euphoria of love. Ultimately, as the passions began to cool, when novelty had run its course and rationality suffused through the haze to become the clarifying state of mind, the polarities in their respective cultures and the expectations each had for the other became stark. The intoxication of her "romantic ideal" of cultural reunification and integration and of marital bliss in that context began to wane.

Falling in love with a man or woman is one thing, falling in love with a conception yet another. Falling in love is not a concept. It is a real thing, but transforming that "real thing" into a lasting acculturational marriage requires physical action, movement, commitment, combination, an enormous adjustment and above all propitiation. By failing to blend these constituents, a marriage of this type will deliquesce and become nonexistent. A concept without proof or evidence of its validity or actuality is an abstraction and unsubstantiated. Concepts, dreams and abstractions only require ideation and imaginativeness, but overcoming the day-to-day practicalities of joining separate and distinct cultures, though shared ancestrally, is far from being an abstraction.

Americans of African descent often make this mistake. We will discuss this issue further on, but there are striking differences between Africans and African-Americans that are not easily overcome without major, significant and sufferable sacrifices. The pallet for integrated marriages between African-Americans and persons from European backgrounds is in some respects easier and more workable, because of common cultural attributes, than in marriages between Africans and African-Americans. Romanticism is fine in its place, but the realities of life always prevail.

It was paramount in Eric's mind that he had a responsibility to his country. The strands of American culture that gave Eric the most pause had more to do with the expectation that because of his advantages in the United States, his loyalty to Uganda, his native land, would thereby be overruled, than with the stuff of typical Americana. Uganda had paid for over ten years of Eric's education, and he had been in the United States for six or more years before his relationship began with Harriett. So, his mind was made up.

If Eric had really desired to make a life for himself in the United States, he was fully capable and credentialed enough to have done so. In fact, Widener University offered Eric a faculty position, as did the City University of New York, where Eric taught some classes. Eric, a man of arresting talent, like Harriett in her department was accepted into the doctoral program in the department of mathematics at Columbia while completing his master's degree. He would have enjoyed success in the United States, but it was not to be.

The timing of his departure to Uganda, for what he imagined would be a routine visit, resulted in his inability to complete the doctoral program. He was unable to reenter the United States because of an event that involved Idi Amin. The United States closed its embassy in Uganda.

"He could not get out," Harriett said. United States immigration policies attributable to the reign of Idi Amin ricocheted through his life, in this instance bringing him to a critical juncture in his marriage and in his education. He had his compatriots—his countrymen, those who favored or those who opposed Amin—to thank for the contribution they mightily made toward the discontinuance of his future in the United States, all of which would foreshadow the ultimate result. After all, if this love was unencumbered by the chains of loyalty and dissimilarity in culture, who would not want to be the recipient of a PhD in mathematics from Columbia University and be married to a member of its faculty, all things being equal?

Eric knew that because of his talent, education and training, his worth to Uganda and the purpose served by his return to Uganda far exceeded his worth in the United States. What's more, to be emotionally settled and at peace with himself required his return. That's how deeply the angst of this predicament penetrated his soul. When compared with the needfulness, the history, the plight and the necessity of his contribution to his country, there was no controversy. African-Americans would do well to emulate Eric's allegiance to the Afrocentric values that informed his decision to stay loyal to his beliefs and not be swayed by the ephemeral attractions of the Occident. He was leaving the arms of a beautiful African-American woman with acquired Afrocentric values—something of a rarity in the self-regarding black American community at that time—for the magnetic and mellifluous alms embosomed in Uganda. Uganda's lien recorded against his person had priority.

Harriett's African consciousness was at an all-time high. The tentacles of her mindfulness had touched the land, her heart, her imagination and intellectual curiosity. So, after receiving her doctorate in 1978, Harriett asked herself, *What am I doing in the US? I'm needed in Africa.* She too felt the pangs of needfulness in Africa. Having gone to Africa to visit her husband's family in Uganda, she knew she could find work and purpose there. As I mentioned earlier, Harriett was invited to join the faculty at Columbia before completing her doctorate and assumed her position on the faculty after the degree was awarded. The tension between her new opportunities and the moral unease she felt by not returning to Widener faded.

As Harriett recalls one of her colleagues, a dean or departmental chair, mentioned an opportunity to establish a nursing program in Botswana. The opportunity to do so arose after Harriett had completed her doctoral studies and was on the faculty. Only by studying at Columbia was she given the opportunity to go to Africa to work in the first phase of a revamping of the nursing program in Botswana—a program that a white chemistry professor, an American professor in Botswana, was establishing.

The opportunity to work in Botswana encapsulated all her dreams: her yen for cultural integration, desires and ambitions. It was a chance of a lifetime to build something from the ground up. To stitch together a new whole cloth that would enable an African country to provide better health care to its people presented her with an Augean challenge. A noble cause. However, as in most cases of *noblesse oblige*, an arduous landscape lay ahead, one fraught with difficulties and many lessons to be learned about cultural chauvinism in Africa and African tribalism and ethnocentrism.[34]

But isn't that what life is all about? Climbing mountains and learning lessons. How could she not take advantage of this *significatif,* this meaningful opportunity? So, in 1979 Harriett made the decision to go to Africa, to go to Botswana. Eric was still in Uganda at that time. Her commitment contractually and to her mother was to stay for only two years, and her mother held her to it. Harriett quoted her mother as saying, "I haven't lost anything in Africa." So, Harriett surmised that her mother was not going. Her mother's views had been created early in her life. Harriett reckoned that her mother felt that way because of American culture—a culture that promoted "hatred of ourselves," Harriett said firmly. In her mother's generation, American and European culture promoted only the bad things about Africa, and Isabelle as well as others of her generation drank deeply from the font. Harriett recalls that it took her one year to convince her mother to go. As a result of that effort, she was exhausted before she began.

CHAPTER THIRTEEN

CHUO ELIMU
SWAHILI FOR "A COLLEGE EDUCATION"

I ask Michelle to tell me how her first day on campus was. She begins by saying that as they casually walked on campus, she and Vixena saw John, the African male student who befriended them the day before and was responsible for obtaining their lodging in Mary Stuart Hall. As he had done before, he volunteered to be of help.

"He took us on our first campus tour. We went by the main campus entrance by the two imposing, tall black wrought iron gates that were supported by stone. The iron gates were not far from our dormitory. We began to walk up the hill, and as we walked up the hill he told us the building on the left was the male dormitory." It had beautiful architecture, she remembers: "It was something like a tropical hotel type of building with a beautiful courtyard in the middle. Several floors of dormitory rooms surrounded the courtyard in an octagonal shape."

All of this was impressive to her since she had not known what to expect from an African college campus. She continues, "John showed us African Hall, where I was scheduled to reside but could not because it was closed when we first arrived, the science building, the political science building and engineering building. He also showed us the arts and mathematics building. I was most interested in the three buildings that I knew would be important to me on a daily basis: the science building, the library, and the mathematics building. Mr. Eric, that is what I called him, had his office in the mathematics building. Knowing that Mr. Eric was on campus went a long way toward relieving my anxieties. When we went by the mathematics building it was closed, but at least I knew where to go next week when I planned to inform him of my arrival on campus. Makerere was a big campus! We walked a few more yards when, suddenly, a gigantic greenish-brown lizard about 9 inches long crossed our path. Vixena and I let out a loud shriek! We screamed, 'Holy cow! What was that?' John and a few other passing male students laughed at us. The lizards were not poisonous or dangerous, we were told, but they populated the area. John said stoically, 'You will get used to them,' but I said to myself, 'I doubt that seriously.'

"After the tour and the lizard moment, we stopped off at a canteen and bought some Fantas, a popular soda brand in Uganda, as well as some meat pies. I enjoyed them both and I said to myself, *Ah ha! I have found my favorite snack*, and I knew I would be enjoying them as each day passed."

Michelle reminisces that while she and Vixena walked about the campus, "my attention was drawn to the color of the soil. The soil was a dark reddish-brown color. I had never seen such healthy and rich earth before. The scientist in me wanted to know more about the soil of Uganda, the soils generally of my motherland." Michelle later found out that the soil in Uganda had a high content of iron and aluminum. The soil is characterized by red and patchy yellow-red minerals, known as a ferralitic soil.[35]

After leaving the canteen, Michelle walked a few feet, bent down in a moment of joyousness, dug her fingers into the semi-arid soil, grabbed some of it into her hand and said to herself, "Our ancestors touched and felt this soil. They depended on the soil for their existence, for the welfare of their families, their sustenance and the well-being of their tribal community." But she now had no reason to imagine these things: she was in Africa, and as she listened to the voice of John, the upper-class student who led them around the campus, she studied the dark ebony hue of his skin, focused on his bright white teeth and gleaming smile. She said she never felt so close to her ancestry as she felt at that moment. She exclaimed fervently, "This is what I have been missing in the States!"

She thought about how in America many African-American students in the white colleges coalesced into a group and mingled together; they were in their own majority. But on those same campuses, the African students were in a distinct minority separated from the African-American students and seemed to want to keep it that way. She wondered why there was a separation by nationality of African peoples. This was for her a "Kumbaya" moment, a moment of surreal consanguinity. *Why can't they all just simply be African people?* she pondered.

Her state of mind at that moment harkened back to biblical or ancient times when black people were only known as Ethiopes, all part of one amalgam. As she thought about her American experience, she felt that she had not ever really connected with the United States. For the brief time she was at Makerere, she was certainly in the minority among all the other African students, but she felt a genuine sense of belonging—no longer a sense of alienation and foreignness in a white-dominated environment.

"We had made the trip and offered a part of our lives to Africa and learned by personal experiences about our ancestral country, and there we felt openly accepted." She was in sheer bliss and open to the many possible experiences that she might encounter. For that brief moment in time, she lost all sense of fear, all sense of anxiety, or the need to overly protect herself.

"Thank you, Jesus! Thank you," she exclaimed, "for blessing me so much to be here. Thank you for loving me so much that you wanted me to have this experience in my life. That among all of the students

I left behind at Swarthmore, that *I*, the least of them, would be given such an award, such an opportunity!"

Michelle tells me, "I thanked God for his gifts and for Swarthmore, because if it had not been for Swarthmore, this experience would not have happened. And I promised to represent Swarthmore and my family well."

Michelle experienced her first tea time: There were several flavors of tea, and there was toast, fruits and other pastries. She had milk in her tea for the first time, but learned to prefer her tea with just a dash of sugar without milk. This is of course a tradition passed on by the British during the days of colonialization in Uganda. Her dinner that evening was fairly standard—with meat, potatoes, vegetables and fruits. And everything tasted good except that the meat was not cooked to her satisfaction. Not wanting to become nauseated or to have a stomach upset, she limited her consumption to the vegetables, fruits and potatoes. She tells me she said to herself, "Henceforth, breakfasts and tea time will be my best meals."

The end of the day was at hand and she went back to her room, sat down and wrote her mother a letter from the heart, explaining to her that she was happy, and that she should not worry. A sense of satisfaction with her decision-making and gratification settled over her person. It was as though she was in a comfortable room surrounded by all her favorite things that she loved, treasured and appreciated. She was comfortable. Her day's activities had been wonderful and enlightening and above all pleasurable. A serendipitous beginning.

As Michelle adjusts her seat on the train to get more comfortable, she describes the registration process at Makerere. She gestures with her hands as she begins to talk. "The pre-semester week began like all pre-semester activities for college students. It didn't matter that my pre-semester activities were taking place in Africa. I could have been on any college campus in the United States. I registered for my classes, which consisted of zoology, chemistry and Swahili. I set up my financial account on campus and made sure that all the important officials on campus that I in any way would have a relationship with were aware that I was present and accounted for. I had a special interest in modern dance. I was a member of a black dance ensemble at Swarthmore, and I wanted to continue that activity while at Makerere, so I inquired about the availability of such a group. African dance fascinated me because it was a polyrhythmic dance employing many rhythmic patterns and themes to tell the stories of tribes, festivals and life experiences. From what I had seen, the vitality and strong ethnic messages in African dance kindled my cultural thirst. And I very much wanted to add African dance music to my dance music tape collection.

"Before the end of the week, I met up with Mr. Eric. We had tea and I filled him in on all of my campus arrangements. I let him know where I was staying and gave him my class schedule. Mr. Eric gave me his office schedule and phone numbers. He explained to me where his apartment was located off campus. Mr. Eric had promised my mother and his wife, Harriett, that he would take good care of me and that nothing would happen to me while I was in his country. I relied on that promise and because of that promise I was reassured. Mr. Eric said that he would not intrude on my privacy or crowd my space. That he would give me plenty of opportunity to experience and learn and enjoy the country. I knew that Mr. Eric was a man of his word, and from that point on he and I talked once a week, and he often took me to tea. Sometimes Vixena joined us. Mr. Eric was a great friend and an invaluable resource. Knowing that I had him on my team made me feel special that I was under the protection of a Ugandan who knew his way around the capital and the university. He knew his country.

"Not long after the pre-semester week ended, I was suddenly awakened from a deep sleep in my dorm room in the wee hours of the morning by an attendant from the front desk office. 'America! America!' he shouted with excitement. 'You have a call from America!' He spoke as though he had done something special, something novel that only he owned the right to tell me. I quickly scrambled out of my bed and put on some jeans and a T-shirt to cover my nightclothes. I ran down the steps to the overseas telephone and picked up the receiver. My mother and sister, Shelley, were on the phone. I screamed with joy. 'Shelley, is that you?'

"'Michelle,' she answered. 'How are you doing? Is everything alright?'

"Before I could answer Shelley's question, my mother chimed in, 'Michelle, this is Mom.' The throaty guttural sound of her voice was easily recognizable. 'How *are* things over there?' My mother said that I sounded like I was so far away, 'somewhere on a mountaintop someplace.' As we talked, I did not want to say goodbye. I wanted to continue to talk so that I would be 'beamed back' like Star Trek to be in their presence. Tears fell again as the reality set in that I was far away from the people I really loved. I felt homesick. I wanted my mommy and I wanted my sister."

CHAPTER FOURTEEN

NOTHING NEW UNDER THE SUN

What is Africa to me?
Countee Cullen, "Heritage"

Michelle began to explore her immediate environment. To get to Kampala she had to travel through Wandegeya, a neighborhood on the outskirts of Kampala, so Wandegeya was a frequent stop of students from Makerere University. Wandegeya was divided into three zones. Each zone was unique in that it housed certain segments of the community at large: a government zone, a commercial zone, and a zone close to the Makerere University campus. Within the neighborhood were old markets, small lockup shops and bars known as *kafundas*. Orange dirt roads bustled with Ugandans on motorcycles passing by mosques, modern finished office buildings, apartment complexes and many partly completed construction projects. Some areas resembled small underdeveloped towns in the American South, many of which still have unpaved roads. There were aspects of Wandegeya that both resembled a shantytown and a small bustling enclave. College students frequented the city because of its accessibility and the opportunity for many young, naïve and uninitiated students to have their first beer, wine, sex and revelry. Small shops were available to purchase groceries and a variety of sundries. Many of these shops had been operated by families for generations.

Kampala is divided into five boroughs. There are many paved roads. Africa is often depicted on American television as being backward, jungle infested, unruly, chaotic and unsophisticated. The reality is that Africa in many of its cities and towns is as sophisticated as any city or town in the West or in Asia. The roads, especially in the busy business districts, have a median strip where tropical trees and plants are grown separating the two sides of the roadway, resembling the boulevards of Lima in Peru. It is certainly true that Kampala and Uganda are underdeveloped, but they are not backwaters as portrayed in Western media. Typically, in a city the size of Kampala there are many banks, clothing stores, movie theaters, hotels, government buildings and numerous business offices.

Perhaps the most striking observation Michelle made when she visited Kampala was that so many of the shops and businesses were run by Asian Indians. Recall that in 1972, one of Idi Amin's main objectives was to confiscate the property of the Indians and expel them from the country. Seeing the Indians as the shopkeepers and members of the middle class was startling. Michelle said she thought that her new reality would be characterized by seeing Africans, sub-Saharan in color, operating the cash registers, being salespeople, clerks and office help. Though the native Ugandans were well represented in these jobs, it appeared to Michelle that in Kampala and perhaps throughout Uganda an affirmative action program for the native Ugandans was needed. But this new observable reality that Indians did all these jobs instead of Africans reminded her of the same thing she saw and experienced in America. Succinctly, Indians have been viewed as occupying the middle ground between colonist of the past and native Ugandans.

Why is this? she wondered. Was it because of the colonialization of the country by the British, who then made the country accessible to the Indians, or was it the illiteracy of the Ugandans that prevented them from being the entrepreneurs that she thought she would encounter? To her, it seemed more of the former than the latter.

When examining this issue more closely, I found that South Asians were brought to sub-Saharan Africa by the British government to do clerical work and unskilled work primarily during the construction of the Ugandan Railway/East African Railway. Researchers note that South Asians had an outsized impact on the Ugandan economy; though they only constituted approximately one percent of the population, they were the recipients of one fifth of the gross domestic product of the country. They were, as Amy Chua expresses in her book *World on Fire*, "members of a market-dominant minority." In her context, Indians extract a disproportionate share of return on capital from the Ugandan economy. The dominance of this population in the economy is buttressed by historical precedent and heretofore government support. This angered Ugandan politicians of the past and still today remains a source of considerable irritation among the native Ugandan people.

South Asian people made the most of their franchise and were sometimes referred to as *dukawallas*, or shopkeepers. They worked as haberdashers, and in banking. The native Ugandans resented these people and their leaders. The Indo-phobia culture began with Milton Obote, Amin's predecessor. The rise of "Africa is for Africans" coincided with the desire to Africanize both commerce and industry in Uganda, which gave rise to a regime of regulatory requirements imposed to restrict accessibility to the Ugandan economy by South Asians.[36]

Michelle went to the Bank of Uganda on one of the large commercial strips in the city to open up a small bank account. Her funds were limited, and she had to be a good manager of her very small budget. She noted that the bank guards wore khaki uniforms and had guard dogs inside the entrances. The guard dogs were mostly German shepherds and were the biggest dogs she had ever seen: "It was quite frightening to see the size and the menacing look of these dogs. I hurried my business to conclusion and left the bank as quickly as I had gone in."

While walking through the city center, Michelle mentioned that she came upon the American embassy. She had not known where it was before she encountered it. The sight of the embassy gave her much ease and comfort. The American flag flew briskly in the azure sky of the Ugandan capital, flapping in the swirling wind loudly as though to remind her of her homeland and the security that she left behind. The stars and stripes, albeit complex for an African-American, was nonetheless a source of pride, familiarity and security to her. She was at that moment proud to be an American. She innately knew that she had never stopped being proud of being an American; she was simply distressed and ambivalent about the history and treatment of her people in America.

She also went into the Hilton Hotel on one of the main thoroughfares, and she recollected that it was a popular place to stay and to dine and was especially popular during tea time. The hotel had a lovely bakery she remembered, and whenever her sweet tooth got the best of her she would make her way to this hotel to get her fix. The songs of James Brown reverberated from some of the shops, reminding her of the sidewalks in Center City Philadelphia where crowds of passersby listened to the soul sounds resonating from shops run by East, West, South Asians and other groups hawking electronic gadgets and other kitsch. As in America, the music ricocheted off the passersby as they looked into the windows pondering whether or not to make a buy. black American music was popular in Kampala. At least this aspect of African-American culture had made its way to "the dark continent." Perhaps other facets were there as well, enshrouded in the overbearing dominance of Western culture.

Next up was the immigration building, perhaps the most important building to a foreigner in Uganda. In this building passports and other travel documents were verified. She relates that she had to check in with these people when entering the country and when planning to leave the country and that she visited this building several times alone and with other students. She says that it was important to know where this building was, among all others, and that the guards that manned the building did not always seem friendly. In fact, many of them had a scowl on their faces as though intending to send a message of unfamiliarity and foreignness.

In Michelle's mind a trip to the city would not have been complete without a visit to a fast food restaurant. Blimpie was a popular sandwich place in Kampala, but Michelle mentions that she never ate there when she was in the States. However, she was not in the States now and she found herself often times eating at Blimpie because of its prices. They served cheeseburgers and fries and you could get a Coke.

Michelle's most compelling discovery was that she was not an African. Though mentally she thought she was, and by heritage her ancestry was surely partly African. In Africa, however, she was considered just another black American. She was easily distinguished from the native Africans by her dress, her walk, her mannerisms, her diction, her language, the way she wore her hair, in this case in an Afro style, and of course, finally, the lighter color of her skin. She says that she could easily be picked out from the crowd and identified as an African-American. There was no escape. "I am who I am," she had said to herself. The fact that she was in her ancestral homeland, "in the motherland," among the indigenous people of her heritage, made no difference. She could not change the fact that she was not "all the way" home but rather "visiting a home alone."

Michelle observes, "Being black was based on what was in your head and not what was on your back or on your head; it is a state of mind based upon a valid hereditary linkage, however tenuous. The woman in the mirror was staring at me in my mind's eye. I was that woman in the mirror. I realized that traveling to Africa would not give me back any lost identity. It only gave me a glimpse of what my ancestors' continent was like, and even that was hundreds of years in the past."

What it was like back then one could only imagine.

"We were taken away," she says, "and we lost our link to our heritage. I was visiting Africa like I would visit any other place, enjoying its monuments, enjoying the cultural differentiation. But the native people on this continent, in this country, in this city, were people of a dark complexion and had an unbroken nexus to their heritage. I was indeed a foreigner, though I did share an ancestral linkage, a commonality long removed."

James T. Campbell in his book *Middle Passages* tells several stories about African-American passages to Africa.[37] In one sequence Campbell talks about Langston Hughes's autobiography, *The Big Sea*, and Hughes's first encounter with Africans. The Africans first encountered by Hughes were the Kru—an African people mostly from Liberia and the Ivory Coast who were noted for their sailing and navigational prowess. These Africans worked on the ship ferrying Hughes to the Windward Coast, i.e. to West Africa from America. Campbell quotes Hughes:

> One of the Kru men from Liberia, working on our ship, who had seen many American Negroes, of various shades and colors, and knew much about America, explained to me,
>
> "Here," he said, "on the West Coast, there are not many-colored people—people of mixed blood—and those foreign colored men who are here come mostly as missionaries, to teach us something, since they think we know nothing. Or they come from the West Indies, as clerks and administrators in the colonial governments, to help carry out the white man's laws. So, the Africans called them all white men."
>
> "But I am not white," I said.
>
> "You are not black either," the Kru men said simply. "There is a man of my color." And he pointed

to George, the pantryman, who protested loudly.

"Don't point at me," George said. "I am from Lexington, Kentucky, U.S.A. And no African blood, nowhere."

"You black," said the man.

"I can part my hair," said George "and it ain't nappy."

But to tell the truth, George shaved a part of his hair every week, since the comb wouldn't work. The Kru man knew this, so they both laughed loudly for George's face was as African as Africa.

Campbell talks about the paradox of misrecognition. He goes on to say Hughes's voyage to Africa symbolizes the attraction and the pull of Africa to African-Americans, how Africa excites their imagination. Campbell says, "Africans have ideas and experiences of their own, which sometimes have little to do with the preconceptions of Western visitors, white or black."

CHAPTER FIFTEEN

A RUDE AWAKENING

Michelle relates additional events that happened shortly after her classes began. She says, "Randy, the other student from Swarthmore, finally arrived. He had been detained because he was mistaken for a spy. He said that the Ugandan security forces roughed him up and took his passport and that he barely made it to campus. Randy moved into the all-male dormitory not far from Mary Stuart Hall. I found out that there was also another black American female student on campus from Kalamazoo, Michigan." It could be said that Michelle and her fellow students were either the Three Princes of Serendip or the four students of mischance. Regardless of how you choose to characterize their experiences, they all had a healthy sampling of both. Michelle says, "Because we all had different classes, we rarely saw each other except at mealtime or on a scheduled outing."

She continues, "I generally enjoyed my classes. In the chemistry class that I signed up for most of the students were male. It was a tough class. Between the electrons, neutrons and positrons, I was totally subsumed by the complexity of the subject. But what was more difficult to adjust to was the body odor emanating from a few of the students in the class. The odor was killing me. The students did not wear soiled or dirty clothes; in fact they dressed very conservatively and their clothes usually looked clean. But some of them simply either did not use deodorant purposefully, perhaps because of the chemicals, or they were not aware of its place in personal hygiene. So, to remedy this issue I quietly sniffed first and chose a seat later. In the scheme of things this was no big deal.

"The Ki-Swahili class that I enrolled in was an attempt to learn the most common language in use in Africa. It was a challenge and also a social event because it required interaction with other students and vocalization of the words. In addition to the Swahili class, I also enrolled in a zoology class."

Michelle had previously taken a zoology class at Swarthmore. Upon realizing that she would not get credit for this class, since she had already taken it, her professor at Makerere, Dr. Kenneth White, was gracious enough to allow her to work on a "special project" on the African lungfish, often referred to as "living fossils." Dr. White, a blond, white Englishman with blue eyes, was very supportive. Michelle remembers Dr. White as being of medium height, always wore a lab coat to class, and exuded a very British persona of uprightness and decorum. The status of her research as a special project would enable her to receive credit for the class at Swarthmore. This kind of accommodation is often extended to exchange students by host universities.

There was much to be learned about this prehistoric animal that has existed for nearly 400 million years. It is known to "reach a length of 200 cm long and has the largest vertebrate genome known to date." The lungfish is eaten regularly by Africans.[38]

This special project afforded her a chance to complete, as she terms it, "a wonderful scientific experience." She recalls that at Swarthmore, she used prepared specimens for microscopic study. For this project, however, she had to prepare her own slides. This meant slicing the cellular tissue, dehydrating and staining the tissue, and preparing the slide for review and study. Michelle exclaims with great enthusiasm that it was a marvelous opportunity to apply what she had learned at Swarthmore. She tells me that a special trip was planned by her class to Lake Victoria so that she could catch an African lungfish. As soon as she was notified of the opportunity, she signed up immediately.

As with many visitors to Africa, myself included, Michelle was advised and received inoculations to prepare her for tropical diseases that she was not otherwise immune to. She had faithfully taken her malaria pills but got sick anyway. She became so ill that she had to seek help at a local clinic.

"My head was throbbing. I felt hot and feverish. I thought I would lose consciousness at any moment and fall to the ground. I walked to the nearest clinic hoping that I would be able to get immediate relief from what ailed me. But when I got there, unexpectedly, there was a long line. Those in the queue had no sympathy in their eyes. Everyone was suffering from something. The looks conveyed a message that said, 'Get in the back of the line. You are no better than us.' So, as I was prepared to do once I realized the reality of what I was facing—that I was not in America—I took my place at the end of the line."

She continues, "I felt so sick. It was only through the grace of God that I was able to stand until I got inside the clinic. I imagined that I was already in the ground dead and buried. When I finally got into the clinic and received medical attention, I was assured that in time I would recover. I went back to my dorm room and collapsed into the bed and slept. I let Vixena know that I was unwell, and she checked on me from time to time and bought me some food from the dining hall. As I gradually felt better, my strength returned. I had missed my trip to Lake Victoria to make my attempt at catching an African lungfish, but with the way I felt, it did not matter.

"Sometime after I recovered my health, a black ambassador who was closely connected to the university invited a group of us black American students to his home for a home-cooked meal."

In Africa many of the elites have cooks and maids in their homes.

"He told us that he had taught his African cook how to prepare delicious fried chicken. 'So be prepared for a feast,' he said."

From what Michelle says, the ambassador's home was beautiful. She describes it as an adobe-like structure all on one floor, constructed of what we would call stucco, but the exterior finish was of a sand texture. The roofing tiles were red terracotta that gave the house a non-native appearance. He had beautiful rugs on top of painted cement floors. There was a sense of Arabic in the furnishings and atmosphere of his home.

Africans and Arabs have an integrated history spanning centuries. African and Arabic cultures are inextricably interwoven. Arabs were some of the first slave traders in Africa and conducted much trade with the Africans. Some have espoused that it was the Arabs, more so than the Europeans, who influenced African culture.

Michelle says, "The ambassador's home was filled with many African artifacts and figurines evidencing both his status in that society and his extensive travels. He was one of the elites in Uganda. And as he had promised, he did prepare a 'feast' for us. The chicken usually served in the cafeteria was boiled and then seasoned, causing it to be tough. But the chicken served in the ambassador's home was scrumptious. In fact, it was the best chicken meal I had had thus far in Africa. During the dinner, the ambassador introduced us to his other guests, who were also living in Kampala at that time. Two of them were women. They were both married to Africans and had lived in Africa for quite a while. The women invited us to visit with them in their homes and we looked forward to those visits, not knowing what their stories would be. I felt a sense of community by virtue of this dining experience.

"The ambassador ended the evening as he had begun, by proclaiming that we were 'Young, Gifted and Black' in the words of Lorraine Hansberry, an American playwright of African descent and author of the play *A Raisin in the Sun*, and as composed in a tribute sung by Nina Simone. I indeed felt special and exalted, and that my potential was unlimited. I was ascendant as a child of Africa living in a world of unlimited possibilities. The song's verse continues, 'There's a world waiting for you.'"

Michelle shares that on one of her solo bus trips to Kampala she witnessed a frightening experience. She saw an old African man running behind a white American man, screaming, "American, American!" The African man chased the fellow with a broom, waving it in the air as though to strike the American with it. She asked the bus driver what was going on, and he told her that the old African man was "not all there." In retrospect, perhaps the old African man was saner than the others. Perhaps he was simply acting out the antipathy or some latent hostility experienced by him or related to him by his ancestors who lived through years of colonialization and abuse by Europeans and their progeny. Perhaps if his African brethren had done the same thing on a grander scale many decades before, much pain and exploitation could have been avoided.

"I decided not to get off the bus," she says. "And I returned to campus. I shared this experience with another black American student and told her, 'Going to Kampala is becoming a risky affair.'"

We pause for a moment to reflect on what has just been discussed. With a heavy sigh, she says, "You know, I never hitchhiked a ride while in America, but I sometimes hitchhiked a ride to Kampala. We felt safe doing it there for some reason. Vixena joined me on several occasions when I did this." Michelle knew that her mother would never approve of her doing such a thing, but her fear abated as her familiarity with her environment and the tenor of the people who inhabited the area grew.

One day, she and Vixena encountered an albino during one of their hitchhiking adventures. Albinism, as it is called by the scientists, is a condition found in human beings or other mammals caused by an absence of pigment in the skin, hair or eyes. The lack of melanin in the skin causes the person to have no color at all. The person's color is pink, not black, brown, red or yellow. Sometimes these people are called "white." Frances Cress Welsing, the noted Afrocentric psychiatrist, whose voice still echoes in the wind entreating those who will listen to heed, put forward the idea in *Cress Theory of Color Confrontation and Racism*[39] that racism is rooted in varying degrees of melanin and the "color inferiority" of white people. She went on to argue that the lack of melanin "led white people to develop hostility and aggression" toward people darker than they. Furthermore, she put forward the theory that "white people are the result of a genetic mutation of albinism and are the outcast offspring of the original peoples of Africa."

Every time she went to Kampala, Michelle says, "One of us would see this albino fella and we would hitch a ride with him." She told me that they got pretty comfortable with him. They ate lunch at the Hilton Hotel with him and on several occasions went on trips with him—to see the Kasubi Tombs, the burial grounds of the four kabakas, the kings of the Buganda. On one occasion, the albino wanted the two of them to go for a ride with him in the country. But they were suspicious and declined to do so. They explained to the albino that they had studying to do, a pretext to shield their anxiety concerning what his intentions may have been. He became agitated, Michelle tells me, and he dropped them off at the main campus and they never saw him again. Who knows how the Ugandans thought of him. Was he a white African in a genetic sense or just a freak of nature in their minds? Perhaps he thought he had found in Michelle and Vixena some friends who looked past his abnormality and sense of alienation and saw him as a person, a chance to be himself. Clearly, the women became uncomfortable because the albino had shown signs of possessiveness.

Michelle says, "On one of my solo trips to Kampala, I saw another frightening sight. As I was looking out of the window of the bus I was riding in, I saw a man running hurriedly down the crowded street holding his ear in his right hand. He was saying something loudly, but I could not hear what he was saying. Blood was gushing profusely from the left side of his head where his ear had been. The horror of the man holding his ear, the startling sight of the dark-red blood oozing from the left side of his head contrasting sharply with the pink of his palm and the deep ebony color of his skin—witnessing this event etched an indelible picture of horror in my mind," she tells me. A tricolor portrait of barbarism exacted on an individual who only wanted food. According to the gossip, one of his ears had been chopped off because he had stolen a loaf of bread. Was this the African derivative of the 1862 French novel by Victor Hugo, *Les Miserables,* but with a much more inhumane result? Evidently, the values on display in this act proved that bread was treasured over parts of the human body. The crime rate in Uganda was certainly kept under control.

"I felt sick and afraid. I planned to exit the bus at the next stop, but I decided to return to the campus. I could not regain my equilibrium. I could not erase the bleeding man from my mind."

Riding the bus to Kampala offered Michelle an opportunity to sightsee yet not be in the crowd. She could look out and not be seen within. Observing from a distance offers an opportunity to see and think at the same time. The incidences of displeasure were few, but those that did happen were riveting.

The next event occurred while Michelle was in Kampala walking down the street to meet her friend Vixena. Upon meeting Vixena, she was immediately taken aback by the fact that Vixena was wearing a miniskirt, a taboo in Muslim countries. Uganda has been known to be anywhere from 10 to 12 percent Muslim. The Muslim community has great influence in Uganda. Idi Amin was a Muslim. The social norms and mores of Uganda reflect many Muslim values, so it was no shock to Michelle, at least, that Vixena's miniskirt attire would evoke a reaction, and it did. Michelle said that the skirt Vixena was wearing was well above the knee, just below her mid-thighs. "I was furious!" she exclaims. Michelle asked herself, *Why in the world would she do this?*

Michelle and Vixena were given instructions on how to behave before they left for Uganda. Chief among them was the admonition that they should be respectful of Uganda's culture, its religion, and laws. Miniskirts, halter tops and other forms of provocative women's clothing was frowned upon and in certain places prohibited altogether. Miniskirts were against the dress code. The campus dress code was more relaxed, so minis could be worn, but not in town.

Michelle emphasizes, "I only had one pair of jeans and I wore them every time I went in town. Vixena knew the dress code." But Vixena, as in Rome, believed in pushing the limits. She feared no evil. And she thought that because of her sexuality, and her nationality above all, that the rules would be relaxed and prohibitions withdrawn, but she was sadly mistaken.

"Why are you wearing that miniskirt?" Michelle asked her.

"Because I want to wear it and nothing is going to happen," she retorted.

Michelle continues, "Not long after we began to talk, some policemen approached us. I could see them coming from afar. The khaki-colored uniforms with their black epaulets and black-and-gold insignia sent a message that could not be ignored. These guys were official. Each officer had a matching black beret with gold insignia on the right side. All of this put the scare into us. Surprisingly, they did not wear sidearms. We had been targeted. From the look on their faces, they were upset. They began screaming at Vixena, pointing to her dress. In response Vixena said, 'I am an American. I am an American!'"

"The policemen responded, 'Is this America? Are you in America? No, you are in *our* country and you must obey *our* rules.' He went on, 'You cannot wear this!' The anger with which the officer spoke was a bad omen.

"They clearly intended to make an example of her. I apologetically insisted, 'She made a mistake!' With my voice dropping in supplication, I said again, 'She made a mistake.' I said, 'She will not do it again!'

"The officer's response was quick and commanding. 'She surely won't; we're taking her in.'

"'Taking her in? Taking her in—what do you mean taking her in?' I asked the officer with tension and turmoil in my voice. I then followed that question with another question. 'Where?' All kinds of wild thoughts entered my mind. I was afraid for Vixena. Had she gone too far this time? It looked like she had."

"The policemen began to grab her by the arms. Vixena began resisting. She tried, in vain, to reason with them and even turned on her flirtatious charms to no avail. I stood there in amazement and disbelief. *She must be losing her mind!* I thought. *This is certainly not the time for winking eyes and batting eyelashes.* One policeman had her by the arm and the other was moving his hands down her skirt. Lust was in their eyes and her skirt was being slowly raised as they were pushing her toward a truck that had pulled up alongside of where we were fussing. A little bit more and her panties would have been visible.

"I saw the terror in Vixena's eyes. I did not want to go with her, but I could not in good conscience let them take her alone. I screamed at the top of my lungs, 'Get your hands off of her! Get your hands off of her! Leave her alone! What are you doing!' Miraculously, out of nowhere Mr. Eric appeared, the guardian angel sent from on high. He began speaking to the officers in their native tongue. After a long argument between them, our melee was over. Mr. Eric grabbed both Vixena and me by the arms and we briskly walked away.

"We got about several yards away from the scene and he looked at me with a frown on his face. An attitude of exasperation prefaced his inquiry. 'What were you doing, Michelle? That was foolish and dangerous,' he said. He was clearly agitated.

"I responded, 'It was Vixena's fault. She wore the miniskirt not me.' I wanted to make sure he knew where the blame should be placed. 'I couldn't let them take her away alone.'

"He admonished us both about following the rules. He re-emphasized the importance to us of obeying the rules. This time I think Vixena learned her lesson. And I never again saw her wearing a miniskirt in town.

"I thanked him for his intercession. We were lucky. He knew the policemen. He had taught them in school. If Mr. Eric had not appeared, this capricious and foolish act of Vixena's could have resulted in a bad experience. My mind began to conjure up our possible fates. I shuddered at the thoughts. I told Vixena, the next time she pulled a stunt like that, she was on her own. I told her I did not come to Africa to become a statistic."

Certainly in America the liberties and freedoms that characterize this society would militate against such a reaction by the police for a trivial act such as described. Nonetheless, people of color in America have lost their lives and been abused by the police for infractions not of much greater importance.

CHAPTER SIXTEEN

THE BLACK AMERICAN'S BURDEN

Harriett Karuhije had a vision of her life fashioned by age, education, and experience. She was a generation removed from Michelle's generation. Harriett was now a faculty member at a prestigious university, married to an African, and had earned a terminal degree in her chosen field of study. She had been approached by a colleague in her department at Columbia, as mentioned earlier, to go to Botswana to start a baccalaureate degree program in nursing. Harriett saw herself as a "nurse educator." She asked herself, *What now say you?* She chose to answer it by asking another question: *What am I doing here?*

The answer: "I was needed in Africa."

The historian James T. Campbell mentions in his book *Middle Passages* that as far back as 1795, during the African repatriation movement, Africa was seen by black people as "black people's 'native country' [...] [T]hese early back-to-Africa efforts also rested on the idea that black people in the United States were no longer like other Africans, that they had graduated to a higher civil and religious status, which equipped them for the task of redeeming their benighted brethren," the Boston petitioners, a group of seventy-five black Bostonians, asserted, "'inlightening [sic] and civilizing those nations which are now sunk in ignorance and barbarism.'"

A return to Africa would be a talisman for African-Americans, a "crook of the arm," so to speak. Africa in many ways would be a stronghold for African-Americans if properly overseen, contemplated, analyzed and developed with their help and surveyed.

Harriett recalled, "In 1978 I was approached by an academic advisor at Teachers College, Columbia University, to apply for the position of nurse educator at the University of Botswana." Unbeknownst to her at the time, she would end up spending three years there. Her faculty advisor had been her EdD sponsor and was responsible for bringing her onto the faculty. Her advisor assured her that this position was "custom made to fit you." Harriett made her initial move to Botswana in December 1979.

Her closest friend in the country was Serara Kupe, a Motswana, a citizen of Botswana and a member of the Twana people, the largest ethnic group in Botswana. Serara had been one of Harriett's master's degree students. She lived across the hall from Harriett in the student/faculty housing building. Harriett explained that she did not want to get too close to Serara because of their academic relationship. Harriett became Serara's sponsor when Serara was enrolled in the PhD program at Columbia.

Harriett remembered that she had much trepidation and doubt about undertaking such an endeavor. She told me that she did much soul searching, and it took a lot of coaching to get her to accept this challenge because she was concerned that Botswana was dangerously close to "apartheid" South Africa. But her fears were allayed somewhat when she reflected upon the fact that Serara was a native of Botswana.

Briefly, *apartheid* was a system of racism and segregation codified into law after the 1948 elections in South Africa. Apartheid built upon existing laws of segregation. Apartheid "cruelly and forcibly" separated people with the legal system and governmental apparatus to enforce it, in effect institutionalizing racism as a matter of law. The apartheid regime was a system of laws designed to suppress, dehumanize, and exploit Africans, Indians and the coloreds of South Africa.[40] The apartheid system was dismantled completely between 1993 and 1996.

Harriett said to me that when Serara learned that Harriett had received the job offer, Serara urged her to accept the position because "a university degree program to prepare teachers for the five nursing programs, one diploma and four programs for enrolled nurses, had been a dream of hers for many years." Serara was ecstatic about the offer. Harriett added, "During my discussions with Serara, I learned that she was the highest-ranking nurse or chief nursing officer in Botswana, and she said she was prepared to give me all of the help that she could to make the program a reality." Serara did not have her doctorate, and they wanted a black person with a PhD to hold the position, and Harriett had the EdD. Since the University of Botswana was a male-dominated university, the men set the terms and conditions of qualification. One thing is for sure: the powers that be did not want a white nurse heading up the program, though one had been identified.

Serara also warned her that there were "powerful forces in the country who did not want an American-style educational program for nurses." Harriett learned that the British system for all education in the country was the existing and preferred model, a model based upon decentralization and minimal expense. The complexity of this controversy between the colonizer and its erstwhile surrogate regarding whose pedagogy would prevail, especially in this nursing program, would prove to be the central conflict that Harriett had to either resolve or suffer through. Despite this contentious issue, Harriett knew that this was an opportunity that she could not let go.

Serara was of small build, a thin woman about five and a half feet tall. She had high cheekbones, short black hair and a small face.

Harriett informed me that Serara had an ancestral connection to, or was a descendant of, the Kalahari Bushmen, otherwise known as the San people: a tan-colored people known to have been the first inhabitants of Botswana and Southern Africa. Serara was truly an indigenous African. This population of African people are also known to be the ancestral progenitor, if you will, of the Negroid race as well as being the "remnants of Africa's oldest cultural group."[41] There was not one scintilla of miscegenation in her bloodline and no Westernization of her native culture. She was an aborigine and an attractive African woman.

Serara and Harriett had a mutual admiration for each other. Their discovery of a shared cultural and philosophical outlook about Africa conjoined them in a collaboration and friendship that endured for decades and still persists today. Serara once asked Michelle's mother, Mary, "When are you coming to my country?" Mary not only could not answer that question but chose to remain silent and let her silence speak louder than words. In the midst of all of this, Mary recalled that she still had no fears about Harriett's safety. "Harriett was older, a great teacher, and her students greeted her with so much love. She was a hell of a teacher and her students were running to greet her."

Mary did not learn for sure that Harriett was going to move to Botswana until it was announced publicly in Chester at a "Who's Who" party, a social group founded for notables in the Chester community by Harriett's mother, Isabelle. Mary said she was shocked that Harriett would actually go. She was disappointed, but she resigned herself to this reality, as she had done with her daughter and with Harriett, by saying, "If you want to go, you should do so." Her heart was not in the words she spoke. She knew that she was powerless to prevent it.

Serara often called Harriett "Sis." Harriett went on to recall that Serara was intensely involved in the affairs of the University of Botswana, and she was passionate about her politics. For example, she vehemently disliked homosexuals and often criticized Harriett because of Harriett's more liberal views toward homosexuality. As a result, Serara was disliked by some but engendered envy and jealousy in others. The intensity of this jealousy caused Serara to gain weight, so she began to run as an exercise to lose the weight and to relieve stress. Harriett discerned that the source of the jealousy was rooted in Serara's upward mobility, aggressiveness to achieve and the economic success she attained because of it.

There was much to be done to make this move to Africa a reality. To start with, Harriett had never heard of Botswana. *Where is this country located?* she wondered. *And what is it all about?* In order to make her final decision, she had to answer these questions and more. As Harriett remarked to me, "Living in another country is vastly different than visiting another country."

Harriett's decision to go to Africa was a seminal moment in her life. This decision would define her as an international scholar in the nursing profession and, in her mind, create the vision of her self-image that she wanted for herself. In combination with her marriage to an African and her assumptive African ancestry, the issue of her commitment and authenticity as an "African" American would be beyond reproach. If she could pull this off, and there was no doubt in her mind that she could, this experience in Africa would give her a cachet not easily found in the academic world. It would distinguish her among equals. Harriett's passion to go to Africa was a valance against which nothing could detract or dissuade.

Her research revealed that Botswana, formerly known as Bechuanaland, is a small country. For comparison purposes Botswana is about the size of Texas in the United States, Madagascar or France. And the Kalahari Desert covers 70 percent of the landmass. This of course limits the amount of arable land available to the population for cultivation and agricultural purposes.

Perhaps the most distinguishing characteristic of Botswana is that it has one of the most stable democratic governments in the continent of Africa. And as measured against other African states, it has a high per capita income as well as a competitive banking and financial system. Botswana has increased its literacy level to over 80 percent and spends over 20 percent of its annual budget on education. Three of its primary sources of domestic and foreign income are mining (especially diamonds), tourism and cattle. The majority of the people follow Christianity as a religious faith. Botswana has approximately two million people and is one of the most well run and least corrupt countries in Africa.

Botswana became independent on September 30, 1966. Botswana is north and east of South Africa, borders Namibia to the west and north and Zimbabwe to the northeast. It also has a northern border with Zambia. Botswana is a landlocked country. From 1886 to 1966 Botswana was a colony, technically a protectorate of Great Britain. Uganda was also a protectorate, for over sixty-eight years, before acquiring its independence from Great Britain. Botswana's custodial oversight lasted for eighty years. During the years of the protectorate, the British model of education, as mentioned above, was imposed on Botswana.

The distinction between a protectorate and a colony lies in the exercise of sovereignty. There is no exercise of sovereignty for a colony. A protectorate normally has something to offer the larger country, and the foreign policy of a protectorate is handled by the country providing the protection, in this case Great Britain. Setswana is the national language, but English is the official language.

A fellow traveler by the name of Ray Hayward, an Aussie, related to me a story he heard while traveling in Botswana in the 1990s that he said was widely known. There is no history supporting the following version of the founding of Botswana. His version was that "prior to its independence Botswana was organized as a trust. The people shared the assets in the trust. Its leader in the late 1940s and early '50s married an English noblewoman and the two of them set up the country where everyone shared the wealth." He said, "As a white man I never felt unsafe when traveling in Botswana," and that he "would go back at the drop of a hat."

What he was alluding to was the story of Khama III, king of the Bangwato people, the indigenous peoples of Bechuanaland, present-day Botswana. Khama was an African of sub-Saharan color, and a converted Christian with a thin face and pointed ears. His hair was knotted in a native pattern of his tribe, neatly arrayed across his head in rows from ear to ear from the nape of his neck to his forehead. Khama fought to ensure that his land and its people would not be incorporated into the Transvaal and the Cape Colony, i.e. South Africa. He was able to convince the British to make Bechuanaland a protectorate, thereby insuring against its annexation and incorporation into the aforementioned British colonies. But for his resolute determination and foresight that prevented the accession, his people and its land would have been subjected to that heinous form of white supremacy and racial separation known as apartheid.

His grandson Seretse Khama, heir to the throne of leadership of the Bangwato people, while studying at Oxford married a British woman—the supposed "noblewoman," of which there is no proof. This event caused much angst in South Africa, resulting in Seretse's preclusion from returning to his native country for six years. However, in 1965 he was permitted to return to Botswana and was installed as president.

The University of Botswana as well as Columbia provided Harriett with assistance in finding suitable housing. Serara offered her assistance as well. She recommended neighborhoods that were close to the university with adjacent shopping available. Before learning that the university would provide housing, Harriett's plan was to rent a house in the city. She owned her existing home in Chester and, not knowing the security or the hospitableness of the environment she would encounter, both natural and unnatural, renting was the only viable option. Harriett was comfortable with her aloneness. She made few friends and confided in me that Mary was her closest friend.

Along with coaxing her mother, Isabelle, to embrace her new adventure, there was much to be done. As mentioned earlier, Isabelle was not of the mind to see Africa as some sort of panacea. Isabelle had accepted America on its own terms and was determined to make it within the existing American system, albeit a racist system. She had no longing for what "might" have been or what she thought she had "missed." She, along with many others of her generation, was whole within herself—without more, she was living a comfortable life. Sure, she knew that things were not right in America and that her people had been much abused to say the least, but age brings on a certain resignation to the inevitable truth of obstinacy when change is sought by people of color to better their condition. During her generation, life had improved for African-Americans. She had lived through the Jim Crow era, predominantly in the North. If her energy and her efforts to change her reality in America in years past had fallen short, she certainly was not of a mind to do it now. At this time Isabelle was approaching sixty years of age. She and Mary, though Mary was a generation younger, approached the issue of their African-ness in much the same way: practical, not fully informed about their ancestral history, but with muted pridefulness.

Harriett went home to Chester to tell her mother of the opportunity not long after she digested it herself. Harriett chose to discuss the issue with her mother on a Sunday evening after they had returned from church. She said, "Mother, I have been offered an opportunity to work in the nursing department at the University of Botswana in Gaborone, Botswana, and I want to do this. This is an opportunity of a lifetime and I promise you, you will enjoy it. It will be something different!"

"Harriett, you know I'm too old and tired to be gallivanting around the world with you," her mother retorted. She went on, "You can stay at Columbia. You have a good job, people like you, and if you don't like New York you can go back to Widener. You still have great opportunities at Widener University. Why not consider that?"

"But, Mother," Harriett responded. "I promise you, you will enjoy it. There will be much to see and enjoy. I understand we will possibly have some servants to help with the housework and to cook, and I want to be close to Eric. Uganda is just across the border from Botswana." Isabelle shook her head from side to side with a sense of resignation. Was this an argument she could win? *Probably not,* she thought.

But she had many questions. "What about my doctors and my health care?" she asked; and she continued, "Does Botswana have enough hospitals in case I need care or get sick? You know I have to have annual checkups because of my condition, and what about my medicines and my prescriptions? Don't they have a lot of military takeovers and killing over there? I don't want to be caught up in that stuff!"

Harriett thought she had better reassure her mother promptly. "Yes, Mother, I know that, and I have been thinking about that. Yes, they do have some of that over there," she said, referring to the military coups and takeovers, "but Botswana is a peaceful country, and we won't have to worry about that." Harriett, though sympathetic, nonetheless repressed her annoyance with her mother's valid objections.

"And," Isabelle added, "What will I do with *my* time while you are working at the university? I don't know anybody over there. What am I supposed to do, sit around and twiddle my thumbs all day?" The questions and comments kept coming, some of which Harriett thought were beyond the pale. But she too had thought of these and other concerns.

As Harriett took it all in, Isabelle thought, *How could I deny my overachieving daughter such an opportunity?* She cleared her throat and looked at Harriett sincerely. "Okay, all right, I will do what I can to make this work for you, but you get some answers for me about these questions I have," she insisted. Isabelle then made her last plea. "I will go as long as you promise me that we will stay no longer than the term of your initial appointment. Two years; is that right?" Harriett neglected to mention the additional year she intended to stay.

Harriett said, "Yes, that's right, and I promise you we will not stay a day later." Harriett breathed a sigh, heartened, and smiled at the discourse. She knew her mother well and knew her inclinations; Isabelle could be stubborn, and there were no guarantees that she would ultimately go. Isabelle had been diagnosed with breast cancer several years before, and as a result, to maintain her health, she had to have annual checkups and X-rays and mammograms and a proper diet to keep the disease at bay. Her concerns were legitimate, and as a loving daughter, Harriett knew the importance of assuring that her mother's health did not deteriorate while she was in Botswana. Her mother loved her dearly and would do anything to help her. Harriett knew that, so her conscience had to be clear. She could not afford those kinds of problems. Having assuaged her mother's ire after much cajoling and debate, Harriett secured the commitment of her mother to go with her.

These were questions and concerns that any prudent person would require answers to before planning a prolonged stay in any country that one is unfamiliar with: in this case, a short-term stay of three years in Botswana. These concerns recall an event that occurred in Liberia in 2015. A three-time Pulitzer-prize-winning photojournalist by the name of Michel du Cille died while being transported from a village over dirt roads to the nearest hospital two hours away. It is reported that a heart attack befell him. Poor and inaccessible roadways, poor transportation networks and an absence of competent emergency health professionals increases the probability of death from illnesses that could otherwise be treated. So Isabelle's concerns were justified.

"It took over a year," Harriett proclaimed. This duty of persuasion was self-imposed since it was she that wanted to go, and she could not go without her mother. Obtaining visas, arranging for the shipment of furniture and other items that she wanted to take with her—books, research papers, computer equipment and all the other creature comforts that would make her feel home away from home, not to mention items that her mother wanted to take—paled in comparison to the effort required to persuade her mother of the efficacy of this undertaking.

By the time she was finished with all that was required of her, Harriett was "worn to a frazzle," as the old folks would say.

Now that her housing issues were behind her and she knew where she and her mother would be living for the next three years, Harriett was able to move forward with the task at hand. But the next question was what to do with her home that she shared with her mother in Chester. She thought about several options: selling the house, renting it, or just simply closing it up and securing it until she returned years later. Ultimately, she decided to sell her home. At least this way she would not have to worry about tenants, damages, maintenance and all that goes with maintaining a home as an absent owner.

Harriett's advent into the African state of Botswana to live, work and to make a life for herself placed her in the company of many notable expatriates who traveled this road to Africa before: *bon secours*, "good help." In James T. Campbell's *Middle Passages*, he tells of expatriates who made a pilgrimage to the West Coast, including Ghana, Senegal, Nigeria, Sierra Leone, Liberia and others, such as W. E. B. Du Bois and his wife, Shirley Graham Du Bois.

I had the pleasure of visiting the home, library and burial site of Dr. Du Bois and his wife in Accra on a visit to Ghana years ago. Also present at the period Dr. Du Bois was there was the auteur Maya Angelou, the writer, poet, singer and actress. Malcolm X and Mohammed Ali also made appearances in Ghana during the Nkrumah era. Mary L. Dudziak, in her 2008 book entitled *Exporting American Dreams: Thurgood Marshall's African Journey*, discusses Thurgood Marshall, the lead attorney in the seminal case of *Brown v The Board of Education*, whose forebears were of Congolese origins. Marshall journeyed to Kenya where he drafted the precursor of the Kenyan

Bill of Rights in the 1960s in the lead up to their independence from Britain in 1963.

Campbell's narrative of the stories of many expatriates is rich and vivid in its descriptions of their struggles while in Africa. As he says, "[T]hree of the defining moments of 20th century history, the African-American freedom struggle, the African independence movement, and the global anti-colonial movement, flowed together [...]"

Perhaps the most poignant example of the expatriate African-American presence in Africa is exemplified by the experience many expatriates had during the post-colonialization era in Ghana, the citadel of the expatriate community, then led by the charismatic Kwame Nkrumah. As Campbell says, Nkrumah was influenced not only by Marcus Garvey but also by Paul Cuffe, the black poet; by Martin Delaney, the journalist, writer and abolitionist; and by Henry McNeal Turner, the minister and politician. "All of whom," according to Campbell, "had dreamed of an Africa remade by the skills, energy, and culture of black people from the Diaspora." The skills brought by black Americans to Africa during this period consisted of contractors who were plumbers, electricians, doctors, law professors, dentists and academics. However, the "largest single contingent were teachers."

Campbell tells us that at the University of Ghana, for example, which I visited many years ago and had the pleasure of purchasing an influential book on African history from, there was "a large contingent of African-American professors and students, several of whom—David Levering Lewis, Nell Irwin Painter, Preston King, Sylvia Boone, Martin Kilson—went on to distinguished academic careers. The dean of the group was St. Clair Drake, who arrived at Legon in 1954." According to Campbell, Ghana had a unique appeal because of its location on the west coast of Africa, the coastline that saw many millions of Africans exported to the Americas to be enslaved. And because Nkrumah was greatly influenced by Marcus Garvey, he was one of "black America's own."

Harriett's mindset was clearly in the same place as that of her past compatriots, but to get there required considerable flying time.

A seventeen-hour flight awaited Harriett and her mother. There would be a stopover in Johannesburg before continuing to Gaborone. This trip would be tough sledding for Isabelle and no walk in the park for Harriett. Both were unenthusiastic flyers.

Upon their arrival in Gaborone, Botswana, Harriett made her way to the house the university provided. She and her mother began to unpack and to survey their new home. Harriett learned that the housing in Gaborone was modern by Western standards, containing all the standard features one would expect to find in a house in the United States or in Europe. In fact, in Botswana you could get way more house for the money than you could ever expect to get in the United States or in Europe. Many of the houses had more than one level but rarely more than two. The colors were soft on the eyes: tanned and varied cement colors, some with pastels but clearly an uplifting color selection. The housing selection was varied: houses built of cinderblock painted white with terracotta roofs, two-story stucco houses painted gray and trimmed in white, brick houses with reflecting glass, two-story houses with driveways and retaining walls, cathedral-like houses with ornamental ironworks, houses with Spanish verandas, orange houses, etc.—you name it, you could possibly find it in the city of Gaborone.

The home of Harriett and her mother in Gaborone, Botswanna, 1979.

Harriett was offered a single-family house built in a community of about ten houses furnished by the University of Botswana. Her house was a brand-new, one-story ranch style with a large kitchen and a patio in the back. The house was painted white with light-green trim. It had three bedrooms and she told me, "It was quite nice." The house had a huge front yard and a large backyard, she remembered. The development had a semicircle in the middle of it with the houses situated around the circle.

She recalled that the source of electricity was a large electrical supply unit located at the front of the semicircle. She was thrown off by the fact that the unit was in front of the development and children would come by, especially during dinnertime, and flip the switch that turned off the electricity.

One memorable aspect of the house was the beautiful parquet floors she loved. There was a living room and dining room combination, and the interior was decorated in an artistic fashion. She also said that she had two housekeepers, one full-time and the other as needed, and a gardener.

Not long after that, she found her way to the university. The University of Botswana (UB) is a modern university by any standards. It has many redbrick one-story and two-story buildings, lush lawns and green shrubs, palm trees and plaza areas with green sitting benches and walkways with ceilings. The university has several statues and man-made ponds with pampas grass or its kindred growing out of the water. Sculptures of cows and yeomen appear on the grounds, emblematic of the contributions of the local people, of cows and chickens and goats, anything that they could contribute to the building of the university. There presently is a state-of-the-art football stadium and a few buildings as high as four stories. There are the occasional sandstone and clay-colored buildings intermixed that lend a variety to the red brick. There is a large student center building. And many of the buildings are very modern, first-world constructions with glistening stainless-steel window frames and beams and large plate glass windows resembling low-rise contemporary technology structures. The campus is clean, well-managed and modern.

The barren dirt grounds are swept daily and offer a striking contrast to the lush green shrubs and grounds. Shade trees are scattered about with their green canopies.

"Grapevines were everywhere. You could eat grapes as you walked through the campus," Harriett recalled. The university was just six years old when Harriett first began her work in 1979. When Harriett worked there, the most common color of the buildings was of classical red brick. Most of the buildings back then were one-story buildings with trellises. Like most universities, the University of Botswana is laid out like a small city. State-of-the-art facilities exist for many of its schools and colleges that would rival any university in the United States. There is the occasional African hut placed in designated areas on the village green to remind passersby of the genesis of it all: a vivid reminder of the rural hinterlands and agrarian past, much of which persists today. One could say that the university is built in an arboretum of sorts. Like Makerere University in Uganda, UB sets the standard for higher education in Botswana. Over 15,000 students attend it. One note in passing: Neither Makerere University nor the University of Botswana is the oldest university in sub-Saharan Africa. That distinction belongs to Fourah Bay College in Freetown, Sierra Leone, founded in February of 1827.

There were quite a few Ugandans in Botswana at the time that Harriett worked there. Her relationship with her husband was still very much intact, and Eric visited Harriett a number of times during her first stay in Botswana. She even tried to convince him to stay in Botswana, knowing that he could easily get a position at the university because of his mathematical talents. Moreover, Eric's standing—in regard to Amin and the powers that be in Uganda—was good, so Eric was able to go to and come from Uganda and to other ports of call in Africa as he wished.

Though they had been married for several years, Harriett revealed that she did not know anything about Eric's politics, especially as it concerned Uganda, his religion, and his views about sex, all of which carried over into his lifestyle in Africa and in America. This cumulative dearth of knowledge about these intimate details about the man she loved and married, though intrinsic to a deeper understanding of the man, were not necessarily fatal. It simply exposed the innocence of her approach and portended, perhaps, an unfavorable outcome. So the battle would now be joined. Harriett was in Botswana and began to take her place at the university. She had undertaken a most formidable task, the success of which would be uncertain, but what she did know was that she would give her best efforts and her memories would last a lifetime.

CHAPTER SEVENTEEN

A WILDLIFE ADVENTURE

Michelle and I resume our discussion of her adventures in Uganda. She reminds me that she has always been skittish, and remains so, about insects, bugs of all types, and wild animals. She was raised in the city where bugs and insects exist, but there are not many animals except in the Philadelphia Zoo less than twenty miles north of Chester, Pennsylvania.

Michelle tells me that she was intent on making the next field trip with her biology class. She took great pleasure in being a student of biology, and to her the entire upcoming outdoor experience along with her classroom work was exciting. She had missed the trip to Lake Victoria to capture an African lungfish, the subject of her research. So, her intent was clear: stay healthy, eat light and make it to the bus on time. She recounts that they began traveling toward the countryside in a van. A white van with the university's name written on the front door. She recalls, "It was suitable enough for us, nine students, four women and five men, to ride comfortably to our destination."

The countryside in Africa was nothing like she ever imagined. This was the outback, the bush, the jungle all combined in one eco-habitat. The road they traveled on was asphalt for many miles.

"On each side of the road there were fields of green grasses and trees as far as the eye could see," she says. "In the valleys and the plateaus that stretched for miles, I could see a mountain range in the background the hue of which was shrouded in a cloudy mist that retained a bluish tint. One could see the occasional hut with a thatched roof and stucco veneer, and in some cases there was just wild grasses six to nine inches high with an assortment of farm animals grazing placidly. And," she says nostalgically, "you had better know where you're going." There was a bucolic feel to it all as she gazed through the van window at the expansive horizon. This was the picture of Africa she had in her mind.

Then the bus driver stopped for the first bathroom break. She looked around for restrooms. There weren't any, not even a "Port-a-John," which would have sufficed. She had anticipated standard bathrooms would be available during bathroom breaks. All she saw was a vast expanse of weeds, woods, trees and ponds. She said to herself, *Where are the women to relieve themselves?* She realized that this would be an outdoor experience when the driver yelled out, "Men on the right, women on the left."

As each student exited the van, the driver passed out sheets of toilet paper. The students walked into the tall grasses and weeds an adequate distance away from the van to find their spot and ensure privacy. Hesitantly, she too walked in search of privacy. Because the driver saw she her lagging behind the others, hesitant to secure her spot, he said, "You better go if you got to go." She had no choice in the matter, so she gathered up her toilet paper and looked for a suitable place in nature's nest to satisfy nature's calling. In retrospect, she says, "It is a real trick knowing how to relieve yourself in the woods and not soil your underwear."

The driver hollered, "Ten minutes! We are leaving in ten minutes!"

In addition to her anxiety over being in this place and having to relieve herself in this manner, she had to cope with being rushed to complete the job. To avoid making a mess of herself, she says, "In the midst of my anxiety about the time and place, I had to calm myself down and take my time so that I could control my bodily functions. I needed to go. I had to go. I had to do this. Who knows when we are likely to stop again!" She then pulled her pants and her underwear down and squatted. Making sure she did not wet her clothes, she slid her trousers and her underwear down around her ankles. Her bottom was exposed, vulnerable to all the creatures in the habitat. She was concerned that she would be a good target for an aggressive bug of some sort, and so she anxiously did her business and pulled her panties and her trousers back up all in one motion, expediting the process. She heaved a sigh of relief that she had not been stung, bitten, crawled upon or scratched by any of the unfriendly elements in that environment. She had survived her first bathroom experience in the African bush.

Since this was her first time, she felt some embarrassment, and she was uncomfortable because she was unable to wash her hands. A fastidious person, especially about her bathroom habits, she says she spit on her hands and used one of her pieces of toilet paper to wipe her hands off. She returned to the van with a commitment to herself: "I'm not eating or drinking anything else today!"

The bus continued on for another hour or so; then it stopped again. And as she looked out the window to find out what caused the bus to stop, she saw baboons all around the bus. This was her first exposure to baboons. The ones she saw were dark brown and she was instructed to be calm. They were harmless. She was also told that the baboons had become somewhat domesticated because so many people fed them, so they felt comfortable around humans, and they walked up to the vehicles all the time for food. She looked at the woman next to her and laughed and said, "I'm glad the baboons feel comfortable because I surely don't." She was glad when the vehicle started up again and made its way to the next stop.

African baboons can weigh anywhere from 50 to 100 pounds.

Their coats are in several different colors: gray, brown, sandstone and dark brown. The natural habitat of the baboons are the savannas and woodlands that Michelle was traveling through with her group. Their pink and often dark faces and long snouts resemble a dog's. Their dark, recessed eyes give them a certain human quality. The most common baboon found in Uganda is the olive baboon, which is large and dark brown, and the yellow baboon, a tan colored animal. Both inhabit East Africa and Tanzania. Among other characteristics shared with humans is the requirement of water and a safe sleeping environment.

When traveling some years ago in South Africa in Cape Town, I encountered baboons around the Cape of Good Hope. Along with the others with whom I traveled, I was taken aback by the friendliness, hyperactivity and the perceived desire of the baboons to get close to humans. We were told to watch our cameras, our bags and any other loose items because, if the baboons got close enough, they would snatch them and run away. It was a fascinating encounter.

They traveled on, Michelle says, and it was not long before they encountered giraffes. "There were several of them." She observed that the lower-hanging leaves on the limbs and branches of tall trees had been eaten in a neat horizontal pattern. They got out of the van and proceeded toward a lake. It was Lake Victoria, Africa's largest lake with a surface area of more than 26,000 square miles. Lake Victoria is located in east central Africa, bordering the countries of Uganda, Kenya and Tanzania. The lake is more than 400,000 years old and has an average depth of approximately 130 feet. Arab traders were the first to record the discovery of the lake and created a map of it dating back to approximately 1160 AD. John Hanning Speke in 1858 was the first European to travel the lake and claimed that it was the source of the Nile River. Lake Victoria is the largest tropical lake in the world and the planet's second-largest freshwater lake.[42]

There they heard the stirring and hair-raising sounds of hippopotamuses in the water. The hippos were jostling among themselves and flapping their heads up and down in the muddy, green-tinted water, frolicking in an element of their natural habitat. She had seen movies and pictures on television of this scene she now encountered in real time, but she recalls, "I could only see a few of them. It was too dangerous to try to get any closer." She thought that she had better not walk alone anywhere because these animals could be roaming around in the bush, and she certainly did not want to face off with any of them. In this same area, a quarter mile away, was a small stream. It was there that she finally washed her hands. She took some pictures. The other female students removed their shoes and waded into the water. Her conservative nature prevailed. The biologist in her was concerned about all of the water species that might inhabit the stream, so she stayed on the strand. But she had a moment of reflection knowing that she would not likely get this opportunity again.

The blue Ugandan couch grass swayed beneath the gentle breezes that flowed from the lake to the grass fields abutting the shoreline. She removed her shoes and curled her toes in the moist tan mush of sand on the shoreline. She wrote the names of her deceased relatives not far from where she planted her feet—those of her two aunts and her grandfather. She also wrote the name of G, her dissociated love. She took a picture of his name as she had written it in the sand and she began to cry. In those moments of cloying melancholy, her attention stayed focused on G and the song "Far Away" by Carol King. She and G had made that song their own. And as she heard the words in her mind, she yearned for his presence.

She also was meditative as she contemplated the entirety of this moment. She said to the Great Spirit, "I have dreamed of this moment, and this moment is here. Connect me, oh God, with the souls of my deceased ancestors and hear them, I pray, Mother Africa!" She was still searching for that elusive connection, that spiritual bond she felt Africa would provide her.

Though she longed for the mystical, she says, she only experienced the corporeal. She inhaled deeply the kinetic sensory perceptions from the environment she was in. She smelled the forest and the grasses intertwined, she heard the sounds and voices of the wild animals back off in the distance; she could hear life emanating from the jungle, the crackling of tree limbs as they fell to the ground, old trees shedding their dead members. She thought of her people and how years of separation from their homeland had caused them to separate from the family tree that they had been attached to.

She could see an unending firmament that for the moment made her feel that she was home in Chester, standing in a field of dreams. She felt the breeze blow through her, over her and around her, reminiscent of "Westwind," a song by Miriam Makeba and sung by Nina Simone. The lyrics of that song captured the moment for her. It said what she would have said had she been the composer: "Guard each gallant warrior's claim 'cause I am the soil from which they came . . . take my people by the hand, spread your glory sunshine and unify my promised land."

As she walked along, meandering at will, sinking her bare feet step-by-step ever so slightly into the wet sand, she felt the loss of the tether. Indeed, the hearts of her people had been broken, leaving only a hollow core filled with a makeshift hodgepodge of Afrocentric trappings: jagged edges of remembrance, shards of memorabilia and affectations of Western culture and civic standards disproportionately inclusive of pop European and American culture, especially in the lower classes. The effect of which is the creation of a new culture, a *fortiori*. The pain of this untethering cannot be filled by artifice and rationality but will forever pierce the veil that drapes the souls of black Americans. What could have been and what can be imagined are of no moment but leave only a haunting reverberation of unrequited love. When the culture of a people is destroyed, so is the identity of that people destroyed.

After a day of exploring, she says, they lodged for the evening. Their lodges were large African huts with thatch roofs. There was one large hut for the women, and one further down the pathway for the men.

Michelle pauses to sharpen her recollection, and then says, "Our hut had nothing inside but some low cots with very thin mattresses, one table, a few chairs, some kerosene lamps and big basins for washing. The toilet was an outhouse, which was only a tiny hut in a state of dilapidation with a hole in the ground with bugs and flies of all sorts swarming around making it their home." In the army, guys are used to digging latrines, which are basically parallel rows of horizontal ditches that are used for the absorption of human waste. Men in the army are used to this sort of thing, but college girls are unfamiliar with it. When Michelle gazed upon the hole in the tiny hut, she told me she vowed to herself that her bottom would not provide the next meal for any bugs on the prowl. "I made sure that I ate very little and drank lightly. I had no intention of going to the bathroom late at night under those conditions."

"I couldn't sleep at all that night," she tells me. "I kept hearing sounds from animals and imagined all sorts of creatures roaming about. Though I did not become hysterical, my anxiety was high, so just like a gunslinger in an American Western movie would have kept his six-gun under his pillow as he slept, I kept my flashlight in my hand as I tried to grab a few winks of sleep. It was tough. After a fretful night, the male students made their way to the female hut and told us that a hippopotamus had poked his head into their hut and that they were able to scare him off by shining the torch light [flashlight] in his eyes and making loud noises."

As an afterthought, she says, "Had such a thing happened to us hysteria would have enveloped us all." The next day was a day of more exploring, and they stopped for dinner at a modern tourist facility. She recalls that "the view from the tour facility of the surrounding terrain was absolutely beautiful." She says she had a scrumptious dinner and was relieved to find standard regular bathroom facilities of which she took full advantage. After a long bus ride back to campus, the tour came to an end. She says, "I was very tired, but I needed a bath. I took a shower, washed my hair and fell into bed. I was consumed with my dreams of Africa. Even though our accommodations in the field had been substandard to say the least, my perceptions were not colored by that fact. Erased from my mind were the caricatures of Africa as portrayed in the American and European media as an uncontrolled web of tangled jungle with wild beasts and barbarous conditions, where serenity and civility, if it ever existed, was only made available by European intervention, not from the innate beauty of the country or the humanity of its people. Dispelled were notions that Africa was unintelligible, unsuitable and unaccommodating to anyone not indigenous to the continent." At this moment, she says wistfully, "All of my concerns drifted away, and I was comfortable in my ancestral continent and in my skin." The realistic yet romantic and idealized reflections expressed by Michelle were those of a naïve young black American female.

For sure, Africa has pockets full of tragedy, mayhem, chaos, barbarism, savagery, despotism, genocide, corruption and megalomaniacal terror. But these characteristics cannot be generalized to apply to all of the countries in Africa. Botswana, for example, has been free of these issues, as have many others.

Historian James T. Campbell describes the experiences of three journalists assigned to cover newsworthy events across the African continent. All of these individuals lived in Africa while doing their reporting, and one married an Ivorian woman. They experienced the good, the bad and the abominable across the continent. Their experiences as delineated in their subsequent writings ranged from absolute disgust to moderate disdain. Certainly, the journalists whom Mr. Campbell discussed were not native to the continent, and all of them brought with them their Western perspectives and cultural expectations. The judgments they made were harsh, but others were framed in a socio-cultural context.

The atrocities that have occurred in Africa have been no greater or worse than the atrocities perpetrated by the Nazis in Germany, the Bosnian genocide perpetrated by the Bosnian Serb army in

Srebrenica and Zepta, the tragedies experienced by the Armenians in Turkey, the genocide perpetrated by Pol Pot and Khmer Rouge in Cambodia, the ongoing Palestinian tragedies under the hammer of the Israelis, the American Indian genocide perpetrated by the Americans, and of course the granddaddy of them all, European and American slavery. And most recently the Syrian crisis with the slaughter of Muslims by Muslims. And the gun violence in America that claims the lives of over 30,000 American citizens each year.

Because the events in Africa are black events, they are made to appear exceptional, but in reality they are not.

CHAPTER EIGHTEEN

THE OMAKUMA

The conductor calls out our next train stop over the loudspeaker system. "Wilmington is the next stop. Wilmington, Delaware. Check around your seat for all of your belongings and exit the train where you see a conductor. Wilmington is next." We are not far from Philadelphia now and will be arriving in "the city of brotherly love" within the next thirty minutes barring any unforeseen difficulties.

Time has gone by slowly, but we have covered a lot of material, and Michelle appears unaffected by the amount of information covered so far. She is anxious to get her story out, and I am just as anxious and interested. Having traveled to Africa myself as an adult, I made the observation that though we, black Americans, relate to Africans by color and genealogy, there is a schism, a cultural divide. Obviously, we do things differently in America than they do in African countries. Though there are many common threads, the African-American view is the Western worldview. I know from my research and reading that the African culture as it relates to children, for example, is based on a matrilineal descent: Africans view children as belonging to the mother, and inheritance descends not from the father but from and through the maternal lineage. In many kingdoms, the mother of the existing king chooses his successor. The Western scheme is patrilineal.

In addition to that cultural variance, African governance in many instances follows the tribal tradition of lifetime tenure, except in those countries that have accepted a postcolonial democratic form of government. The tribal king or leader of the clan rules until he dies or is killed in battle.

Michelle begins this next round of discussion by talking about the luncheon she had with the two African-American women she met at the ambassador's house during the dinner she attended. She says, "The two black American women who were married to Africans invited us to lunch." When she and Vixena found the house, they perceived that a solid middle-class environment surrounded the home. She remembers that the house was a two-story modern home, quite comfortable. She recalls, "I noticed that there was an exterior bolted door leading to the second floor. I was told it was there for security reasons." She learned that these middle-class houses were frequently broken into, so the door protected the family members as they slept upstairs. "I thought that was a good idea" she says. This was not a practice she had seen in the United States, but her security-conscious leanings embraced the idea. The income disparity in Africa is a contributing factor to the high need for this type of security; in America we have gated communities and homes with iron bars all around.

Through my experiences, some of those that are considered middle class in Africa would in most cases be considered lower or upper-lower class in America. The way some middle-class Africans live would not be acceptable to middle-class African-Americans. In fact, what Americans consider middle class is, in all probability, the upper class in Africa, especially with regard to living conditions. Some writers and academics have written that Africans making two dollars a day are middle class and that only two percent of sub-Saharan Africans can be classified as middle class.

The home that Michelle and Vixena entered was a white, stucco two-story, split-level house with modern rectangular windows. The house was set back ten feet or more from the curb and had been well kept, she says. One could see that regular maintenance to the house was ongoing. Inside, Michelle saw a decor characterized by using brown colors and earth tones. Drapes ran across the front windows with white shears available to let in the sunlight. She noted that the different blends of African wood—poculi, African cherry and sapele—gave the tables, ottomans and chairs an assortment of nativist hues. Prominently displayed were hand-carved figurines of giraffes and other wildlife on a lovely bookshelf made perhaps, she thought, of zebrawood and shedua. African urns and statuettes sat on the end tables and coffee table in the living room.

Michelle says she did not get an opportunity to view the sleeping quarters as they were considered off-limits, but if the sleeping quarters in any way resembled the style of the living and dining room areas, it was certainly decorously furnished. Africans will often hang rugs of various African designs on their walls similar to the way Western homes use portraits. The colors of Africa are often reflected in the tonality of furnishings and overall texture of the living environment. The dining room table was rectangular and made of wood. Wood chairs with low backs faced each other on either side. The table was made of a darker wood, perhaps of African teak. The bowls and serving dishes the hostess used were characteristic of African tableware, a blend of Egyptian and tribal design motifs. And the room was painted in a beige color that seemed to bring all of the tones and the ambience of Africa together in one place. Michelle has a great interest in interior design, and she was quite observant of the way this hostess lived.

For lunch the hostess served grilled fish, rice and a salad. For dessert there was an assortment of fruits, pineapples, melons and mangoes. Michelle continues, "We appeared to have the house to ourselves. Both women were present at the luncheon and both had children. The hostess was pregnant with another child. After we exchanged pleasantries, we ate lunch and brought them up to date on our experiences thus far in Uganda. I asked them what it was like being married to an African and living in Africa."

From a woman's perspective, Michelle wanted to know as much of the intimacies as these women would be willing to share. She knew there were limits to what they would reveal, but women often share much about their private lives with each other, a kind of sisterhood.

Michelle sought to gain more insight into Harriett's marriage to Eric. "Our hostess was very happy. She loved her husband and children and felt her life was very fulfilling." The hostess told Michelle that her life involved the community of the university, university professors and their families as well as noted Africans and black Americans, ambassadors and the high-end black social elite. To her this was a charmed life. She had a beautiful home and family. She had servants to clean the house, cook their meals, do the laundry and run errands as needed. The hostess understood she would not have such a grand living style in the United States without a hefty price tag.

It is indeed passing strange that Michelle would have to travel to Africa to be free of overt racial prejudice and to see other members of her ilk living middle-class lives without the racial prejudicial element. Why should she have to go to Africa to witness this relief? Wasn't the point of living in the US that this type of freedom should be available to all, whether they were middle-class?

The husband of the hostess worked as a university administrator at Makerere and was a part-time faculty member. The other woman's husband was a government official working in the justice ministry.

Michelle's eyes widen and her face contorts into a frown. "The other wife was not happy." The woman told Michelle, "All we are to them are baby machines. I refuse to be a baby machine. He thinks he is Omakuma."

In Ugandan history, the title *omakuma* refers to the king of the Bunyoro. According to Paul Briggs and Andrew Roberts, authors of the *Bradt Travel Guide Uganda*,

Bunyoro was the largest and most influential of the kingdoms until the end of the 17th century. It had a mixed economy, a loose political structure and a central trade position on account of its exclusive control of the region's salt mines. Bunyoro was presided over by an Omakuma, who was advised by a group of special counselors. The Omakuma was supported at a local level by several grades of semi-autonomous chiefs, most of whom were royally appointed loyalists of aristocratic descent.[43]

This kind of governing structure contrasts greatly with the stereotype of African society. Lugard, the British general referred to earlier, also found an operating governing structure when he defeated the kabaka in Kampala around 1890.

Michelle recalls that the discontented woman became somewhat hysterical: "She was fed up with her husband and she was returning to the States, to Baltimore." She had four kids and said her husband wanted more. She refused to give him more. She would leave him and return home. But she did not want to leave her children, and her husband told her if she left, she would have to leave alone. This was a terrible dilemma for this woman.

Michelle says, "I watched as the hostess consoled her friend. I became a little uncomfortable and thought they would want some privacy. The crying woman apologized for spoiling the visit, but we told her it was a great visit and we thanked our hostess for her hospitality. 'Don't let it happen to you. Go home,'" was her parting admonition to us. This was a haunting and sobering statement that separated the idealized and romanticized from the actuality of marrying some African men.

"I felt sorry for the disconsolate sister," Michelle says. Then she mentions a story about a Banyoro ruler who was "stated to have had about 2,000 kids." However, the story does not end there. Briggs and Roberts tell the story that in 1731 Omakuma Duhaga took the Banyoro throne. Traditions remember him as being "light-skinned," hairy and difficult—perhaps he was an albino, which could make sense—and as having the second greatest number of children of any omakuma. The authors regard as a dubious and incredulous history the notion that Omakuma Oyo I had 2,000 children. Nonetheless, Briggs and Roberts have written that Omakuma Duhaga died in battle fighting alongside of his seventy sons.

A point of history: historians who have written about Uganda make mention of the fact that the various kingdoms in historic Uganda and the people who occupied those kingdoms—e.g., the Baganda in Buganda, the Banyoro in Bunyoro and the Banyankole of Ankole—each had a king. Each king was known by a different title. The Baganda king was known as the *kabaka,* the Banyoro king was known as the *omakuma.* And the king of the Banyankole people of Ankole was known as the *omugabe,* "the strong one." Each kingdom and people of that kingdom had their own governing structure. To the south and east of these historic kingdoms would evolve modern-day Uganda, as well as Rwanda, Burundi and Northwest Tanzania. To Europeans, these governing structures mattered little and were not respected. Europeans looked upon them as relics of an ignorant and uncivilized people, but in fact these governing traditions preexisted for centuries and kept order among the people. And these traditions moved the African people through the Stone and Iron Age, well ahead of European society during those same time periods.

Many scholars have written about the effect of the destruction of African traditions, in governance, family structure, and geographical tribal boundaries following the imposition of the "nation-state" by colonialism. See Basil Davidson, *supra*. Plural marriage and multiple offspring have survived these changes. Many African women, because of their cultural familiarity with these traditions, embrace much of it, but it is foreign and, in some cases, unacceptable to American women of African descent.

After experiencing this episode Michelle says she thought about her friend Harriett and whether Harriett had considered all of this before marrying Eric.

We have talked about the cultural issues that underlie a traditional African marriage that Harriett, in the midst of her love and affection for Eric, failed to consider. Key among them is the practice of polygamy. Plural marriage in Africa is widespread. The practice is a result of history, religion and culture. Polygamy is practiced in Islamist countries in Africa. Polygamy is deeply rooted in the African continent, and its origins have to do with the definition of wealth, which is defined by the number of children a man has, similar to the way that wealth is measured by number of cattle, cowries and wives a man retains. Having many children was considered a way of building an empire.

European colonists in certain regions of Africa fought against the practice, and it is postulated that Europeans fought the practice because it conflicted with their notions of real property ownership and inheritance. Having many heirs complicates the distribution and diffusion of wealth. It is reported that one man in Kenya has over 100 wives, and that in South Africa, Jacob Zuma, the president, supports the practice and has over three wives and more than twenty children. The Sudanese president, Omar Hassan al Bashir, supports the practice as a way of populating his country.[44]

Two scholars, Yasuko Hayase and Kao-Lee Liaw wrote a persuasive, detailed study about polygamy in sub-Saharan Africa. In Kenya, for example, a law legalizing what had been a traditional practice, known as the Marriage Act of 2014, was enacted. Outside of Africa, in Arab countries, the practice is also quite prevalent. And Sarah Barringer Gordon as well as others have written about Mormons of the United States, to whom polygamy historically has been an important tenet of their religious culture.[45]

After this encounter with the two women, Michelle reasoned soberly that all marriages were different and that each had distinct goals and objectives. A mature thought for a woman of her age. Perhaps her view of marrying an African had been forever changed. She was not involved with an African man, nor was she contemplating marriage in the near future, so perhaps she felt a sense of immunity from the immediacy of this poor "sister's" plight. Michelle remarks that maybe she was only seeing illusions and not the real world, her *new* real world.

I think Michelle is right. I ask Michelle what, if anything, had she gotten out of her African experience up to this point.

She looks me in the eye as though to say, "That's a ridiculous question!" She responds sarcastically, "Are you kidding? Of course, I got a lot from my experiences over there!"

My question is not intended to be rhetorical but designed to elicit a definitive recitation of what she took from the experience. I want her philosophical truths and principles as well as her empirical observations arrived at from her experience. After all, this had been one of the seminal events in her life up to that point. Clearly, I know that she benefited from the experience. Who wouldn't have? But I want some general conclusions about Africans and African-Americans, the cultural deficit issue and that whole dichotomy, if it exists. I raise my eyebrows as if to say, "And so what do you think?" I'm anxious to find out, but she is irritated. I shrug and smile, trying to encourage her to continue.

After exhaling a bit, she says, "Well, Africans are not African-Americans and don't want to be African-Americans. They are proud of who they are. They are from their own countries, their own tribes, their own cities and are members of their various religious faiths. Africans have no desire to be us. What they want is what they perceive us to have, the abundance of America. They want what all people want and that is a good life for themselves and their families. They are no different than any other people on this earth. Africans are chauvinistic about being African, and they clearly understand who the colonizer is and was."

She also observes that Africans are relatively uninformed about the severe impact of slavery on the lives of black Americans and the price black Americans have paid for the freedoms we enjoy in abundant America. They lived through colonialization not slavery. Their culture was sustained; ours was disemboweled save for what little we could salvage from memory and oral traditions.

She contrasts Africans with African-Americans, or Americans of African descent, as we should be properly known. She explains, "We are Americans and only know Westernized customs. Americans of African descent know only capitalism and Western civilization. We salute the red, white and blue and honor the red, black and green," the flag colors of Pan-Africanism. "To survive and enjoy Africa you must be ready to adapt to their customs with no hesitation or regrets. But you must also know yourself. You must see yourself as who you really are, and not your illusory self. Decide for yourself where you want to be in this world," she emphasizes.

I sum up her statement by saying, "You must decide what place in the world is best for you in light of your orientation, the long and short of your history, comfort zone, familiarity, tolerance and psychic needs."

"Yes," Michelle says. "I was learning that for myself." Michelle alludes to the image of the African woman in the mirror incident: "That moment helped shape my thoughts."

To end her thoughts on this matter she philosophizes for a moment that "moving to Africa, wearing African clothes and an African hairstyle, learning African languages, having African friends, absorbing yourself in all things African and even marrying an African man do not make you—regardless of how earnestly you may desire—an African. The same can be said if one married a European or an Asian or any other person from a foreign continent; you will still be a non-native."

She adds, "We heard later that the unhappy wife returned to the States, alone."

CHAPTER NINETEEN

OREM'S THEORY

De winter days are drawin' nigh
An' by the fire I sets an' sigh;
De no'the'n win' is blowin' cold,
Like it done in days of old.

De yaller leafs are fallin' fas',
Fur summer days is been an' pas';
The air is blowin' mighty cold,
Like it done in days of old.

De frost is fallin' on de gras'
An' seem to say, "Dis is yo' las' " –
De air is blowin' mighty cold
Like it done in days of old.

Waverly Turner Carmichael, "Winter Is Coming"

The rich green whorls of Pennsylvania pachysandra that bloom in the spring with yellow-tinged leaves and pink and white spears were a harbinger to Harriett, a native Pennsylvanian, as she approached the winter solstice of her years. She wondered who would remember and who would care about the efforts she made, the energy she expended and the costs she bore to upgrade the nursing program at the University of Botswana. Unlike in America, her African compatriots may have no memories or give scant recognition, if any, to the large accomplishments reflected in and through the achievements of the many students she trained. When she began, she had only seven students who completed the program she inaugurated, and all seven earned doctorates in nursing from colleges in the United States.

Harriett and I had been sitting and talking in her living room for a while when she asked, "Would you like a cup of tea?"

I said sure.

"What kind would you like?" she continued.

I replied, "Do you have any chamomile? It's my favorite."

"Uh, I don't think so," she responded as she looked into her cupboard to see if, by chance, she might have some. "What about some Earl Grey?"

Not wanting to be difficult I said, "Yeah, that'll be just fine as long as it's decaffeinated."

"Yes, I have some," she said.

There was silence for a few moments as Harriett worked around her kitchenette in her well-appointed yet modest apartment and prepared the tea. Cups and saucers sang a song of clatter as she readied them for the teabags and hot water to follow. It took a while, but it was not that long in the scheme of things, before she brought the tea to the living room on a rectangular brown porcelain tray with yellow etching around its four sides. The off-white cups and saucers appeared to be made of thin bone china—what I would characterize as "the good stuff," historically known as "white gold" because of its perceived value. This collage of tableware epitomized Harriett: quality, discretion and moderation. In my judgment, she sought not to live a life of gaudiness and ostentation but rather one of circumspection and understated elegance. When she and I resumed our discussion, we now had the tea for lubrication.

Harriett related that hers was not an easy task once she was ensconced in her office at the University of Botswana. Her office was less than 120 square feet. She had a wooden desk, an executive chair and a credenza. The walls were painted in a faded gold color that was showing its age. The ceiling was painted white and the wood baseboard was four inches high with a dark stain painted over it with no adornment. The baseboard matched the wood floors that creaked every so often to remind Harriett that she was not the first to occupy the office.

She began by getting to know the existing staff, faculty, administrators and students. Serara had certainly given her "intelligence" on the key players in her department. But Harriett knew she had to make her own assessments. She quickly discerned that a turf war would ensue between the American program she was trying to establish and the existing British program's cultural underpinnings. Harriett remembered, "The new American program was very unpopular with the students, the administration and faculty. That's why it took a lot of coaching from Serara and others to get me there. It was all very stressful, a new culture, new attitudes toward women that I was not accustomed to, and trepidation about American education."

One question she often encountered was why women needed a bachelor's degree to be a nurse. She recalled that a male faculty member asked her, "Would a woman with a bachelor's degree be a better mother?'" Harriett replied with a sense of pique, "Would a man be a better father with a bachelor's degree?" Harriett noted to me, "Of course there was no response, just a quizzical look."

"The problem was," she said, "they had never had a degreed nursing program before. You see, the British had already written the nursing school curriculum." Harriett soon found out that she was the only black nurse in Southern Africa with a nursing degree, not to mention a EdD, in curriculum development in nursing education. She was in fact "reinventing the wheel" for these people. She noted that the South African and British faculty all had PhDs. Then she said with astonishment, "The dean even made inquiries to verify that I had an EdD!"

Overcoming disbelief, skepticism and European colonial history was the essence of her struggle. As Kwame Nkrumah noted, postcolonial Africa mirrored the image of colonial culture as evidenced by the fact that the black bourgeoisie imitated and installed the systems of their colonial masters rather than revert to their historical patterns of lifestyle and governance. This of course is no accident. Imitation is not always the best form of flattery; it may in fact be an indictment on the effectiveness of exploitation. Harriett reasoned that though the existing system was flawed, it could be built upon—in effect integrating the concept of Negritude and a fight against institutionalizing permanently a neocolonial set of educational policies that she was there to change.

As black expatriates from an earlier era had done, Harriett was bringing, through her mission, an African-American black liberation educational ideology. The British colonial system and its postcolonial residue intended to make the Botswana nursing corps subservient, and dependent on it or other first world entities—a corps with limited horizons and an underserved population. This was classic colonial methodology: exploitation of resources, denigration of native culture, and dehumanization of the population. In the "Scramble for Africa" between 1874 and 1914, also known as the "Partition of Africa," the European countries of Belgium, Germany, France, England, Italy and Holland all sought to bring light to a dark world, to defeat the poorly defended, to civilize the uncivilized, to Christianize the unchristian and to humanize the degenerates of their colonies.

In academia, the study of colonialism and postcolonial disciplines seeks to explain what this practice was all about. Briefly, writers such as Franz Fanon, Edward Said, Derek Gregory, and others postulated theories, all of which are true in my opinion, about the contrived notion of Western and European cultural superiority. The theories advanced by proponents of European colonial realism is indeed a fiction. The fallacies inherent in the doctrines all emanate from one basic proposition: that the Western world and its systems and culture are superior to all others, and as such gives rise to a divine right, if not a "calling" on the Western world, to bring the heathens to bear. It is a discharge of the "white man's burden." The colored world is a prospect for "the subaltern"—not necessarily in the language of Gayatri Spivak,[46] but they *are* the oppressed. Without going beyond the purpose of this writing, suffice it to say that the Occident versus the Orient, the West versus the East, and "the Other" are all terms associated with colonialism and postcolonialism; terms meant to differentiate and stratify hierarchically the West from "the Other."

Many noted writers have opined on this subject—too many to mention here. Working to change the nursing education system Harriett encountered brought her into contact with most, if not all, of the theories put forward by the writers and scholars mentioned above; Fanon's concept of double consciousness, Said's theory of imperialism being represented in high culture, which the elite in Botswana wanted maintained, Spivak's plight of the subaltern, and Gregory's application of colonialism to the modern-day status of third world countries at one time or another all abounded in her new world.

Had it not been for her tenacity to overcome these ingrained colonial constructs, she and her program would have succumbed to them.

Harriett said that she often walked to the university but that it got so hot she could not continue to do so. One of her neighbors saw her walking in the heat one day and volunteered to give her a ride. To solve the walking problem, Harriett bought a stick shift Toyota Corolla from a dealership in Gaborone and drove to the university daily from that point on. Faculty members got a discount, and the dealership provided assistance to help faculty members learn to drive on the opposite side of the road with the steering wheel on the right side of the vehicle. She remembered that the roads were very bad, there was only one stoplight in the city, and that not many people had cars. Over time, the government helped to improve the life of the people, as "dirt roads were the only roads in the rural areas, but there were some asphalt roads in the city." She said she could not get a license to drive without driving a stick shift. It proved one's ability to drive.

Harriett recalled that there were shopping markets very near the university: "There were African markets and an African shopping mall within walking distance of the university. It was quite modern." South Africa was only five miles away, and many of the expatriates did their shopping there. "Asian Indians were there as well as Chinese," she said. "The Chinese had a huge embassy in Gaborone. The Indians had butcher shops and plenty of money, but the Chinese built the university, and I remember that they worked twenty-four hours a day."

Every day, Harriett was up at 5:30 a.m. She started her day early at the university, usually between seven and eight. She said she began each day with a couple of meetings with her faculty and staff, discussing curriculum changes and course offerings. She usually taught a class from 10 a.m. to noon, then took lunch from noon until 2 p.m. because "the Africans always took a two-hour lunch, their largest meal of the day, and then they slept for an hour and then began the workday again." It was a kind of "siesta," she came to learn, common in hot countries as well as in some European countries. After that, her day resumed. She taught classes from two to four and then from four to six in the evening. She worked long and she worked hard teaching in the program and preparing lectures for the next day, along with finding time to draft the outlines of a new nursing curriculum program. Slowly but surely, she began to earn the credibility in Botswana that she had already attained in America.

Harriett went on to elaborate that "it took about a year before I was able to get textbooks and the classrooms I needed. It felt like Management 101 was always in play." She said there was a stratified hierarchy at the university level. The administrators and deans of the university were at the highest level, next was the department level, and the faculty level was the last rung. She discovered that in her department many faculty members were related to other faculty within the university, a clear display of nepotism throughout. She thought that what went on in her faculty meetings would remain private and not be disclosed, but to her dismay that was not the case. Harriett said that each discipline within the department had its own faculty meetings, and just about everyone knew what her faculty was doing, and they blocked it at every opportunity. She called these experiences "the curriculum wars."

Harriett continued, "I had expectations that I wanted to fulfill and that I thought would be greeted with open arms." But she was not. Another "shock and awe" invasion gone awry on a smaller scale. For the most part she felt the fetters and the headwinds of resistance. In spite of it all, she spoke loftily of what she was able to accomplish installing a program that she was educated in at Columbia in the nursing program at the University of Botswana.

While Harriett was there, the US ambassador to Botswana was invited to speak at the university convocation. He asserted, "Ambassadors are otherwise nice young men who go abroad and lie for their country." She thought those remarks were a poignant and particularly befitting description of American and European ambassadors in Africa.

Harriett then rattled off an additional litany of issues that confronted her once in-country and on the job. She referred me to a paper she had written that said,

> [A]t the center of many international controversies over the appropriate education for nurses are the two major nursing education models that prevail worldwide: British and American. Britain exported hospital diploma programs. The United States created and exported AD, Associate Degree; BSN, Bachelor of Science in Nursing; MSN, Master of Science degree in Nursing and Ph.D. programs!

She went on to say that questions typically arose over which of these programs was most useful for nurses. She asked me rhetorically, "Which one is more efficient in producing effective and efficient nurses?" Harriett subscribed to the view that "although the kind of nursing care may differ from one country to another due to the sociocultural context and/or economic situation of the country, the domain of the 'discipline of nursing,' its *raison d'être* and its development cannot and should not be drastically different in one region of the world." She had adopted the view of Dorothea Orem, one of several authorities she admired on the subject of international nursing.[47]

In an animated tone, which often characterized Harriett's frame of mind, she told me, "So, when the University of Botswana selected me from a number of other candidates to help develop the first baccalaureate program for Botswana nurses, I was not only thrilled but eager to translate my American beliefs about nursing into a program of study that would utilize a nursing theoretical frame of reference." She talked about Orem's self-care framework that provided an approach consistent with not only her ideas but also her beliefs about the education of nurses: a theoretical framework suitable for meeting nursing care needs of individuals worldwide, including Botswana.

A "theoretical framework" is a set of interrelated concepts and theories promoted by one individual to prove a hypothesis or a belief. This notion was certainly high in the weeds of academic dogma. But Harriett cared deeply about the academic as well as the practical side of nursing. She said she abhorred the view that patients were just a passive recipient of nursing and medical care. She thought that nurses should embrace patient participatory care. In other words, the patient should be very much involved in their care, and I certainly agree. Those of us that have been in the hospital know that to receive the best care from health professionals requires that you know as much about your condition as a layman can. This allows you, the patient, to ask intelligent questions and to challenge those approaches that you feel are not appropriate. I am interested in all of this history because who among us has not or will not, at some point in the future, be the recipient of health care?

As Harriett spoke, my mind drifted away and imagined what it would be like receiving health care in Botswana during her time. If anything serious were to happen, I am sure I would have had to go to a medical facility in the West or at the very least to South Africa.

Harriett's approach is clearly understandable, and I am in agreement. Her support for the "self-care theory," she said, "strongly supports my view of the value of self-determination, self-control and self-fulfillment; values that were and are still very strong following numerous wars for liberation on the African continent." In this context Harriett was analogizing one of her academic theories of nursing with the political struggle of African countries to free themselves from their colonial past.

This is a broad vision and expansive view of the context in which she operated. African peoples, both black and brown, are weight lifters. Just like a weight lifter who struggles to lift and thrust a heavy weight above his head and hold it there for a sufficient time to show he or she has lifted the weight, African peoples have struggled since the fifteenth century to lift the weight of white supremacy above their heads long enough to clear their subconscious and conscious mind of the scourge of the fiction.

She went deeper into her philosophies and mentioned another nursing pioneer, by the name of Virginia Henderson, a renowned nurse educator. To some, Henderson was known, Harriett said, as "the Nightingale of modern medicine." Harriett liked Virginia Henderson's approach because Henderson's philosophy focused on nursing practice. Harriett said that Henderson emphasized patient independence, human needs and the need to shorten hospital stays. Harriett said that Henderson's definition of nursing had been adopted throughout the world. She went on to say that Virginia Henderson's definition guided her practice, her teaching and her approach to the development of a nursing curriculum. And, as with Orem, Harriett introduced these theories of nursing and their philosophies to her students, faculty and anyone else who would listen. She felt that Henderson's philosophy incorporated Orem's "self-care" framework, and both were of American derivation.[48]

Harriett said that, amazingly, "prior to 1978, neither a college education nor any facility for training nurse educators existed for nurses in Botswana; all advanced education for nurses in the country required travel abroad. Most nurses who sought higher education traveled to either Great Britain, Canada or South Africa." Harriett told me, "Nursing in Botswana, as in much of Africa south of the equator, had a very slow start. Formal training for nursing started in 1925 when three local women were admitted for training at the Seventh Day Adventist Hospital in Kanye in Southeast Botswana. By independence in 1966, forty-one years later, approximately seven hundred nurses from the country had been trained, a production of only about eighteen nurses per year." Serara told her this information.

Fourteen years after gaining independence from Great Britain, which of course installed its educational, legal and cultural system in the country, and three months after Harriett arrived, the university senate of the University of Botswana established the Department of Nursing Education. She stated with much pleasure, "I was appointed its first chairperson. My new department consisted of four faculty members. Three were full-time, including me, and one person part-time; two from Botswana; an African-American, me; and a Caucasian American." She went on to say, "Since the British colonial system was firmly entrenched in Botswana prior to me entering the country, a nursing curriculum had already been developed and accepted as a program, but the program was structured without the assistance of any nursing faculty." She disapproved of this lack of insight and the condescension that it connoted. To exclude the nursing professionals from participating in the formulation of a curriculum that impacted them directly was the height of arrogance.

Harriett related that in 1977 an American non-nurse faculty member in the science department of her alma mater, Teachers College, Columbia University, was appointed and accepted the position as head of the new program in nursing. This faculty member then proceeded to implement her vision. All of these top-down approaches were paternalistic and exclusionary.

As Harriett continued to expound on her nursing activities, she said, "Pioneering the development and implementation of a radically new nursing curriculum in the Republic of Botswana and in Southern Africa would be quite a challenge intellectually, physically and emotionally." To implement a new successful nursing program required knowledge about the land, its people, the language, its government, the currency, the societal image of the nurse, major health care problems, health manpower needs, and respect for the culture's beliefs about health, health care and the causes of several indigenous diseases. Harriett said that her major interest had always been and continues to be curriculum development and instruction for nursing education programs. She thought that her graduate education had specifically prepared her to teach nursing students and create nursing educational programs that reflected nursing's global purpose, which for her is simply stated as "caring for, caring about and taking care of people wherever they may be in the world."

Harriett went on to say, "To my amazement, my ideas about the appropriate educational curriculum for student nurses were considered heresy and were vigorously opposed by most of the university faculty, especially the British and British-educated faculty." She quoted Machiavelli, from the sixteenth century: "It ought to be remembered that there is nothing more difficult to take in hand, more perilous to conduct, or more uncertain in its success than to take the lead in the introduction of a new order of things. Because the innovator has for enemies all those who have done well under the old conditions, and lukewarm defenders in those who may do well under the new."[10]*

Britain colonized both Uganda and Botswana, and as mentioned above, it imposed its colonial system on each country. Harriett's challenge to install an American form of education for nurses was an uphill climb because her task, among others, was not only to convince her compatriots but to prove her credibility for the job.

She told me again, as though still suffering from disbelief, "My doctoral credentials were challenged primarily because few of the university faculty had heard of a doctorate in nursing education and therefore did not believe one existed, accusing me of falsifying my credentials. The reasoning being, if my credentials were false, by the same token my ideas were without merit and did not require serious consideration."

She said, "The fights in the faculty meetings were like hand-to-hand combat. The back and forth unending battles were just about unbearable. Minefields were set all around and the nursing curriculum wars seemed as though they would go on forever."

The situation in Botswana, with its high rate of poverty, communicable diseases and its multiple-sector health care delivery system, required a "supportive educative nursing system." She said, "In fact, the majority of the communicable and lifestyle diseases were preventable and the result of ignorance."

Harriett explained, "In my opinion it wasn't necessary by itself that the nursing curriculum I was fighting to install would emphasize that the student was not only being prepared for living as an informed citizen of Botswana but also for earning a living as a nurse with a university degree."

She reminded me, "The health of a nation is the wealth of a nation; a healthy people are an imperative to create and maintain a productive society," she exclaimed. "There is a distinct difference between an educated rather than a trained nurse." I liked what I heard when she said, "I differentiate between training and education

---

10   * Nicolo Machiavelli, (1469-1527) *The Prince*

in this way; animals such as horses and dogs are trained, humans are educated." Wow! That really nailed it. For a moment I imagined that I was in one of those meeting rooms that Harriett spoke about, and that I was witnessing the age-old debate in the American black community between Booker T. Washington (1865-1915) and W. E. B. Du Bois (1868-1963)—the debate whether black folk should be trained in vocational skills or schooled in the higher-level academics of university training. The "great debate," it was called. Were we better off, as Americans of African descent, having had this debate a century ago?

However, one cannot generalize because this particular debate only concerned Botswana and its nursing program. Clearly other departments in the university were long past these issues, and many other African countries established universities without these issues arising. Harriett's experience was just a microcosm of the debate, a cross-cultural replication. A debate that took place not only in the black community but included many white philanthropists instrumental in establishing black colleges and universities in the nineteenth century. Harriett of course was an entrenched academic, as was Dubois. Her opposition—the existing faculty, both African and English and some American—supported the position of Booker T. Washington.

Is this irony or neocolonial thinking? A debate on these issues taking place in the twentieth century in an African country where slavery did not exist seems ironic, but the effects of colonialism resulted in black Americans and Africans confronting similar questions with a similar people a century and a half later.

Harriett was animated as she continued to relate the tough academic battles, she fought with the entrenched power structure in the university. Old habits die hard. "I tried to get my colleagues to understand that an educated person must be able to think and write clearly and effectively; an educated person should have a critical appreciation of the ways in which we gain knowledge, and an understanding of the universe, of society and of one's self." Never a truer statement could be made.

Harriett's approach relied upon intellectual experience in literature and the arts. An educated person within her theoretical framework, and in terms of the universality of her approach to nursing education, was an educated person with an informed acquaintance with philosophical analysis, ethical dilemmas and concepts of the nursing discipline.

In effect Harriett was trying to break up the British closed system of limiting the training of nurses to learning just the jobs of nursing. Harriett wanted to expand their horizons to include chemistry and biology, of course, but also the arts and philosophy to give the student a worldview of the field of nursing, not a closed shop.

Our tea cups were now empty. Harriett gathered up the cups and put them on the tray. She gingerly walked back to her kitchen and placed the tray on the small kitchen table in the center of this small room. Both she and I began to think about dinner and where to go to eat. She suggested Clyde's, a local sophisticated eatery within walking distance from her apartment building. I liked the food there and the service, so we decided to go there. I did not expect her to cook. At her age and with my inclination, a meal out was quite appropriate. Before breaking for dinner, though, she said, "The nursing curriculum therefore must be structured to prepare a graduate who can consciously plan to make a difference in the health and well-being of society; a graduate who understands the crucial connections among health, wellness, global progress, technology, education and economic advances."

In the final analysis, she said, "Without a responsive nursing education curriculum, which is key to a healthy workforce, neither national nor international progress will occur." She recited a statistic that I thought was very interesting: "During the height of my career there were more than seven million nurses in the world and almost fifty percent of them were in the United States." Harriett reminded me that nurses all over the world operate in diverse cultures yet serve the same healing function. Harriett again recited from one of her authorities: "We can no longer have a lofty contempt for people whose culture is different or seems strange."

I was impressed with Harriett's thoroughness of knowledge and her broad approach to her field. She had been in Botswana to get something accomplished, to reconnect with her continent and to make a contribution. She had been an erstwhile member of the expatriate community of old and sought to make things better where she could, using the expertise she had gathered in America. She said, "I have emphasized Africa because my ancestry is there, so the need in Botswana was for a response; a relevant nursing curriculum resonated and continues to resonate with me. There are, in fact, several ways to expand one's global perspective. A student can achieve a broader perspective from the education they receive that does not require them to leave their country."

CHAPTER TWENTY

THE SMOCK AND THE DUFFEL BAG

Harriett and Michelle—the exchange student and the expatriate finding out that Africa is not easy, worthwhile but complex, drawn together by their common yet separate quests to find the grail of African culture.

As we continue our discussion on the train, Michelle reminds me that Africa is not hot all the time. The nights can be very cool and pitch black.

She says, "There were no lights except the dotted lights seen from my balcony and the adjoining dormitory windows. When I walked on campus at night, I always carried a torch. The campus would lose electricity from time to time, but in spite of that our meals were served and life otherwise appeared normal. Not everyone had a torch, and those with torches, including myself, were often asked by male students to lend them the ones that we had. I always said, 'No, brother man; your sister needs her torch.'"

She tells me, "On one of those nights, I walked to the dining room for tea. It was quite dark and romantic as the lights flickered on and off and candles burned in the windows and dim lamps illuminated the immediate area where they were placed. The low power limited the area the light covered. When blackouts occurred, I normally did not eat because I wanted to forestall the need to use the bathroom. Others kept eating as though things were normal and kept using the bathroom. To me that was an errant, haphazard and onerous thing to do, see or smell. As for me, I just simply refused to use the bathroom until the electricity was restored.

"On another such occasion when the electricity was out, of which there were many, a group of us decided to catch a movie, thinking that we would take advantage of the darkness. It did not seem like a bad idea at the time since it was dark outside and that would make it darker inside. As we watched the movie we were told that the electricity had been restored on campus. I was happy to get back on campus. I was delighted to see the lights back on. My sensitivity to my safety was always present, so whenever the electricity went out or there was a power shortage my concerns about my safety were heightened. We returned to the campus, and I immediately went to use the bathroom. To my surprise the bathroom was sparkling clean and a long tree limb was placed in the corner to absorb the bathroom odors that we all are familiar with. The tree limb had a minty smell, and I thought that was simply grand—to use a natural deodorizer for something that was also quite natural."

Trees are known by many ecologists and people in rural communities to be useful in biodegradation and odor absorption. The fact that Michelle encountered a tree limb in the bathroom would not be uncommon in Africa, since in Africa the people are acutely aware of the value of trees and other plants to aid them in their daily lives, providing everything from fruit to medicines and psychic benefits. Trees in Africa, as in other continents, carry many medicinal properties and are important in folklore.

Michelle did not know the name of the tree, but one African tree that is known for its mint fragrance is the peppermint tea tree, also known as the oil tree. The shea nut tree is another candidate. It too has multiple uses. And finally, the African cedar tree, which is treasured for its fragrance and is used in shoe molding. Uganda is a small landlocked country, as I have noted, but it is rich in biodiversity with an abundance of species of birds, various habitats created by glaciers, and many tree species.

Michelle describes an event that cascaded into her eventual exit from the country:

"A couple of days later, after the latest lights-out incident, while I was in Kampala I saw a large group of students marching in green smocks. The students were joining the parade and marching in town to see Idi Amin." As mentioned before, Idi Amin was the dominant and preeminent leader of the country. He came to power through a political coup. And though Michelle had not met him—fortunately for her, as it had been for Harriett—she says, "I had seen many pictures of him." Michelle continues, "I grabbed the green smock and joined the parade, laughing and joking and enjoying the revelry of the moment. We marched in straight lines laughing and talking along the way."

Michelle says she began thinking about Amin. His persona had gotten her attention, and she was curious to know more about this man and what his presence in Uganda might mean for her and others. So, she read something about his history. She knew that he had served during the Obote regime, that Amin had fought the Mau-Mau in Kenya and that he was a product of the British military system in East Africa. Michelle says she knew nothing about the Mau-Mau except what she could recall from an old movie entitled *Something of Value*, starring Sydney Poitier and Rock Hudson. "What an irony! There I was in Africa to discover for myself what Africa was all about, but I was referring to an American movie to recall something about a very African event." She reminded herself, *Why am I here? To see and discover what the truth is about Africa, not to rely on American movies.* The movie *Something of Value* was released in May 1957. The movie is about a white man and a black Kenyan who form a close relationship over many years and the conflict that is inherent between African traditions, the Mau-Mau and colonialism.

The term Mau-Mau at first glance may sound like a disease or some other foreign or exotic thing. But the term is defined as "a member of a revolutionary society in Kenya, established in the early 1950s. The group engaged in terrorist activities in an attempt to drive out the European settlers and to give government control to the native Kenyans." The origin of the term is *kikuyu*, which means "to threaten or intimidate."[49]

The Mau-Mau revolt between 1952 and 1960 was an attempt by the native peoples of Kenya, mostly the Kikuyu people, the dominant ethnic people in Kenya, to dismantle the British colonial system. Jomo Kenyatta, a reputed member of the Mau-Mau, became the country's first president after independence in 1963. Amin, as a British military officer, fought on the side of the British colonialists against the Kenyan rebellion. In putting down the rebellion, Britain used its Africa corps to fight the battles against indigenous people in East Africa, both in Uganda and Kenya, rather than use its white citizens to fight African wars of liberation. The old divide-and-conquer strategy. Among many things of note, the Mau-Mau instituted an "oathing ceremony," requiring the adherents to pledge allegiance to the struggle. The Mau-Mau guerrilla fighters referred to themselves as the "land and freedom army."[50]

When it comes to examples of good African leadership, there are many striking leadership contrasts with Idi Amin. Consider Jomo Kenyatta, for example, who was an African leader of great dignity. He looked like a mythical African leader and was well educated and dignified in his carriage. He was ruggedly handsome. Kenyatta and Thurgood Marshall collaborated in the drafting of the Kenyan Constitution. Two stalwarts in the fight for black liberation. However, Kenyatta continued the Kikuyu tribal tradition of female genital mutilation.

Then there were others, such as Nelson Mandela, the first African president of South Africa, and Kenneth Kaunda, first president of

Zambia, who tried to straddle the fence between the West and the East. Julius Nyerere, the first president of Tanzania, argued against using the Western model of capitalism and argued for a form of African socialism. And then there was Patrice Lumumba, the first prime minister of Congo. Lumumba had the courage to say in a speech in June 1960, in front of the Belgian king, the murderous colonizer, that he would not be cowed by any country as he sought to free Congo from the yoke of European colonialism.[51]

There are many others, including José Eduardo Dos Santos, president of Angola. Dos Santos, a democratically elected president, led Angola out of an East-West proxy war to destabilize his government. Both Dos Santos and Lumumba were assassinated by a shadowy group of Western conspirators led by America and Belgium. According to Seymour Hersh in *The Dark Side of Camelot*, the CIA played a significant role in plotting Lumumba's assassination.[52] Kwame Nkrumah, the first president of Ghana, is yet another example of an impactful African leader who resisted colonial government rule.

Finally, Samora Machel, first president of Mozambique, whose wife Graca later married Nelson Mandela, led his country out of the grip of the Portuguese during Mozambique's fight for liberation. However, he collaborated with South Africa against the African National Congress, a political party that ultimately liberated South Africa for its native African population. There were many other freedom fighters that I have failed to mention. The point of this brief recitation is to make mention of some of the many good leaders in Africa who were in no way similar in style or action to Amin.

Michelle recalls, "As we rounded the corner, everyone became silent. We marched a couple of yards ahead, turned and looked to our left up a clay-colored hill. There were patches of grass all around the hill, but the grass did not cover the entire area. Right in the middle of the hill was a large, burly, dark-skinned African man. The darkness of his skin was striking yet beautiful in texture and tone, reminding me of black onyx. The richness of his complexion defined his African genealogy."

In fact, the electrical outage on campus foretold of a darkness that would envelop Uganda during the reign of Amin, a shaded era that cast a pall over the entire country. His presence was imposing and menacing. From what Michelle describes based upon what she saw, and from what I can remember of Amin from pictures showing him in full military regalia, his uniform was usually filled with military decorations on the left and right breast as well as on the epaulets. He wore a narrow, dark-brown belt that extended through his left epaulet and across his stomach, connecting with a large, wider belt that extended around his waist with a holster on it. He was, in military parlance, wearing a full-dress ceremonial uniform. His adornments glittered in the bright sun. His peaked military cap was green with a red-and-gold patted weave around the crown band. There were leaf-shaped embellishments sewn on the visor, known as "scrambled eggs" in military parlance.

"Amin," she says, "was giving a talk, and after a while he sat in a chair that looked like a throne fashioned in a Queen Ann style. The seat and high back were upholstered in a dark-red fabric. The frame of the chair was made of wood. The arms and legs were painted in a gold veneer with a black strip in the center. If nothing else, one could tell that we were in the presence of 'the king.' The king was surrounded by soldiers dressed in green uniforms who carried big black guns, perhaps Kalashnikovs. They positioned themselves as though they were ready to fire. The young students, including myself, who had put on the green smocks were unwittingly wearing the colors of the soldiers' uniforms—soldiers who could destroy us.

"There were other soldiers who held onto large military dogs with a portion of the leashes wrapped around their hands to keep the dogs closely positioned by their side. Some of the dogs sat on their hind legs while others stood on all fours. They were panting, their pink tongues wobbling. The white enamel of their teeth shone brightly." She thought that most of the dogs were German Shepherds and Doberman Pinschers, and she says, "Those were the largest dogs I had ever seen. They were as big as lions and leopards. Suddenly, I felt very vulnerable. A sense of fright invaded my being: if the soldiers unleashed the dogs, we surely would have been mauled and devoured. And what if the other soldiers opened fire? We would have been mowed down as if we stood before a firing squad.

"I knew that Amin was there to speak, but I was transfixed by the crude display of military force—a show of raw power. I am sure that was his message to all assembled." She remembers, "I was simply in a daze. I had never seen or even thought of anything like what I was witnessing at that moment. It was as though everything was in slow motion. I could see Amin moving his mouth and I saw him raise his fist in the air. The dogs were looking down on us and the soldiers were pointing their rifles at us. It seemed that all that one had to do was to make a false move and pandemonium, hell, and abomination would ensue.

"To me it was a most frightening experience. At that moment, I had no love for Africa. Africa was not where I wanted to be on this occasion. I felt as if I was in a long dark tunnel holding onto a rope as I was dragged over an abyss. I imagined that the air was dusty and I was suffocating, gasping for air to breathe. In my daydream, perspiration poured down my face. My heart beat rapidly as though I was running to save myself from an unanticipated fright. Tears streamed down my face.

"*What in hell is this?* I asked myself. Was this a bad dream, or was this simply the reality of living in an African country with an unstable government with little or no regard for the value of human life or human rights? Was this an aberration? Whatever the purpose of this frightening show of power, it shocked me to my core, and the concussive effect was to knock me out of my idealism once and for all.

"I immediately left the crowd and threw off that green smock that had covered my clothes. The discarding of the smock was tantamount to shedding the idealism, romanticism and naïveté that I had about Uganda and Africa in general. I was just a young black American female student unaccustomed to the display of crude military power. I was scared to death. I went back to the campus in an attempt to put it all in perspective and to calm myself down."

When she and the others returned to the dormitory, she went to a friend's room for comfort. A few other students were also there. "I shared with them my experiences that day." She asked innocently, "What if there is a coup? Will we be safe on campus?" The students looked at one another as they confronted this unexpected reality.

"We all looked at each other and they looked back at me. One student said that during the last coup, the soldiers came on campus. They captured and raped the female students. It was a horrible experience, she said. A simply horrible time.

"The student also admonished us that we should have an escape route: 'There will be no alarms or warning. Only the screaming of the students. If you hear the screams, leave your room immediately and don't return,' she said. 'Many of the soldiers know where the American female students are, so you will not be safe.'

"I returned to my room," Michelle says, "and I cried and said, 'What the hell have I gotten myself into?' This was not the Africa that I imagined. But it was the Africa that I had to survive in, and I had to protect myself from grievous harm. So I devised an escape route from my room. I walked around the back of my dormitory and looked at my balcony and then turned around and looked ahead. I saw nothing but brush and trees. Under some large underbrush I found a large hole that could definitely shelter me in the night and possibly during the day if I wore camouflaged clothing."

Michelle tells me, "I knew I could not rest that evening until I had perfected a sound escape route, but then I asked myself, *If I use this escape route, I will not be able to return to my room, and then where will I go?* I would not be able to go to Mr. Eric's house because his house was in the direction of the front entrance. The soldiers would be entering the campus through the front gate. I would not be able to make my way safely to his house, if he was even there. My paranoia had arisen to levels I was not used to, but in this moment of perceived crisis, my better self and my survival instincts took control. I had to come up with something.

"My sense of abjection made me deal with the prospect that this reality could happen. So, I made myself an emergency kit. In it I put my passport and any other identification that I had, malaria pills (since I might be outside), some aspirin, some dried fruits, hard candy, some soap because I would have to take a wash in the nearby Bayer River. I also packed toothpaste, a brush, a washcloth, bug repellent, socks, a sweater, a torch and batteries, toilet tissue, pen and pencil and a small calendar.

"In retrospect, most of these things were probably impractical, but at the time those were the items that I thought I would need. I put all these things in a duffel bag, folded the duffel bag, tied it at the top and put it under my bed." She then says, in a state of deep reflection, "I had no idea if I would ever need those things, but at least I felt better knowing that I had done something to save myself if it came to it."

"Whew!" I say. "Let's take a break; so much to process."

Michelle agrees, and we take a pause to regroup.

"Want a soda from the café car before we get to Philadelphia?" I ask.

"No," she says. "I'm alright."

We pull into Philadelphia, a stop that I am quite familiar with. Our last stop will be in New York City, about an hour or an hour and a half away. I'm surprised that listening to her story is so taxing.

I say, "I think I will go to the snack bar and get a glass of wine and some chips."

"While you're gone I'll go to the bathroom."

As she crosses over me to get to the aisle, I say, "Good luck with the bathroom." She looks at me skeptically. Anyone who travels Amtrak on a regular basis knows that the bathrooms are usually a mess. After so much talk about bathrooms in Africa, one wonders if African bathrooms might not be better after all!

I make my way to the snack bar, which is two or three cars ahead. I order my wine and some chips and make my way back to our seat. Of course, both going and coming, I'm thrown from left to right. I walk through the connecting cars each time wondering whether I will make it from one car to the next, but, holding onto the iron railings for support out of necessity, I make it.

By the time I get back, Michelle has returned to the seat. She makes no comment about the bathroom, so I assume that the conditions must've been negotiable.

"Michelle," I say. "May I share an observation with you?"

She looks at me quizzically, as though expecting another fatuous question. She nods hesitantly and says, "I guess so. What is it?" She responds with a sense of irritation, yet she still wanted to be cooperative.

"You did a lot of crying on this trip—crying en route to Africa and while you were in Africa. Why so much crying?"

"Well," she says pensively, "I was frightened a lot of the time. I had only myself to depend on for my survival, and it was a good way to relieve the stress of my fright." She reminds me that the title of her Africa manuscript was *Crying All the Way Home*.

I jokingly mock the line that Tom Hanks says as a baseball coach in the women's baseball movie *A League of Their Own*. Instead of "no crying in baseball!" I say, "There's no crying while traveling in Africa." I'm not unsympathetic—just a moment of light banter on my part.

She looks at me with another imponderable expression and does not respond.

CHAPTER TWENTY-ONE

NEEMA KWA MAHARGE

SWAHILI FOR "A FAVOR FOR BEANS"

Michelle tells me about an incident that was comedic, interesting and frightening. One morning at breakfast she observed an African female student being served by an attendant while in the "chow line," a term the military uses to describe cafeteria-style food service in a kitchen or lunchroom. Michelle recalls that the attendant was nondescript. He had no distinguishing facial features, but he was of thin build. She said that the usual protocol was that each student would get one tablespoon of baked beans. The beans were tightly portioned.

But on this occasion, she observed that this female student got a "heaping" serving of beans. By her account the student got three tablespoons of beans! So, Michelle asked the girl in front of her, "Why is that student getting the extra helping of beans?" The student next in line said, "Favor, favor." As the student uttered the words to Michelle, she winked. The student continued by saying, "This woman gave out some favors last night."

"Ooohh, I see," Michelle remarked to the student. Michelle reacted to both the student's reply and her own awareness in amazement.

Michelle tells me she clearly understood what the deal was. "Sex for food favors." That was the exchange; a tacit understanding between the male employees around campus and the willing females. The cafeteria attendant as well as the other male functionaries around the campus traded extras for a "romp in the hay." When Michelle's time came to be served her portion of baked beans, she says, "I quickly placed my hand over my plate and said, 'No extra beans, please. No favors. No favors here!"

She wanted to make sure the attendant knew that she was not available for the bargain. She said the attendant gave her a quizzical look, as though he could not understand why she would not be approachable for this deal. Her friend Vixena, the other black American student, had a large portion of beans on her plate. Michelle knew how Vixena behaved from their interaction in Rome and thus far in Uganda. And she quickly put two and two together.

"Vixena probably had traded or would trade her favors for the beans, but I could not be certain," she says. Michelle did not know which end of the transaction Vixena was on: the "gotten" or the "to-be-gotten." Michelle asked Vixena, "Do you know what you're doing?" And Vixena reacted in her usual coy manner, and said in a devilish tone, "Hey, I know what I'm doing." She followed that up by saying, "A smile is all he's getting."

The African female students and African male students often dated each other, which was to be expected. In essence, the black American students at Makerere were in the same position that the African students were in at Swarthmore. They and their white counterparts were minorities. At Swarthmore, the African students were minorities within a minority.

Michelle reveals that an African male student befriended her and asked her to go on a date and she obliged. She describes him as "a nice-looking short man who did not look entirely African. His skin was not as dark, and it seemed that he had some European features." She says, "He was a nice guy and very respectful." Still, she felt obligated to tell him not long after they met, "I just want to be friends." She wanted to make sure there was no misunderstanding. After that he understood that her date with him would not lead to anything further. She mentions that the African student showed her his dormitory room, but she made sure that the door was kept wide open. He did not object.

The African student made mention of the fact that her features reminded him of a certain African tribe. Michelle was thrilled to make an ethnic connection. She said that she felt to some extent that she had been authenticated. The male African student had many questions about America and wanted to know how it was to live in America. She recalls that she took her time before answering the question, knowing that her answer would possibly form a real impression in his mind. Being asked this question by an African caused her momentarily to reflect on how *she* felt about America.

During her stay in Africa, Michelle had many opportunities to reflect on her feelings toward America. Campbell reminds us, in his aforementioned book *Middle Passages: African American Journeys to Africa*, that African-Americans discover more about their feelings about America while in Africa than they do when in America. This is a paradox. Why would it take a journey to Africa by an African-American to sort out his or her feelings about his homeland? Did it have something to do with a loss of inheritance, a feeling of alienation or the lack of a solid sense of inclusiveness? This of course goes back to the Frantz Fanon "dual consciousness" of a post-colonized person of color.[53]

To some African-Americans it is not an issue; to others it is. Michelle explains without further hesitation that she loved America. What she sought to balance was the impression that many African students had—that America was a paradise—with the reality that people of color faced living in the United States. She told him that in many ways America was like Africa. That America was a wealthy country but not everyone had wealth. She said that Americans went about their daily lives like all people do, trying to make a living, to get ahead and to do the best for their children.

In her judgment, most Americans lived fruitful lives. She said that there was no difference between what people of color wanted in America and what the white people in America wanted. This response addressed the mistaken belief that somehow black people wanted something different out of America than white people wanted. As she explains to me what she said to this African student, my mind drifts back to my experiences in Chicago at the Harris Bank, my first professional position as a lawyer. One of my male coworkers asked me during lunch, "What do black folks want?" And I responded to him almost automatically: "black folks want the same things that white folks want."

Why is there this misperception, if it truly exists, between the races about wanting a certain quality of life?

Michelle said to this fella, "Laws and practices in America make it difficult for people of color to advance. It's a struggle," she told him, "it's a fight. But, that's life."

She says, "He grabbed my hand and said, 'But together, we can make a difference.'"

"I said, 'Yes, we can.'"

"After our brief talk in his room," she continues, she and the student "went to the canteen and ate meat pies and drank orange Fanta sodas." She recalls, "We talked for several hours about Africa and America, about brotherhood and sisterhood, about our mutual connections, racial and ethnic inheritances."

She says he wanted to know about certain sports personalities, but Michelle was not up to speed in this area. He was curious also about how large her home was. Whether she lived by herself or with family. What did her parents do for a living, and what were her ambitions after finishing school? What type of music did she like, and who were her favorite movie stars? She says that he walked her back to her dormitory, and they shook hands. There was no kiss. She realized that, in earnest, "I had made a friend."

For the black American females, there was always a concern for their safety. Michelle recounts that there was a man who had raped a young student on campus. "When he was caught, he was violently beaten and his life was threatened if he returned to campus," she says, but she goes on to say, "He kept returning to campus, was beaten again, but still he was seen on campus." Apparently, this person had heard about the black American "sisters" and wanted to meet them. Michelle says that she was thankful the male students did not tell him where they lived. But her bigger question was, why wasn't this man in jail, if what she had been told was true? So, she always made sure that whenever there was a meeting between her and an African male student, they met in a public place where her security was not a concern.

Such acts in America would not go unpunished. The perpetrator would at least be jailed and brought up on charges. An American university would not tolerate such an act on its campus and if it does can be subjected to lawsuits and other civil penalties. Does the tolerance of this behavior, if these events are true, say anything about the status of women in Africa and about the priority of security on Makerere's campus, especially for women?

CHAPTER TWENTY-TWO

A RETURN TO A LEGACY

*I feel the capacity to care is the thing which
gives life its deepest significance.*

Pablo Casals

When Harriett arrived in Botswana in 1979, she found that a nursing curriculum had already been developed and accepted. The science department of the faculty of education at the university created, designed and developed the program. It was a three-year nursing curriculum that had been fully approved by the university administration. Her task, an Augean one, was to change the mindset of the university administrators, the white and African faculty and staff. And to sell, as well as implement, an American-style educational nursing curriculum, the benefits of which she was a recipient.

Harriett showed me a presentation she made to a group of American nurses after she had returned from Africa. The presentation about her experiences in Africa said that the existing nursing curriculum for a bachelor of education in nursing had very few courses related to "nursing education." This new and fledgling Department of Nursing Education that she was the chairperson of required, among other things, a change in the erroneous concepts about nursing,

nursing education and nursing practice which was reflected in the existing program. What she was proposing was considered a radical new concept, educating nurses to be professionals rather than just technicians, and that concept was and had to be reflected in the new nursing curriculum.

"After all," she said, "nursing is a discipline, a legitimate branch of knowledge, and it has to be that this knowledge is unique to nursing and that nurses required specific nursing education courses. Nursing students needed to know about nursing administration, nursing practice, the legal aspects of nursing, nursing history, ethical issues in nursing, and they needed classroom and clinical teaching strategies as well as nursing research to broaden their base of understanding about the career they sought." American education, in contrast to that of the British model, mandated a professionalized nursing program. Harriett wanted her nurses to be treated as professionals, not as para-professionals.

During colonialization, the British were interested in education on the cheap. As a result, they used non-governmental organizations to provide schools and to recruit teachers. The British sought to federalize education in the sense that it was left to the cities and towns and local districts to provide for the education of their people.[54] When African countries became independent, they took control of the schools and they adopted the educational system established by their erstwhile colonizers. It is, however, postulated that the British system, as opposed to other European colonial systems of education in the postcolonial era, increased enrollment and literacy in the British colonies. According to Cogneau and Moradi, British colonialization was commercial in nature: "The flag followed the trade." In essence, political accommodation in the politics of imperialism occurred after business interests were protected.

As a result of this commercial orientation to their colonialization policies, education was important. Consequently, education grew faster than in other European colonies. A student's geographical proximity to a school also had a lot to do with access to education. In essence, the aforementioned scholars came to the conclusion that British colonialization in a postcolonial setting resulted in higher literacy rates than in other, non-English colonies, and the likelihood of gaining an education had much to do with the system of distribution and geography. The British had more schools because they did not rely solely on government to provide them as a single provider of education, but rather used missions as well as other charitable organizations in addition to governmental entities to provide education.

The United States and the United Kingdom are home to half of the top 200 universities in the world. Both countries have a rich tradition in providing comprehensive and substantive qualitative education. They are in effect competitors when it comes to who has the best educational system and philosophy. It should be noted that one of the main differences between the educational systems in the United States and the United Kingdom is the amount of time it takes to complete their degree programs. Some authors have indicated that in the United Kingdom courses of study are shorter because the programs are more focused than in the United States. This rivalry can be seen in the struggle against British influence Harriett faced implementing her system.

Harriett's dilemma was that the existing nursing program was too narrowly tailored and needed to be broadened and expanded. In the United States the emphasis is on "breadth." This is achieved through the use of "electives" to broaden the student's exposure to many disciplines. This can be contrasted with the English system of education where the emphasis is on "depth," singularly obtaining knowledge about a discipline or chosen subject. A typical bachelor's degree in Britain takes approximately three years; in the United States it takes four years. In Britain a master's degree can be finished in one year; in the United States it normally takes two years. The PhD in Britain usually only takes three years; in the United States it can take from five to seven years to earn a PhD.[55]

The ever-clamorous spectrum of debate that ensued from Harriett's promotion of this "radical concept" was to be anticipated. Harriett thought, *How can a student be a nurse without a knowledge of literature and of chemistry?* The Department of Education in which the nursing program was housed had a three-year bachelor of nursing in education degree program. The introduction of a new Department of Nursing Education that Harriett introduced was unorthodox, disruptive, and, to some, an apostasy. The existing program required the completion of 103 credit hours, 70 percent of which were outside of the nursing department and the nursing major. The remaining 30 percent of the credits required for graduation were split between the sciences from the science department, an educational foundation from the Department of Educational Foundations, and the new Department of Nursing Education.

The existing program supported by the science faculty did not embrace the broader concepts of nursing education and nursing practice. In the new curriculum that Harriett proposed and implemented, the total credit hours required for the degree was 112. Fifty percent of the total credits under the new curriculum were devoted to nursing, and the remaining 50 percent were distributed between general education and liberal arts courses. So, the new program had a greater emphasis on nursing, and the remaining credits required completion of general education and science courses and liberal arts. In the liberal arts, she proposed that students take statistics, African literature, and political science that involved the politics of contemporary Africa, to gain an understanding of the structure of Southern African societies.

Harriett sought to have her students' horizons expanded. Not only to prepare them to be competent nurses but also to enfold that nursing competence into a wider appreciation of the societal environment into which nursing practice takes place: "The nursing environment," I would term it. Harriett wanted her students not only to be exposed to the hospital wards; she also wanted her students to work in women's prisons, in the elementary and secondary schools, as well as in the university health service, something she knew personally about. She also advocated for her students to work in the various daycare centers and in various health screening programs that existed from time to time. Her mantra was "nursing as a discipline." Harriett was a disciple of Du Bois whether she knew it or not. Harriett was spreading the notion that black people, in Du Bois's case African-Americans, and in Harriett's case Batswana, should be educated in the broadest sense— not narrowly focused. Her compatriots had to be dragged kicking and screaming into the new world of nursing. They had to shake off the shackles of a colonial mentality. They had to move beyond the strictures of neocolonialism that Britain and the European influences sought to continue, especially in nursing education in Botswana, and move bravely, with courage and foresight, into a truly postcolonial era of education. For Harriett this was the stuff of a life's work.

I am reminded that Nkrumah, whom we have mentioned previously, felt that neo-colonialism was the highest stage of colonial exploitation an artifice. Finally, on the point of the legacy of colonialism in education in Africa, the experts make a distinction between the British postcolonial legacy in education, which had as its objective "individualism" in citizenship and social and political interaction known as "cultural adaptation," contrasted for example with the "assimilationist" doctrines promoted by the French, which deemphasized individualism and sought to "homogenize" the culture of its colonies.[56] These viewpoints represent a significant segment of the underpinnings of colonialism in Africa. Overlay these approaches, *status quo ante* with a postcolonial status in the heretofore colonies, and you can see the truncated program that the British installed would result in more nurses as technicians but not as professionals. As I said earlier, the experts have said that the British system resulted in a greater diffusion of educational attainment. So there you have it; this was the crux of the conflict to be resolved.

Harriett related an incident that illustrated her dilemma. She said it rained heavily the night before her curriculum meeting with her faculty. The rain had cooled the air temperature the following morning, so she wore a green paisley serape around her shoulders. In her satchel were copies of her draft of a proposed new curriculum, entitled "We are educating them to be nursing professionals."

The four faculty members gathered in a vacant classroom in the late afternoon. Everyone was tired. It had been the usual long day. The squeaking of the floors and desk as the faculty members filed in and took their seats was a preamble to what would soon follow. With her serape around her shoulders, Harriett distributed copies of the new curriculum. The curriculum talked about the humanities, chemistry, literature, ethics and nursing education as areas to be incorporated into the new course of study. Harriett wanted the students admitted to other departments for humanities and the like. After the faculty had taken a few minutes to read the paper, immediately one of her faculty members, an African woman asked, "Why do our students need to know chemistry? They will not be prescribing medicines."

Another faculty member asked, "Why do they need courses in ethics? They are not doctors and they will not be making life-and-death decisions." They continued to hammer away with one objection after another. Harriett rejoined by explaining that nurses needed to know something about chemistry so they could explain the side effects of drugs to their patients and communicate to the patients' physicians what, if any, side effects the patient experienced. "This," she said, "is essential."

She went on to say, "I do not want my nurses administering medicines without knowing what the consequences to the patient are likely to be." She then looked straight at the questioning faculty member with a steely determination to win the point. "Wouldn't you agree that that is important?" Logically, the faculty member had no choice but to relent and accept Harriett's logic.

Harriett then took on the faculty member that thought ethics was not important. She asked that faculty member, "Don't you think it's important for nurses to know whether a patient is tolerating a treatment regimen? She should have enough knowledge to discuss these issues with the patient and communicate her concerns to the treating physician."

She then asked a follow-up question: "Isn't it the nurse's duty to discuss issues of efficacy with the treating physician and to disclose harmful reactions a patient might be experiencing? Isn't it important for nurses to be able to judge the efficacy of a proposed treatment, especially when she knows the patient's medical as well as social history?"

"Patients," she continued, "often feel more comfortable talking to nurses about their conditions than they do their physicians. Nurses are not as intimidating as doctors and as such, patients often feel freer to confide in their nurses what they are really feeling. Nurses are nurturers as well as caregivers. So, the nurse must be able to bring these issues to the attention of the physician involved, and to balance his or her caregiving with the personal relationship. We do not want our nurses to be just 'order takers!'"

The faculty member who was a white male responded, "We are not training nurses to be doctors!"

Harriett retorted, "Of course we are not training them to be doctors. We are training them to be professional nurses!"

The tension among all of the players in this meeting was rising. Then a faculty member asked another question.

"Dr. Karuhije," she said, "I hate to say this, but why do our nurses need to know about African literature and history? This is a waste of their time when they could be concentrating on their nursing education courses that save lives."

"Do you know who Wole Soyinka is? What about Nadine Gordimer, or Chinua Achebe?" Harriett responded. The faculty member, not wanting to be caught flat-footed, replied cheekily, "Of course I know who these people are."

Following up, Harriett said, "Well, if you know who these people are, shouldn't our students know who they are as well? Shouldn't our students know something about them? They are their countrymen."

She felt like asking, "Well, who are they?" But because she did not want to condescend, she held her peace. Her point had been made. All of the persons mentioned above are highly acclaimed African writers. Gordimer and Soyinka are Nobel Peace Prize winners in literature.

Harriett's experience in this fight was analogous to a salmon swimming upstream to spawn. She was caught in a crosspatch of competing ideologies, traditions and myopia about education in Africa in this particular program and in the University in Botswana. Not long after that exchange, the meeting ended.

These conflicts arose frequently as Harriett sought to win over the established hierarchy to accept a new direction. She tried, though she failed on many occasions, to be *de rigueur* in her approach, but that did not always work. The fact that a proper approach did not work was revelatory in that it demonstrated the biases built in to the neocolonial mentality in Botswana. She thought at times that these conflicts were indissoluble and that she would be unsuccessful at doing something she really loved and felt committed to. The opposition and the politics had been visceral, a "take no prisoners" approach. The elephant in the room was and remained the British educational dogma. But in spite of the headwinds, Harriett persevered and submitted her new bachelor of nursing education curriculum to the higher-ups for approval, and it won approval.

After the faculty exchange, Harriett's day ended, and she made her way back to her home. After a day of teaching and advocating so often repeated to the point of exhaustion, she sought quietude. She kicked off her shoes after closing the door behind her, greeted her mother and collapsed onto her living room sofa. She said she felt like the blood had drained down to her feet. She was exhausted. After a pause, she lamented to her mother, "These folks are driving me crazy! They block everything I try to do. They oppose every suggestion I make, and they don't believe a word I say. I have to fight for everything! This is ridiculous!" she groused.

Isabelle, knowing her daughter well, responded patiently with a soothing texture to her voice: "Harriett, be patient. Don't let these folks frustrate you. Give them a chance. They are not used to these ideas. They will come around. Fix yourself a drink and let it go for today." Harriett was known to enjoy a good shot of good vodka every now and then, and she did just that.

After a blood pressure screening exam not long after this event, Harriett learned that her blood pressure was high. Additional stress was added because, in her home, she did not have the usual creature comforts that she had gotten used to in America. There was no telephone, or TV, or coffee. Gasoline was only sold on Wednesdays, and there was simply no public transportation. Her concerns about health care became more and more acute as each month passed. She thought that the health care treatment issue would be determined by where she lived in Africa. In this she was correct.

There was much to be concerned with on a personal level, and chief among them was her mother's health. Before Isabelle left for Africa, she was diagnosed with breast cancer. She had had breast cancer surgery in the United States. During this first pilgrimage, if you will, she was required to have her yearly breast exam. This exam was not available in Botswana, so Harriett was required to take her mother to Johannesburg, South Africa, which was not far from Gaborone. The exam revealed that her mother had a recurrence of the cancer. Harriett and her mother discussed her treatment options and where it was best to pursue those options in that region.

Harriett had other concerns of a lesser nature. She did not like the clothing or the shoes that were available to her in the stores, and the haircare that she had been used to as an African-American woman was nonexistent. Fish and chicken were the main staples of the diet, and she introduced turkey for the first time to her cook and housekeepers. She mentioned that cleanliness of the food, especially meat, was a big issue for her personally and for her mother. And that it was always hot!

Her return to the United States in 1982 was not only contractual but bordered on being a medical necessity. Her mother required continued treatment and close medical supervision. Although treatment was possible in South Africa, her preference was treatment in the United States. Irrespective of all of this, her mother passed in 1993 in Chester.

In addition to everything else Harriett had to deal with, she learned that the Kellogg Foundation had been a major funding source for the Botswana nursing program. Because Harriett was hired by the university, the Kellogg Foundation lost the ability to run the nursing program. This was more than an annoyance to the foundation, so agents for the foundation set about to sabotage her efforts. If they could not run the program, no one would. And since they were paying significant money, they wanted their people in place. Also, the United States Agency for International Development (USAID) was a funding source. USAID wanted to fund a short-term nursing teacher diploma program in the department. Harriett said she was able to get some funding from the university, albeit a small amount. She recalled that she was able to live on her university salary and apply the USAID money to the faculty.

Her contract was up in 1982. "I would have liked to stay," she said, "but the conflicts simply were too great." She intoned, "The British did not want nurses enrolled in liberal arts courses. Their vision did not embrace it." Members of the British faculty thought they were the doyens of education, especially in this university and in the discipline of nursing education. The British were aided by the Batswana because the Batswana were, like the British, purblind, at least in this context, and unable to visualize a more progressive future. And they did not want to credit "American education" for improving the nursing curriculum, not to mention crediting an African-American educator with making such improvements. It was not until she returned to Botswana, which we will get to later, that she had her fights with the Kellogg Foundation operatives.

In this first tour, she had to prove her bona fides as a specialist in nursing curriculum and design. Her mission was to set up a bachelor of education degree program in nursing, and she accomplished that objective. When she returned years later, her charge would be to construct a master's degree program in nursing.

CHAPTER TWENTY-THREE

THE ENCORE

Sweetest of the flowers a blooming
In the fragrant vernal days,
Is the Lily-of-the-Valley
Well, you chose this humble blossom
As the Nurse's emblem flower
Who grows more like her idea
Every day and every hour
Like the Lily-of- the-Valley
In her honesty and worth –
Oh! She blooms in truth and virtue
In the humble works of earth....

Paul Lawrence Dunbar, "Lily of The Valley"

Harriett returned to Botswana in June 1993 after serving for three years as associate dean of the Howard University School of Nursing, but this time she returned by herself. In spite of her apprehensions about departmental politics and living conditions, she realized that she really loved what she had been doing and where she did it. In the intervening years, her mind often returned to the enchantment of Africa. The struggles had been difficult, but sometimes difficulty is what makes something attractive, especially years removed. "You begin to relish the combat, and you feel emboldened because you survived it," she said. "In effect, I had been validated."

The pain in her heart from her mother's passing to some degree could be leavened by the new challenges that awaited her. And she could not resist the allure of a second tour. During her first tour, she had been naïve and underestimated the opposition. Her frustrations affected her health and created an ulcerative condition in her psyche. The anodyne approach she took when she first went to Africa in 1979 was scrapped and exchanged for a strategy to be more hard-nosed and less plaintive. She had nothing to prove to these people, so she sought to convey an attitude of expectancy. She expected her lead to be followed this time around, and she did not tolerate fools too gladly. She had earned her "stripes," and her baptism had been cleansing. She had been schooled and educated in the politics and prejudices of a neocolonial state and passed her course.

"The conflict remained," she said ruefully: the British educational system versus the American system. She went on to explain that when she returned for the second tour, Serara, her former student from the doctoral program in which she served as a faculty member, was now the chairperson. "It was she who invited me to create a master's degree program," she emphasized with justifiable pride. She reminded me, as if I had forgotten, that she had been the "founding chairperson" of the nursing program in that department.

As a part of Serara's employment with the university, she had been given a house. Serara used that house to start a real estate business and she became rich. Serara was resourceful and entrepreneurial. But in a society where everyone took the measure of each other within a closely-knit elite clique, Serara created many enemies by her success.

"As her friend and former colleague, that enmity spilled onto me. The paint splattered," Harriett said. "This time, none of my moving expenses were covered under my second contract." Times had changed. When she returned for her second tour, many of the buildings that were under construction when she left were now completed. The Chinese had continued their construction and put in air-conditioning, and many of the buildings were now modern buildings. However, she felt that the prevailing paternalistic attitude of the medical community in Botswana was still the same: As a matter of nursing practice, the patient could not refuse the recommendations of medical staff, and men were always in charge.

During her first tour at the university between 1979 and 1982, the British educational system was her main opposition. Her opposition during her second stint, between 1993 and 1996, was compounded by the Kellogg Foundation operation.

The Kellogg Foundation was funding the master's degree program in nursing education, and obtaining funding for these various programs was essential, but the foundation did not run the program. Harriett, on her return, set up the master's degree program. She wrote the curriculum, and it too was accepted by the university administration and faculty.

Two black women associated with Wayne State University in Michigan represented the Kellogg Foundation in Southern Africa and engendered an invidious form of infighting. They fought to get their people in place through one artifice or another. One of these ladies was in charge of the Kellogg Foundation operation in Southern Africa, and the second woman was her deputy. Their discourse with Harriett was tendentious to say the least; as a result, little agreement was reached on issues each felt passionate about, such as who did what, how and when.

Harriett said she was shocked, if not taken aback, that these women of color would fight her, a fellow African-American woman, as much as they did. As a consequence, residential privileges for native Botswana students on campus while attending the nursing program at the University of Botswana became uncertain due to inconsistent funding. South Africa was the only country in Southern Africa with a guaranteed residence program for native Africans of their country.

The government in Botswana, newly enriched by the diamond trade, wanted to educate their people with the new resources, and Harriett was one of their representatives. After all, again she had been hired by the university to implement her vision. Even though the students loved the program of study in nursing and many were trying to get into the existing program, that enthusiasm did not move the needle for Harriett. In spite of the popularity among the students, Harriett continued to make enemies. She says she spent ten to twelve hours a day intensively working to build the master's program.

Why weren't the Africans receptive and accommodating to Harriett's attempts to help them improve their program as she thought they would be or as they should have been? She was an American black woman who earnestly wanted to help. The reasons are complex, perhaps a mixture from the vestiges of colonialism, neocolonialism and simply African pride. You would think that the African faculty and administrators would be falling all over themselves to accept and incorporate Harriett's ideas into their program, but instead they resisted, rejected, obfuscated, obstructed and circumvented most of what she tried to do. What she achieved she did in spite of these barriers. This was what disillusioned Harriett. Her optimism had been clouded over.

Harriett intended to make Botswana her permanent residence, but because of the stress and immigration issues, she had to leave to protect her health and safety. She wanted permanent residence status, but it was denied to her, she concluded, because of the jealousy about her and her close friend Serara: "The Botswana immigration authorities taking orders from higher up made sure that my status was impermanent," according to Harriett. A line had been drawn in the sand by the United States regarding Eric's attempt to resume his doctoral work in New York and be reunited with his wife. The Botswana immigration authorities had similarly drawn a line for Harriett. Therefore, she had to leave, this time for good.

Harriett at farewell dinner for a departing faculty member, May 6, 1995 in Gaborone, Botswana. Left of Harriett, Miriam Sebego, one of Harriett's first students now a PhD in nursing, next left, Sheila Tlou, now a PhD in nursing, all Botswanans. Across from Harriett is a faculty member from Nigeria when Harriett first arrived in 1980.

The thought of returning was a phantom. She believed her requested permanent residency was also denied because she was not British. Harriett said, "I was disappointed, not so much in the situation, but disappointed in my expectations of Africa, especially during my first tour. I misinterpreted Africa." She went on to explain that it was not anyone's fault. She just had preconceived notions.

Harriett explained that she thought she was "pure African" and "thought that I would be welcomed with open arms. But I was not," she confessed. She explained that she did not know African culture. That she was unfamiliar with how the strong sinews of politics, history, indigeneity and Afrocentricity connected African society. A common mistake of Americans. She explained that she thought that because of her ancestry, her path would be made easier. She perceived herself as being an African, but she was seen by the Africans as an American. That was disappointing to her.

She also said, "Africans did not see African-Americans as special. They were just jealous of the privileges that African-Americans had." She said she was wearing an Afro, but her hair had been "treated" and teased so much over the years in America that her hairstyle just made her more obviously non-native. "I just wanted to be one of them, but they did not want any part of me." She was crestfallen. "Just as I Am" is the Baptist hymn "without one plea[...]," but her pleas fell on deaf ears.

Once, when going from Botswana to South Africa to take her mother there for treatment, her mother went through the American embassy to gain an entry visa into South Africa from Botswana. Harriett, however, sought to use the Botswana immigration facility for her passage that would not require a visa. At that time, natives of Botswana were not required to obtain a visa to enter South Africa. Embittered, she said, "They knew I was there at the university, but they said that according to their records they had no one in Botswana by my name." Harriett became mad and angry about "a lot of things"—chief among them, her treatment during her final tour. Harriett reiterated, "I thought that because I was of African ancestry that I was African, but I was not, and the Africans let me know it."

In the old days before "black is beautiful," children had an old rhyme: "The blacker the berry, the sweeter the juice." It was used as a comeback when one black person teased another black person about the dark color of their skin. The Africans Harriett encountered require that the "berry" be grown in Africa. Her bubble had been burst, her preconceived notions destroyed. She was told she had to go through Botswana visa control which meant applying for a visa to enter South Africa, if required, as an American citizen. Again, she pleaded, "Officer, I'm an African." He responded matter-of-factly, "Madam, you are *not*." She was required to prove she had entered Botswana legally by obtaining a work visa; then she was required to obtain a visa to enter South Africa, like any other foreigner.

• • •

Her relationship with Serara hastened her departure from Botswana. There was too much jealousy of Harriett's relationship with Serara, so much so that she felt her well-being was in jeopardy, especially when Harriett served as an "external examiner" for the school system in Botswana.

The British during that time had a system in place called external examiners. It was a system to ensure that there was consistency and equality in the education that people under its system were receiving. The administrators of the system chose experts in the subject matters being evaluated, and this team went from school to school, university to university, college to college and examined the curriculum, test scores, examined students and graded their results. They reviewed faculty credentials and test-passage rates on regional and state examinations. It was hard work being an examiner, and the pay was modest compared to the responsibility.

Harriett served as an external examiner during her time in Botswana. We will examine this concept a bit further, but it is one that I find attractive and if applied properly would be beneficial in America. Americans, however, have preferred standardized tests, both state and federal, as a leveling-out platform to evaluate the quality of performance, instruction and student proficiency.[57]

Harriett concluded that African-Americans simply do not know African history. And because of that, African-Americans have many misconceptions about Africa. She said, "We should be proud of our African history, and every African-American should go to Africa." She went on to say that most African-Americans do not embrace Africa. They are somewhere between being on the other side of the wall and sitting on the ledge. She said the African elites were highly confident in themselves, but not necessarily arrogant. She declared that black Americans have been "sold a bill of goods about Africa." In retrospect, she avowed without being prompted, she did not perceive of any problems marrying an African; she was motivated to marry Eric because of her very high degree of respect for him.

• • •

Her decision to divorce Eric came after many decades of separation. No children were born of the marriage. As she got older, she was urged to file for a divorce to protect her estate from an absent and errant spouse. She finally initiated divorce proceedings with much sadness. She did not want to close this chapter in her life that had meant so much to her. She had given her love sincerely, willingly and without reservation. Reservations blemish sincerity, although in retrospect perhaps there should have been some. Joining their two cultures was enabling, empowering and authenticating. She had, and still retains, an *Afrocentric* perspective and takes pride in what Campbell calls "the essential *Africanity* of African-American people." Matters of this type are complicated issues and do not yield to simple answers or explanations.

The paradox in all of this is that immigration policy had a significant impact on the lives of these two people. American immigration policy kept Eric out of America at a crucial time. And Botswana immigration policy sealed Harriett's fate in that country. Both she and Eric were kept from doing what was important to them by the cultures that played a vital role in their lives.

Harriett in 1992; Associate Dean in the College of Nursing, Howard University

In the intervening years she had only sparse contact, if any, with Eric, she recalled. Her information was more gossip from contacts in Botswana than from personal interactions with him. Eric did not attend her mother's funeral; he may not have known about it. The chasm between them had been growing for many years now.

Finally, one can surmise that Eric may have fallen under the sway of his family and culture and perhaps had remarried and felt no further obligation to Harriett, but this is only speculation.

Surely, if he cared for her and loved her, his efforts to reunite with her would have been manifest.

In July 2013, seventeen years after Harriett left Botswana and Africa for the last time, her divorce hearing was scheduled to begin. The master who presided over Harriett's divorce proceedings asked Harriett a series of routine questions to prove the elements of an uncontested no-fault divorce under Maryland Law. Harriett took her place in the witness box after she was called and sworn in. She then proceeded to answer the master's questions. To those that knew her, it was obvious she was nervous and uncomfortable.

Firmly but without arrogance the master commenced the examination. How long had they been separated? What was the nature of the separation? Had they been separated from each other for at least three years both from bed and board? Were there any marital assets that had to be divided? Were there any minor children born of the marriage? Had her husband been given proper notice of these proceedings? Had Harriett satisfied the residency requirements? And did the court have jurisdiction over the matter? The latter two questions would be satisfied by a review of the court file, not by Harriett's responses to the master. Since Harriett had not seen or been in contact with Eric for many years, her answers were simple and direct. She was uncomfortable with the intrusiveness of the questions, but with courage and dignity she answered them truthfully and to the best of her knowledge.

The master, as the trier of fact in the case, must judge the credibility of each witness to determine whether the witness is testifying truthfully and that the court record is complete. The master does this by judging each witness's demeanor and answers to the questions. In effect, have the requirements of the law been satisfied? This master could easily discern that Harriett was a mature woman of substance and her plea to the court for a divorce was not a frivolous matter. The master was satisfied.

Michelle was called to the stand by Harriett's lawyer shortly after Harriett completed her testimony to corroborate some of Harriett's testimony as far as she could about their separation. Both Harriett and Michelle made good witnesses. Harriett's lawyer's job was made easy. Glancing down at the transcript, the court satisfied itself that the record was complete and in order.

After Michelle's testimony the master announced in open court that the moving party, Harriett Karuhije, had proven the necessary grounds for a divorce and that he was awarding her a divorce. An unceremonious end to a resounding troth made by these two people. The judicial relief Harriett sought but had avoided for a long time was granted.

Outside of the courtroom after the case was over, Harriett's lawyer asked her whether she wanted to retake her maiden name and she replied softly, no. She loved her name: it was the last vestige, other than what she still held in her heart, of Eric. Her married name was an extension of who she was. It represented her state of mind and self- image.

Many people seek in a name a definition of self, but very few find it. In today's world some names are a concoction of what sounds hip or novel, a meaningless label solely for identification. Some in our community come up with quasi-sounding African names, fads that mean nothing, given to a child without regard to the importance it plays in that person's self-image. Many of us, myself included, accept the name of a former slave owner somewhere down the genealogical line, wholly unrelated to who we are ancestrally. A name without ancestral meaning except for its immediate significance to the family is hollow and without character definition or identity. A name matters. It stands for something and should not be given lightly, but rather with care and an attention to meaning. The recipient of the name grows into the name; they become as one. He or she will wear that name for the rest of their lives unless later changed by court order, so it warrants and requires careful consideration and should mean something connected to family, not just a collage of words.

So Harriett's retention of her married name was a badge of

honor. A cherished possession. It encapsulated a significant segment of her persona.

Two weeks after the hearing, an envelope arrived in the mail for Harriett from the Montgomery County Circuit Court. After she retrieved the envelope from her mailbox, she returned to her apartment and opened it slowly. The white parchment was stapled to a blue backer, often used to highlight the importance of a document. She read it carefully. The paper was her divorce decree. The decree was an award of an absolute divorce written in legalese with a few Latin phrases added for dignity, including *Vinculo Matrimoni*, a release from all marital duties and obligations of marriage. She folded the letter neatly and put it back into the envelope and filed it away with her other important papers. It was over. This epoch in her life was now determined. All that remained were memories and matters of the heart. And so it seemed at this particular time that Oscar Wilde's comment was right: experience in this case had triumphed over imagination.

CHAPTER TWENTY-FOUR

A LEOPARD FOR MOTHER

The experiences Michelle has recounted so far, with Idi Amin and her male African friend, caused her to appraise much about her purpose for going to Uganda. But there was more to come.

As the train leaves Philadelphia's 30th Street Station, Michelle resumes her story.

"Things were going along smoothly," Michelle says. "I felt very much engaged in campus life." She explains that when she worked on her African lungfish project, she was able to relax and to clear her mind of all of her anxieties. So she began to work frequently in the lab on the lungfish. She wanted to study its various cells, its organs and characteristics. Michelle tells me the name of the lungfish is actually a misnomer.

"How's that?" I ask.

"It does not have a lung but uses an air bladder like a lung," she explains. "It can breathe in both air and water."

"That's pretty nifty," I say. I quip, "That kind of flexibility would be helpful to a lot of people, including myself."

She says that when she first saw the fish she was going to use for her experiment, it was alive in a fish tank in the laboratory.

"Tell me something about the laboratory," I say.

"The lab was on an upper floor in the science building. It had several horizontal rows of long counters with black countertops with large wood cabinets underneath. Microscopes were all around and lab coats were left folded over some of the chairs in the room. On some of the shelves in the back of the room were large jars and bottles of various preserved reptiles, plants, insects and animal parts. The room smelled like formaldehyde." She jokes, "When you entered the room you were either there to study something or to be preserved."

We both laugh. "Some of the counters," she continues, "contained water spigots that flowed into small, stainless steel sinks. The sinks were used for various purposes: to wash and rinse off specimens of one kind or another and for students and faculty to wash their hands if need be."

She says that she prepared a timetable for work on her project and that she contemplated working over her next holiday break. She was aware that some of her fellow students were planning to go to Nairobi for the semester break, but she had made arrangements with a fellow student to go to Tanzania and Mombasa.

"I had plenty of time to travel. I had a whole year," she says.

The next time she went to the lab to see the fish, the fish was dead. She does not give me any explanation why the fish died. She simply says she began the dissection process. She used a scalpel and some other instruments to isolate certain tissues and to begin the dehydration and staining process she needed for her slides.

"I was really busy and enjoying every moment," she tells me. And she says, to my disbelief, "I began collecting bugs and storing them in tiny bottles of formaldehyde for preservation." I'm in disbelief about her bug story because for many years Michelle has shown a strong aversion to bugs of any sort. She says that she planned to compare the insects on Makerere's campus with those on Swarthmore's campus.

"If you couldn't find me in the lab, I was dancing with students preparing for an upcoming school program. I was fully engaged. I was in a tranquil state of mind," she says. "I went to the market and bought some beautiful orange cloth for our performances. I even attended some Christian programs on campus, and I felt the loving spirit of peace and beneficence." She felt like she was becoming a part of the university and wanted to make the exchange program a success for herself and for future students.

There was a leopard in one of the big crates in the far-left corner of the lab where she worked. A lab assistant told her that her professor, Dr. White, had captured it for a friend. The leopard had been sedated, and for a long time while she worked, she even forgot it was there. The lab assistant left the room and she continued to study and to make her slides. She was making copious notes and observations, drawing cellular structures on graph paper, her colored pencils strewn about haphazardly on the laboratory countertop. When one of the pencils fell on the floor, she moved her stool to pick it up. Before returning to an upright position, she noticed small movement coming from the crate.

She says, "I took a second take, picked up my pencil and resumed my work. Then I began to hear a low moan and the sound of something moving in the crate. I then looked seriously and carefully at the crate. The low guttering tones and moaning of a wild animal captured my attention. I was alarmed, but I knew that the crate, as the lab assistant had said, was securely fastened, so I did not panic. The lab assistant had said that the cat was probably waking up from the sedation and that it would be fed soon. The lab assistant assured me of my safety and told me 'not to worry,'" she remembers.

But then, "the lab assistant left again, and I felt more vulnerable. Intellectually I knew I was safe, but emotionally I felt unsafe." Michelle tried to concentrate on her work, but the leopard began moaning again and its movements quickened in pace. Michelle says, "That's when I began to think about my mother. The leopard was her favorite cat. She always wanted a genuine leopard coat. I smiled to myself and thought, *Well, Mom, here is your leopard!*

"Shortly after that, my studying was interrupted by a loud roar," she said. "The sound startled me. I felt my hairs standing on the back of my neck and my pulse rate skyrocketed. All I could think about was what the lab assistant said: the cat was probably getting hungry. Those were the last few words she uttered. 'Getting hungry, getting hungry' was all that I could remember. Was the cat smelling my scent? Was I supposed to be the food that satisfied his hunger?

"I lost all concentration. There was no need to even think about my lab work. The leopard kept roaring. He clearly was out from under the sedation and was uncomfortable in his confinement. I quickly gathered up my belongings, made sure I had no more pencils on the floor and immediately l left the lab. I left the leopard's fate solely in the hands of the lab assistant. I always followed Murphy's Law. 'Anything that can go wrong, will go wrong.' I was looking forward to my own dinner, not being someone else's."

CHAPTER TWENTY-FIVE

CAUGHT IN OBETE'S WEB

The conductor calls out the next stop. "Trenton, New Jersey, in twenty minutes." We pass through the North Philadelphia stop. Some trains stop there, but others don't. This is one of the few times in over thirty years of traveling on this train that I am not getting off the train in Philadelphia.

As we move briskly along toward New York City, the scene is all urban industrial cityscape. I am trying to do three things at once, an impossible task. I continue to read Michelle's manuscript, I record my notes and observations in my Moleskine, and I glance attentively out the train window at the skyline of Philadelphia, my erstwhile home. I look out the window at the parkways, boulevards, streets, row houses and walk-ups of Philadelphia. I am reminded of the joy and the pain, the sacred and the profane, the flutter and the wow of it all when I lived and worked there thirty-seven years ago. I experienced all of these emotions individually at any given time. Each emotion, quality and vibration was felt and to some extent internalized. My experience was both monumental and enriching, personally and professionally.

But those days are in the past, gone forever, a bygone era. I am in another phase of life now. Long after Michelle's African trip, our lives became interwoven in this city of brotherly love, or as some would say, the city of the "jugular vein." Just like our revered first president, George Washington, who in 1776 crossed the Delaware River, and as many of my ancestors who were enslaved along that river and those that escaped from the tyranny of the North and South using that river, I too had crossed the Delaware River in pursuit of freedom. I went to Philadelphia many years ago to practice law and ended up staying there for twenty years. This is what happens when life-altering experiences recast the template of our lives. You are changed by them. You are no longer the same.

After a few minutes of multitasking, Michelle and I resume our conversation.

By far the most startling event that happened to Michelle was completely unforeseen. It takes a long time for her to tell me this story, but she finally gets through it. She starts by saying, "A day of tranquility, I thought. I had been in Uganda for three months. My first semester was at an end. Time had passed quickly. We were at a semester break and I was instructed to clear out of my room. All of the students had to do this because the university rented out the dormitory rooms during holidays and school breaks. So, I had to pack up everything," she says. "There was a basement in the dormitory, and I stored most of my belongings there. The remaining items I carried with me. Mr. Eric arranged for me to stay in his apartment. He had a two-bedroom unit and a houseboy to cook and clean daily. Mr. Eric was seldom there, so I had the place to myself most of the time. On this occasion, he was returning his brother to school and arranging for his brother's travel.

"My plan was to stay in Mr. Eric's apartment and work in the science laboratory on my lungfish project. I was in the laboratory most of the day, and when I returned to the apartment, the houseboy, a young African lad, slender in build with a bright smile, usually had cleaned the apartment and prepared dinner. His usual routine was to hang around for about an hour after I returned. We would chat for a few moments and he would tell me about the food he prepared. Shortly thereafter, he left for his home. I did not know where in the area he lived, but he must have been able to walk from his home to the apartment without much trouble. He returned each morning with the same objective to cook and clean. This sort of arrangement was quite prevalent in the university community. The middle class often hired help. It provided jobs and also was a class distinction."

Michelle pauses momentarily, then resumes: "As far as I could see, all was well on the African front. I was comfortable in my routine. My anxieties were under control and there were no unsettling times. Blue skies were all that I saw. During these moments, I momentarily forgot that I was in Africa, in Uganda, much like I felt when we visited Lake Victoria. At times, I felt more at home in this community than I did in America except for the absence of my mother and sister. I think my feeling of tranquility had a lot to do with a feeling of being home, the commonality of spirit, of blackness, of ancestry and a feeling of communal integration.

"The only unsettling aspect of my routine occurred when I had to walk past a community of bats. The bats lived on the way to the apartment building, so I had to walk by them twice a day. The bats were clearly visible, and over there in Uganda they were of enormous size. On one occasion, I noticed a bat had fallen to the ground and died. The biologist in me wanted to gather the remains and take it to the laboratory. I would have dissected it, as I was doing with the lungfish, and before long it would have ended up in one of the large jars filled with formaldehyde to be preserved. But my conservative sensibility won out. Mainly because I thought of the various diseases that bats are supposed to carry."

Michelle sighs. Then she says, "The troubles began when rumors circulated on campus that a bloody military coup was in the offing. Unfortunately, in certain parts of Africa this sort of rumor is not uncommon. So, my inclination was to ignore the talk, to disregard it and focus on my work. For the most part I was apolitical. I was not a student of public affairs or politics: not in the USA and certainly not in Africa. Why was there a need to? After all, I felt safe and I was comfortable in my surroundings. Nevertheless, the rumors continued to swirl about a pending coup. I was told that people were leaving the country, that some people were being assaulted, women were being raped, men beaten and some even killed. People's possessions were being confiscated and homes looted.

"It was not long before I got the shivers and the worries. I cornered some of my professors on campus and asked them what they made of it all. They said they feared for their safety and said that I should consider leaving. I was having the best time of my life, so why would I think about leaving? It was the farthest thing from my mind. *Just when things were getting good,* I thought, *this has to happen!* The experience of a lifetime was being sullied by events beyond my control, by events that one only hears or reads about, a forcible change in government. Idi Amin was in power, so who was deposing who? I was not a supporter of Amin and was uninformed about his despotic tendencies."

"I did not have time to answer that question. Rumors continued to churn about Asian Indians being killed. And an atmosphere of alarm invaded the community outside of the campus. Since at the time I lived off campus, I felt safe. I thought about the warning that the female African student had given me and the others when we returned from the Idi Amin rally: 'Have yourself an escape plan and don't expect any warning; just listen for the screams.'"

The dreadful beckoned. It would appear, based on the timeframe, that Michelle was caught in Obote's failed attempt to take back power after his ouster by Amin in January 1971. Remember, Obote was a graduate of Makerere University where Michelle was studying. After Obote was forcibly removed from office by Amin, Obote took refuge in Tanzania. The president of Tanzania, Julius Nyerere, offered him sanctuary. When Obote left Uganda, thousands of refugees and some military men followed him. There was an attempt by Obote and these exiles, with the tacit support of the Tanzanian president in 1972, to mount a countercoup. This web of intrigue, the result of a poorly organized coup, failed. Subsequently, a violent purge by Amin and severe recriminations were exacted upon Obote's loyalists and tribal members, many of whom died or were killed. It is estimated that between 80,000 and 500,000 people were killed, including Frank Kalimuzo, the vice chancellor of Makerere University."[58]

She continues, "It became personal when I received the cable from Swarthmore College advising me to leave the university. It was not a suggestion; it was an order. There was no room for indecision. The professors back home had decided to get their students out. So, I had to leave. I rationalized the situation by thinking that whatever was causing this convulsion would be over soon, and I would have only a brief absence, a hiatus, that could quickly be forgotten. Not knowing what the timetable would be, however, I packed as if there would be no return. The cable from Swarthmore instructed me to inform the other students of this preemption. But I did not know where the others were. Some of them I had not seen for a few days. All I knew was that they were somewhere in Nairobi for holiday, but where in Nairobi I knew not. I could not focus on the other students. Self-preservation required that I focus on getting 'Michelle' out of this country.

"I went to the front of the university and boarded a bus to Kampala. The bus was filled with passengers, everyone looking and talking feverishly. There was standing room only. The rickety multicolored bus arrived in Kampala a short time later. I had in my mind three destinations: the American embassy, the immigration building and the bank. All of these offices were in the business district of town. I went to the embassy first and spoke to a young white American and explained my situation to him. He agreed with me that I should leave. He offered me the option of leaving with an embassy staff person and his family. I was unable to make an immediate decision, so I told him that I would get back to him. My hesitation was because of my disbelief and need to talk with Mr. Eric.

"The feeling of panic in the wider community now informed my state of mind. I walked quickly; I did not look at any passersby. The noises and sounds of cars and trucks moving and people talking with a look of wonder on their faces, all looking for direction, was not my concern. I was in my own world, oblivious to the needs of others at that moment.

"I proceeded to the immigration building. It was only a block or two from the embassy. Since they both shared a common purpose in some of what they did, it made sense for me to go there next. The immigration building was a gray marbled structure of several floors with ceramic-tiled hallways. Some floors had painted walls divided into two shades of color. As I walked down the hall, I saw many soldiers. I held my head up and walked past them, when one of them yelled, 'Where do you think you're going? Stop!' When he ordered me to stop, I simultaneously heard the cocking of his rifle. I froze.

"When I turned around to face the soldier, I saw that he had his rifle pointed directly at me. Never in my life had I had anyone point a weapon at me, not to mention a rifle. I was at a loss for what to do. I was paralyzed with fright. My attention was squarely on the rifle. The soldier yelled out again, 'Where do you think you're going?' Nervously, I looked at the soldier and replied that I was going to the visa department. The soldier was clearly agitated. There were other soldiers around and behind him. I tried to stay calm, and initially I did not look him in the eyes. I let my body movements indicate submission. I answered the soldier's question by saying, 'I know where I am going. I have been here many times.'

By talking I gained some confidence, so this time I did look at him in the eyes. The firmness of my voice was meant to convey that though I was under his control, I was not going to be easily subdued. The soldier and I peered into each other's eyes. After a few moments he said, 'Come with me!' He was authoritative, and I could discern that he meant for me to follow him. The soldier was a dark-skinned African dressed in a green military uniform. His rifle and his boots were black.

I didn't see any insignia on his breast pockets or shoulders as I had seen on Amin's uniform. He seemed like an ordinary soldier, one of many.

The soldier directed me to go in a direction that I was not heading. The office I was accustomed to going to was just around the corner from where we were standing. The soldier led me down a flight of steps and I thought the worst. My anxiety level was high and my heart was pounding. My worst vision was of me being thrown to the floor and raped behind or underneath the stairwell. The soldier kept yelling at me to 'hurry up!' Inertia acted to slow me down against my effort to follow him. I felt as if I was carrying an additional hundred pounds. Everything slowed down. As I went down step by step, I began to chastise myself: *Why did I look this man in the eye? Who do you think you are dealing with? This was a stupid, stupid, stupid thing to do!*

When we got to the bottom of the steps, I heard a door opening miraculously near me. I had actually made it down the stairs. The soldier opened the door, a wood-frame door stained in a mahogany finish with a large window extending from below the top of the door to the middle panel. As I entered the room I looked around. I saw other people lined up around the walls.

Then I saw a familiar face, a staff person that I had dealt with over the last three months. This young Ugandan, an educated man, wore a short-sleeve white shirt and beige pants. His shoes were black. He looked and acted like a bureaucrat, which he was. He was not in the military, but he had an officious style to his manner. He occupied a position of importance, but he too probably wondered what his fate would be in this new reality. He looked at me and asked, 'May I help you?' He smiled as he asked the question, indicating that he recognized me from before. Periodically I had to check in with this fellow to let him know I was still in the country.

International Driving Permit 1972. This permit was used by Michelle in addition to her passport as as an Identification document.

"'Yes! Yes, you can help me!' I replied thankfully.

"The familiarity of our association and the friendly words we exchanged relieved what had otherwise been a heavy load of anxiety. The clerk said to me that the location of his office had been moved to the lower floor and he apologized for the inconvenience. I quickly gave him my departure information, my passport and my other immigration papers. He stamped them and I left.

"I had one more stop to make. I had to go to the bank. I did not have much money in the bank, only enough to sustain me from month to month. Our allotment from Swarthmore was paid in US dollars, and the Ugandan exchange rate extended the purchasing power of the money. I wanted to close my account. To do this I had to declare my assets and my liabilities. In effect, I had to prepare a financial statement.

"As I began to fill out the paperwork, a crackle of gunfire erupted! A loud scream echoed across the banking floor. I looked around to see what had caused the panic. There had been one shot after another, a cavalcade of life-threatening sounds. There was an incessant chorus of yells and screams. People began to run toward the doors. But the guards prevented them from leaving.

"More gunshots rang out outside of the building and the screams increased and people dropped to the floor. The lights went out. Out of my body came an uncontrollable scream. I was screaming and yelling to the top of my voice. The soldiers were shooting outside the building. The teller windows were old world with iron bars that ran from top to bottom in front of the glass, with a circular opening in the middle through which the teller spoke as she or he completed the transaction. A horizontal opening at the bottom provided space for the teller to complete the transaction. The tellers behind the windows left their counters and high-back chairs. They too dropped to the floor.

"I was unable to see anything of consequence. I sat on the floor with my knees drawn to my chest, my head down and my arms tightly wrapped around my knees. More gunshots rang out! I was unfamiliar with the sounds of gunshots. I had never heard the sound of a gun being fired nor been in close proximity of gunfire. My mother did not have a gun, Daddy Kake did not have a gun, my grandfather, to my knowledge, did not have a gun.

"Each burst of gunfire startled me. My pocketbook and my papers were crushed in between my legs and my stomach. The atmosphere was simply unbearable. An ambiance of terror replaced what had always been the business-like normality that characterized my bank visits. I was in disbelief. I couldn't imagine that this was happening to me, that I was in the midst of some sort of gun battle. Someone began banging on the front door. His banging became louder and louder and the screaming became more shrill. 'I want my wife! I want my wife! I want my wife!' the voice pleaded. Those behind the doors with me ceased to talk. The sad, continuous demand of the husband for release of his wife was spellbinding. A woman inside cried and screamed.

"Then some lights came on. That same woman dashed to the door and screamed to the guards to open the door. Her words burst in squalls of screams. The husband screamed as she screamed. Everyone was yelling back and forth. The husband's appeal had been ignored until at last the guards relented and opened the door. The bank guards were not soldiers. Most of them wore gray pants, black shoes and blue shirts with a broad black belt around their waist. I do not remember seeing guns on their belts, but they may have worn them. Since the bank guards, in all likelihood, were not trained in the military arts, their responses were more humane, and their temperament was more suitable for civilians. For that brief moment, when the guards opened the door, everyone including me immediately ran to get out. People were running in front of me, people were running behind me, people were running beside me, but I made it through the door.

"I cannot describe the sheer horror of it all. People were running everywhere, trucks of soldiers were speeding up and down the roadways. And perhaps the most frightening aspect of it all was that the soldiers had their rifles pointed toward civilians, regular people in the street. I thought that the soldiers existed to protect the people; perhaps that only applied in America, but even then this might not apply under certain circumstances. A military coup had taken place, and I was right in the middle of it.

"Once out of the bank, I walked hurriedly toward the bus stop. As I got closer, I caught a glimpse of a shiny yellow metal object about an inch in length lying on top of an iron manhole grate in the middle of the street. I didn't know what it was at first, but after a few moments it came to me that this 'thing' was a shell casing from a rifle or a gun that had been discharged nearby. I saw many other shell casings as I walked. The sounds of gunfire that I heard from inside the bank were confirmed to be real.

"As I moved along, I saw an African woman carrying a baby on her back. The baby was tightly held in the pouch of a red tango cloth wrapped under the mother's armpits. Most often this cloth is called a *capulana* in Mozambique, a *leso* in Mombasa or a *kanga* in Kenya. I was told that African women measure their wealth by the number and color of the cloths they own. The color and design of the cloth was striking. But more arresting was that every time a truck of soldiers passed this woman, she turned her body inward toward the building she was closest to, in a real submissive manner. I mimicked her body gestures. I kept my head down and never looked directly at anyone.

"I had to walk back to the apartment. The bus service was no longer available. It was a long and frightening walk. Tears streamed uncontrollably down my face. I don't think I stopped crying until I reached the apartment. When I entered the apartment, no one was there. I could see that the houseboy had been there earlier. A bucket of cold water was left in the middle of the kitchen floor, and cleaning rags were thrown around as if scattered in a hurry. No dinner was prepared. Clearly, he left in a rush. I went to my room and cried. I prayed to God! I yelled, 'Oh! God deliver me!'

"When I awoke the next morning, sunlight and clear skies greeted me. Now it was time to face the reality that my stay in Uganda and study at Makerere had been violently and perhaps irretrievably interrupted."

CHAPTER TWENTY-SIX

THE RETURN

As the train pulls out of Trenton after a brief stop, just long enough for the New York commuters to board, Michelle explains to me how she was able to leave Uganda: "The next few days I feverishly began to pack up everything that I brought with me and had acquired. I remained at the apartment and hoped that Mr. Eric would soon return. I needed his help to get out."

Everyone she knew and talked to spoke of the trouble they were having trying to leave the country. Michelle realized that the rampant rumors were true. "I was made a believer," she intones. "I went to the university and visited my chemistry professor and said my goodbyes. The campus was deserted. It had an eerie and absent atmosphere. It was like a plague had been contracted nearby and the university had been quarantined," she recalls. "Desolation" is how she describes it. "I called my mother to let her know I was coming home. I did not share my troubles with her because I did not want her to worry. I could have won an Academy Award for the acting I did during that telephone call. I convinced her that I was fine and that the news reports in the states were exaggerated. I told her that I would get home safe and sound. When she spoke to me she sounded so far away, yet I wanted her to be close to me at this time. I needed her embrace and I needed to hear the assurance of her comforting words. I wanted her to make me safe. But she was helpless to intervene."

She remembers feeling self-pity and inadequacy: "I questioned my whole reason for coming to Uganda. I became despondent, helpless. This was not how things were supposed to be."

For a moment, it seems as though she is reliving everything. This episode was a traumatic event in her life, and retelling it brings back all the pain she lived through. She withdraws to another place momentarily. She just as quickly reengages, and her voice lifts when she continues: "When I gathered myself for the morning, Mr. Eric had returned. I was so glad to see him." Mr. Eric told her that he had a tough time getting his brother out of the country. That everything was breaking down. She told him of her experiences, and he told her, "You have to get out tomorrow."

She told him, "I am packed and ready to go." The day passed uneventfully. After they ate dinner she retired to her room.

"What I wanted was a smooth departure," she adds, but "I doubted that possibility." It seemed to her that everyone had left the country. But those that tried were being thoroughly searched and their belongings confiscated. She says, "I think the soldiers were looking for money and valuables that people were attempting to take out of the country. If your papers were not in order, you were not allowed to leave." To lighten her load, she decided to take only the essentials. That required "that I leave all of my bedding and household supplies with Mr. Eric. It broke my heart that I had to leave the souvenirs I had purchased during the course of the semester, which included a wonderful small stool and some black vases with white carvings.

"To help me sleep, I made myself a cup of tea. I decided not to take the mail I had received during the semester. I did not want to be stopped or interrogated about the contents of my mail, so I tore it all up. Before doing so, I reread each letter and postcard and quietly reminisced and reflected on what it was that I had been doing when each letter arrived. My trash basket was filled with torn letters and postcards and some mementos from Rome that I purchased while I was there. Along with the mementos, souvenirs and keepsakes that reminded me so dearly of my stay in Uganda, these were all material objects that could be replaced, but I had grown attached to them. I kept saying to myself, 'It doesn't matter as long as I get out safely.' I repeated it to myself over and over again, to intellectually lessen the effect of the pain of leaving things that I treasured. I took refuge in the thought that I would have my memories indelibly etched in my mind that no one could take from me." This was her personal, real-life untethering from Africa, an enzymatic breakdown, dissimilar only in degree multiplied many times over from what her ancestors had experienced tragically centuries ago.

She says, "Melancholy had taken its place among the fragile mood swings that I was experiencing." She turned off her lamp light (the electricity was still on) and prepared herself for bed. She could hear the sounds of gunshots in the far distance. And she thought of the shell casings she had seen when leaving the bank. She repeated to herself, "As long as I get out safely. That's all that matters."

"I cried for my mother and for home, but I was far away. As I cried, the gunfire was a constant reminder of my predicament. It was a searing reminder of my last night in Uganda."

Michelle relates, "The next day Mr. Eric took me to the airport. Roadblocks were everywhere. People were trying to leave the country any way that they could. The soldiers stopped the panicked locals on the roads, on the buses, on the trains and, as you would expect, at the airport. In my naiveté I could not identify any subversives among the innocent-looking civilians that they harassed. These were just people panicked for their safety and for the safety of their families. Their future was not in Uganda.

"The soldiers rummaged through the bags and belongings of the people they stopped. They tried to confiscate the jewelry that I had, including a watch. I saw Mr. Eric get into a terrible quarrel with one of the soldiers. The intensity of their disagreement frightened me. I became afraid for Mr. Eric and for myself. People were pushed and jostled as though they were cows being herded for slaughter. The soldiers took whatever they wanted. It was open season on the people. If there was any resistance by the person, he or she was slapped across the face. You could hear the sound of the clap as the blow landed. That would then be followed by a rifle butt against the chest, and the person fell prostrate to the ground.

"I thought that I had made myself safe by disposing of my letters, but the soldiers could care less. They took my Ugandan money, all my course-books and notebooks but surprisingly allowed me to keep my tape cassette recorder and my tapes. Mr. Eric got us through three roadblocks. Most importantly he kept me from being body searched. At the roadblocks, the soldiers were at great liberty to do what they wanted. I saw women being body searched and molested right in their cars with no one there to stop it. Few of the native Ugandans were able to get through the roadblocks; their journeys ended on the road. Abandoned and empty cars of all kinds, mostly small dilapidated European cars, were scattered on the sides of the roads. I had told Mr. Eric that I would control my emotions and not cry even though my emotions were right below the surface. The terror of getting through the last roadblock broke down my resistance and I wailed uncontrollably."

Michelle continues, "We were finally at Entebbe, the airport. Because of our encounters at the roadblocks, I missed an earlier flight. Fortunately, another flight was scheduled in the next hour. Again, my bags were searched, my papers scrutinized, and harsh unrelenting stares were fixed on me. You could never know what these people were thinking, and I thought that they were thinking the worst. The loud cacophony of yelling and screaming at the airport continued unabated. People were standing in long lines to go through immigration, and the soldiers seemed to enjoy the power that they held over us.

"At first I was told that I could board the plane and then I was told that I could not. My bags were on the plane, but I was not. I looked at Mr. Eric and he looked at me. I could tell that he was at the end of his magic. He seemed to be losing control. He knew he had a responsibility to get me out. He had promised my family that he would protect me. I'm sure he thought about Harriett and my mother, whom he met at the wedding shower, as well as the tranquil times he had spent in America. I could feel his sense of desperation. He knew this was my last chance to get out of the country, and he could tell from my face that I was terrified that his best efforts might fail.

"Emotionally, now, I was stripped down to the sinew of my being. There was very little left. I stared blankly out of the windows in the airport as we made our way through the lines. We continued to negotiate our way through the morass of confusion that was all around us, but from time to time my vision was obstructed by the high anxiety and panic I felt from what was going on in front of me. I was about to care no more. I no longer cared about my bags or my belongings, as long as I could get my body unharmed aboard the next plane with my ticket and my passport.

"An argument between Mr. Eric and an airline official became so heated that no one but Ugandans would ever understand what was said between them. The red lips, tongue and gums, bits of saliva and the white enamel of their teeth against the backdrop of black skin flashed in staccato sequence in my mind. I was now standing at the gate waiting to board the plane. A pilot walked past. Mr. Eric instructed me to stay put and then he disappeared. Fifteen minutes later he reappeared, grabbed my arm and said, 'Time to board.' He cracked a smile for the first time and said the pilot was an old student of his and that *he* had gotten me on the plane.

"I looked at Mr. Eric with astonishment, amazement and exhaustion. Tears of gratitude ran down my cheeks and the tracks from them, I know, created a pathway to my heart. How could I ever thank him for all that he had done, both for me and for my family?

He was a man first and an African second and then a Ugandan. He had kept me safe from harm while I was a guest in his country. I thanked him like I had never thanked anyone in my life. And I gave him the biggest hug I could summon from the energy that remained in my exhausted body.

"As I walked toward the stainless steel, silver-colored stairs to board the plane, I looked over my left shoulder and waved a goodbye. I saw him standing behind a wall of plastic sheeting that separated the airport structure from the runway. He saw me and waved back, and even from the distance I could see his smile. I boarded the plane. And I never saw him again."

CHAPTER TWENTY-SEVEN

EN ROUTE TO SAFETY

Michelle's ruminations have not ended. "My route out of Uganda took me through Nairobi, Kenya. I was not leaving on my own terms. This was not a brief holiday on the shuttle and then back to Kampala. I left Uganda never to return to complete the school year I was so looking forward to. I had mixed emotions. On the one hand I was breathing many sighs of relief at having gotten out of Uganda, but I regretted most heartily the interruption of my school year, the unfinished lungfish project, my planned visits to Mombasa and Tanzania, the planned biological trips, the dance concert that we were planning and my Swahili classes. I knew I would not be fluent in Swahili by the time my year ended, but I had hoped to show off some of my Swahili-speaking skills to the pretenders at Swarthmore.

"The sadness I felt was soon overcome by my thoughts of the other American students, and the immediate prospect of going home. I was able to find lodging at the University of Nairobi. It too rented rooms during semester breaks and holidays. There was only one other person on my floor. The university was deserted, but not for the same reason as Makerere."

Apparently renting out rooms when students are not attending class represents an economic subsidy for some African universities, evidencing a real need for revenue. This practice is unlikely at an American University, though dorm rooms are occupied by new students during summer breaks attending various summer programs sponsored by the university.

Michelle said that she went downtown and began to buy more souvenirs for herself and her family. She would stay in Nairobi for a few days before flying on to Europe. She remembers purchasing a brown leather pocketbook with the fur of a leopard on the outside for her mother. The memory of the leopard in the laboratory was still crisp. For her sister, Shelley, she bought a handsome jewelry box, and for herself some ivory earrings, two African drums and a few dresses.

At this time when Michelle purchased her leopard-skin bag, leopards were not covered under the Endangered Species Act. By now, because of hunters and poachers, this animal is protected by some African countries and is a potential protected species.

Self-preservation looms large when an existential threat is made real. Life and freedom and safety are no longer taken for granted, and small things drop away like debris.

All of this is getting quite emotional, and I tell Michelle we need to take another break. I did not think I would get caught up in her story as much as I have. So, we sit back in our chairs, look ahead to the seats and the baggage lying on the shelves several seats ahead of us, and share a moment of quiet. Neither of us speak for a few moments.

While we were talking, the conductor had announced that we were approaching Newark, New Jersey. As we pull into the station, I see beige-colored office buildings, high-rise apartments that appear to be of the luxury type, and a phalanx of large government and private office buildings. Newark has a dubious reputation, a mixture of urban decay and downtown promise. A city plagued by crime but, because of its proximity to New York City, full of potential. The city's black mayor, Cory Booker, has made a name for himself attempting, with some success I would say, to reverse the order of decline and to sustain and rejuvenate the promise. Since we will shortly be coming into New York City, in a half hour or so, I urge Michelle to continue on.

She agrees. "As I was walking down the street in Nairobi, I kept thinking how I was going to find my friends. Where could they be?" She says it dawned on her that a group of black students from Kalamazoo had rented a house and maybe they would be there. "No sooner had I thought about the house than I walked a few steps ahead, looked up and to the right, and saw Randy walking across the street. He stood out because, like me, he did not resemble native Africans. His lighter complexion, Afro hairstyle and wire-rimmed glasses branded him an African-American. Gleefully, I yelled, "Randy!" He walked across the street, making sure to avoid the oncoming traffic.

"As he stood in front of me, I told him about the cable from Swarthmore. Since he had been in Nairobi, he knew where the other students hung out. It was not long before we caught up with the others. Everyone had heard about the upheaval in Uganda. And after much discussion, a few of the students said that they were staying. Some of them said that if they could not stay at Makerere, they would transfer to the University of Nairobi. After my experience, I felt compelled to return home. Swarthmore had instructed us to do so. I knew that my mother wanted me home and that Mr. Eric expected me to go home. The other students had not experienced what I had in Uganda. They were in Nairobi when the worst of it happened. So most said that they would take their chances.

"I had done what I was instructed to do. I shared the information with them. It was now up to each individual to make his or her choice. It came as no surprise to me that Vixena was not returning to the States even though her school, the University of Pennsylvania, had requested that she do so as well. She was the type to slither through any crevice or crack in the system; her conduct in Rome had demonstrated that. I wished her and the others my best, continued my souvenir shopping, and went to the American embassy to get my tickets for home. I said goodbye to everyone and spent a few extra moments with Randy, reminding him again of the cable from Swarthmore. I bid him farewell and said to him that I would see him back at Swarthmore. I had discharged my responsibility.

"I did not see Vixena anymore after our meeting in Nairobi. We had little in common beyond our adventure in Uganda. Our relationship had none of the ingredients needed to sustain an enduring friendship. So, we let what we had in common end on the continent where our common interest converged."

She continues, "It was time to board another plane, but this time my journey home would begin in earnest. I retraced my route back by stopping in Rome again. There would be a few layovers, so there was no reason not to stop there. After I boarded the plane and buckled my seatbelt, we experienced a rough and nerve-racking path to takeoff. The takeoff was abnormal," she says, "and the ascent was rough. We were bumping up and down in our seats, then finally the plane slowed down, turned around and flew back to the airport. It was announced that we were returning to the airport.

"The plane taxied down the runway toward the terminal. Everyone was asked to leave the plane. The reason given was that the tires had blown out and if we had continued, our flight would be problematic. We were told that we would be flying out tomorrow. The airlines paid for our food and overnight lodging. We could eat anything we wanted. There was a large smorgasbord, and you had the option of ordering off of the menu as well. I decided to eat some delicious lamb chops, which I had not had for quite a while.

"After dinner I retired to my room, which was of average size with the usual furnishings, to rest for the night. I did not realize how the stress of the last few days had depleted my strength and put my nerves on edge. I was really tired. I slept for several hours until I was awakened in the middle of the night by noises coming from the hallway. I got up, looked through the peephole, checked to make sure my door was locked, but I saw no one. I was a bit unnerved after having gone through the Ugandan turmoil. I was determined to get home safely, and I was taking no chances. I propped a chair up against the door and placed it so that the door would be difficult to open. I looked at the door for maybe an hour before concluding that no harm was imminent.

"I was at the airport the next day on time for my flight to Rome, but because the prior day's flight was canceled, I had missed my connection. When I arrived in Rome, I was given the option of staying in the airport all night or going in the city and staying in a hotel. My connecting flight to New York City would not leave until the following day. The meager sums of money that I retained were dwindling fast. And though I did not feel the insecurities I felt in Nairobi, my anxiety about getting home made me decide to spend the night in the airport. Besides, I was tired of dragging my luggage around."

Michelle says she met a young white French girl whose name was Fifi. They became fast friends and kept each other company during the night. "Fifi had been a dancer and stopped her dancing due to an accident. She had moved to Rome to be with her lover, but things were not working out, so she was returning home."

The next day Michelle gathered up her luggage to prepare for boarding and said goodbye to Fifi. "Suddenly, I heard some screams. I turned around to see what was going on. I saw Fifi embracing and kissing a young man. He gathered up her luggage and they walked toward the exit. I thought about my relationship with G and whether my heart would be saved. I glanced at them a few minutes more. I smiled to myself and boarded my plane for home."

Chapter Twenty-Eight

A FINAL SIGH

I have been in Sorrow's kitchen and licked out all the pots.
Zora Neal Hurston, "Dust Track on a Road"

"I was mentally and physically drained as my plane made its way to New York," she tells me. "My exhaustion for the moment overcame my need to be embraced by G. But I still had a need to see him and to be embraced by the man I had kept so close to my heart during my travails in Uganda. When my mother and I had talked on the phone, I asked her to contact him and to give him some idea of my flight arrival plans."

The time was something past 1 p.m., she says, when her plane, a 747, landed at La Guardia International Airport in New York City. She had been flying for more than twelve hours. As she exited onto the tarmac with a theatrical sense of triumph, G was there and nodded with assurance that all was well. They folded into an embrace. She looked back at the plane and exhaled deeply, forcing a Mona Lisa smile in the process. Her dream, which began favorably, had become an ordeal. It all was now at an end.

"I was not expecting it, but G met me at the airport. I was glad to see him. We hugged each other as though we had never hugged before and we kissed like we had never kissed before. Yet, there was something that was not quite right; something was missing. Our relationship had been platonically modulated. The quality of the relationship we had before I left no longer existed.

"Upon reflection, there had been a metamorphosis. I had grown and so had he. I had shed my timorous disposition that was overlaid by a veneer of vulnerability.

"In its stead grew a hardened shell of thicker skin. I was no longer the naïve sheltered college student from Chester, Pennsylvania. My horizons had been broadened. I felt more confident in myself. We both had changed and it was difficult to ignore it. Our needs, dependencies, expectations and aspirations were no longer the same. The novelty of love between us was no longer enchanting. I thought my lack of energy toward him was because I was extremely tired and worn out. I gave him the small African drum I purchased for him in Nairobi.

"Though my feelings for him had changed, we still spent a few hours in the airport catching up on things before my next departure to Chester. It was great seeing him. I am sure I blathered nonstop because I do not remember hearing much conversation from him. As boarding time approached, we held each other's hands. He gave me what would be our last kiss, on the cheek, and I boarded my final plane, destined for Philadelphia. I told him before boarding that I would be in touch.

"My next stop was Philadelphia airport. From there I boarded a Septa train, a local southeastern Pennsylvania commuter train. I knew my mother would not be home because her friends were giving her a surprise birthday party. I freshened up a bit and took a taxi straight to the party from the train stop. I walked into the party and ran into my mother's open arms. When she hugged me and called me 'Mikie!' I knew then that I was no longer 'crying all the way home.' I was home. Not in the motherland but in my homeland.

"Back at Swarthmore, it was catch-up time. Registration for the next semester's classes was immediately at hand. The school newspaper, *The Swarthmore College Phoenix*, ran a big article on our adventure in Uganda. They had a picture of me and Randy in the article. I later found out that the program we were on was not a true exchange program because Makerere University had no students studying at Swarthmore while we were there. The article said the following:

> The future of the exchange with Makerere is at this point uncertain. Ironically, the University had been selected partly because no students had ever been killed there and the situation was considered fairly safe [. . .] The risk and problems of some kind of disruption on an African campus are far greater than on an American campus [. . .] It can be a very fascinating and very different experience than attending an American university, but the possibility of the school term being disrupted for one reason or another is all too real.

"The phrase 'no student had ever been killed' and 'the possibility of the school term being disrupted for one reason or another is all too real' was a ridiculous understatement. I had enough close calls with death and maiming that I could have become a statistic. But for the grace of God and the character of one man, Mr. Eric, what would the outcome have been?"

• • •

Alas! Our train ride is at an end: The Crescent slowly pulls into Pennsylvania Station in New York City. It is curious that the train station in Philadelphia is known as 30th St. Station but the train station in New York City is known as Pennsylvania Station. But that question is for another time. The conductor gives us his instruction. "All passengers must exit the train. Check around you and make sure you have all of your belongings. Exit the train where you see a conductor."

As I gather my belongings and help Michelle with her luggage, I feel I'm leaving something behind. I have been on a whirlwind of an adventure and I wonder, without even trying to answer the question, what is the greater meaning of Africa to me? And how a young, unsophisticated woman had the nerve to take on such a trip as that. *As an African-American, I think we have much to be proud of, much to work on, and much to overcome.*

Michelle and I are in New York for a long weekend. We plan to see a Broadway show, enjoy the cuisine of New York City and visit a few monuments. I have been to New York City many times but never really had a chance to explore and "enjoy" the city. This time will be different.

There is a momentary silence when Michelle finishes telling her story. She looks wistful. I busy myself closing my Moleskine and packing away her manuscript papers. Her story for now has come to an end, but I have yet to begin writing her story anew. It will be several years before that journey begins.

CHAPTER TWENTY-NINE

DENOUEMENT: THE LAST TRAIN FROM DJIBOUTI

You know who people are by the language they cry in.

Mende Proverb[59]

In 1974 Michelle graduated from Swarthmore College with a bachelor's degree in biology. A few years later she and Harriett would share an apartment in New York City. It was during this time that Harriett worked on her EdD while Michelle pursued a master's degree at New York University. As mentor and mentee, they were friends forever. Their families were interwoven by long-standing friendships and shared local experiences in Chester. Michelle and Harriett were conjoined by their relationships with four common dominators: Mary, Chester, Africa and Eric. These associations had enduring consequences for their lives and made indelible memories each of them carry with them today. Their mutual relationship with the same man was a pivotal coincidence.

My daydream on our train trip about a journey on the last train from Djibouti had me pondering many questions about Michelle and Harriett while staring out of the window. I imagined the vast deserts and pastures where long, green stalks protrude out of the marshlands that house the roots of rice plants. I visualized wild forests, swamps, lakes and rivers as the train traveled west to Addis Abba. These scenes flashed by my window in video-graphic detail like scenes in a movie. In my daydream I was looking as far into the horizon as I could see; my gaze was endless and my thoughts were just as expansive. The savannahs of the African plain are indeed beautiful, mysterious, mystifying and awe inspiring.

Operated by the Ethio-Djibouti Railways, the rail service from Djibouti to Addis Ababa, Ethiopia, was built in 1897 by the French and opened in 1929. The British government put together a company to complete a section of the line as well. Hailie Selassie, the emperor of Ethiopia, opened the train station in Addis Ababa in December 1929. The rail line was closed in 2009 for repairs. The train was a creation of Alfred Ilg, a Swiss national, who at the time was an advisor to the Emperor Menelek II of Ethiopia. Menelek II is renowned for saving his country from colonialization, and he objected to the French government's involvement in the construction of the line. The rail line was built to provide landlocked Ethiopia with a port for the export of its goods through the Port of Djibouti. The rail line is a conglomeration of several rail companies beset by financial disruptions and lack of funding that evolved over the years to build the complete line to Addis Ababa. Initially the line only went as far as Dire Dawa in Ethiopia.

Train cars of the Addis to Djibouti train taken in 2019, in the train yards of Addis Ababa.

The word *Djibouti* has a mixed derivation. Some say that it comes from the Afars and Issas people who are indigenous to the region. Other authorities give it Somali roots. And there are those who say the name comes from the name of a French general whose last name was la Djibouti, the conqueror of the Afars and Issas people. He is said to be the founder of Djiboutiville.

Yet for many African-Americans, Africa is a paradox. In my dream world of riding this train within my chimera, what did I see? Was I looking out at the last resort to soothe the disquiet of Americans of African descent with Western civilization? That's questionable, but aside from looking at the beautiful terrain, what else was I thinking about? Contemplating as I was during this moment of idleness, the stories of Michelle and Harriett raised issues beyond the lessons learned by the two of them during their experiences in Africa on an individual basis. There is no magic elixir to cure all ills, nor is there a panacea, or an idyllic country that we as African-Americans can live in. The "best of all possible worlds" does not exist. We must make our existing world the best it can be. To paraphrase an aphorism, "The perfect must not be the enemy of the good." Our dreams are infused with our realities. Oftentimes our dreams reflect our fears and the joys that we have experienced.

I dream of Africa. What is the fascination? If I had my druthers, I would want Africa to be a place of tranquility, successful, modern and in many ways a duplication of states and nations in the Western world without white people in the majority. Diversity of the races is my preference. I want to find my ancestors in Alex Haley's mythical "Village of Juffure." I want Africa to be what I have imagined it could be. Many times, when I visited Africa, I felt that I was in a land of kindred spirits just like Michelle had experienced. When I visited Africa many years ago, I stayed in fine hotels, ate good food, and my safety was not an issue. Based upon my experience, I could have been in any Western country in the world. But I was a tourist on the tourist track and not imbedded in the culture.

• • •

My departure metaphorically on the last train from Djibouti speaks to the departure from Africa of two educated black women as measured against their expectations after a series of disconcerting events in Africa. They arrived with one frame of mind and departed with another. Between the two axis points, a passage, a journey took place. And the sights and sounds seen and experienced along the journey made the journey what it was. There is growth, maturity, self-examination and perspective gained between the terminals. In many respects, it was their "Last Train" from Djibouti.

In effect, the loss of innocence, the destruction of a dream, and the failure of aspiration can be a "last train." Our imaginations often make us think that life would be better and more agreeable elsewhere. But the reality is that life may not be better elsewhere. The grass may actually be browner after the rain stops falling. African-Americans operate in an America plagued by what psychologists would describe as a Munchausen syndrome by proxy—a syndrome that is defined as a disease that is, to some degree, self-inflicted in an otherwise healthy individual that now seeks treatment to cure the same.

African-Americans are adversely impacted by an America that has caused its own syndrome, its own disease, that of racism that did not have to exist. Racism was not preordained for America but became imbedded into the founding documents of the republic because of actions taken by the founding fathers and perpetuated by subsequent political leaders. This infirmity has festered and metastasized to the point that it threatens to destroy what could otherwise be that "shining city on a hill," if there is such a place. America finds itself grappling to find a treatment or solution. Racism is a cultural adaptation, according to anthropologists. And those inflicted with the disease must find a treatment. Some Caucasians, and other people as well, often suffer from historical prejudice rather than allowing enlightenment and personal experiences to dictate actions and belief.

We know from our discussion that the decision by both women to go to Africa was a seminal moment in their lives. For Michelle, it was a decision she made to strengthen her maturing identity and to give form to an amorphous personage still uncongealed. Michelle found the beauty she had dreamed of, but the other imaginings were tenuous or transitory. For Harriett, it was to establish a nexus with Africa and to claim her African heritage. As a mature professional, she knew that her stay in Africa would shape the vision she held of herself and would or could confirm that self-image.

So, what are the parallels in the stories of these two women? To find them, I look back to what caused Harriett to be in court in Montgomery County, Maryland. And I think further about Michelle and her term of study at Makerere University. Several questions come to mind. The answers to some are quick and easy, but others require more explanation.

Did expectation turn into disappointment? For both women it did, but not completely.

Did identity affirmation turn into reaffirmation? Yes, the identity of both women was reaffirmed as African-Americans, not as Africans, though their ancestry was not in dispute.

Did excitement turn into exasperation? Yes on both counts.

Did purpose turn into achievement? Yes, I would say so. Both women had a purpose in going to Africa and achieved, for the most part, their objectives.

Did heritage turn into identity? No! *Random House Webster's Unabridged Dictionary* defines *identity* as "the state or fact of remaining the same one or ones, as under varying aspects or conditions; the condition of being oneself or itself, and not another."

Both Harriett and Michelle were Americans of African descent when they left, and they returned as Americans of African descent, albeit with a greater sense of self and an enhanced appreciation of their heritage. How could they be anything else? That is who they are innately. Harriett sought consciously to change a geographical fact into a new nationality; all Americans of African descent are genetically descended from African ancestry, but we are not Africans incarnate because we are not native, in our current state of being, to the continent of Africa and never will be.

Who you are connects to identity. *What* you are connects to character. *What you are* is more important than *who you are*. Dr. Martin Luther King spoke of this when he espoused that African-Americans should be judged by the "content of their character not by the color of their skins." Identity is indeed important, but character is more important.

Was the myth equal to reality? It never is. For these women, some elements were equivalent and other parts were not. Both women had their idealisms about Africa—the people, the terrain, weather conditions, state of modernity and ethnic atavism—recalibrated to attempt to recombine within their present physical being African ancestral inheritances they felt they were missing. They discovered that the people, Africans, were not as accommodating as they imagined they would be, especially in Harriett's case. The weather, land and temperatures as well as the state of modernity in the cities were in line with what they thought it would be. Not up to Western standards in many cases, but sufficient to accommodate most of their needs. But the genetic recombination from an ancestral form was not all there. The atavism or the lack thereof was surprising to both women.

And finally, was ignorance converted into enlightenment? Unquestionably there was enlightenment. There was tremendous growth in both women. Vision, maturity, insight, invaluable experience about life in Africa and a broadening of their perspective were the enduring benefits gained by both women.

Harriett said, in a moment of remorse, "I became disillusioned with Africa." To become disillusioned, one must be operating under an illusion—an illusory construction of what Africa was about. She had imagined Africa as something that it was not. Michelle was not disillusioned because she had hopes, not expectations; nevertheless, she was shocked at times and dismayed by some of her encounters and what she had to overcome. She expected new experiences and was open to many of them; in that regard she had no unfounded expectations. Michelle expected to cope, for the most part, with what she encountered. She was made to accept the reality of living in some states in Africa, in her case Uganda.

Harriett confronted a clash of cultural values in education and in family life: African culture versus the black American experience in America. Harriett, because of her age, had formed a prevision about Africa. Harriett looked for cultural adaptations that were nonexistent. Her expectations extended beyond the reality of her personal as well as professional involvements.

• • •

Neither of these women were delusional. They accepted the reality of what they confronted and tried to cope as best they could. Michelle at once was enraptured in the beauty of Africa and its meaning to her identity but was frightened to death by the harsh realities of its politics. Being apolitical, she had no perspective to bring except to react to what was unfolding before her. The fact that the politics of Uganda threatened her personal safety changed rapture into retreat. Africa was the *gestalt* of it all, in one continent.

Life by definition is conflicted. It operates in a conflicted environment. There is no unilateral affirmative or negative: a blend is what we have, a comparative in most instances. Sorting out the proportions of each is a life's work. The joy and exhilaration both women felt at times during their sojourn was tempered by the downside of chaos, fear, rejection and dissemblance. Africa in conflict was experienced by both women, but those conflicts did not obscure the deeper meanings that both women sought and found. Separating from Africa for however long is a long goodbye.

The variability of its many cultures—including skin color, though generally united by dark skin color—is one among many essential elements that make Africa so unique. Harriett had been besotted by the wiles of Africa. Were native African peoples more accustomed to unstable governments, illiberal democracies, dictatorships and military strongmen than Americans of African descent? Yes, of course. All these forms of governance are foreign to Americans. Harriett said she was at any one time confounded as well as disillusioned but not overly disconcerted by Africa.

Harriett reminded me, though I was already keenly aware, that we are a part of the diaspora, that African-Americans are a part of the African Diaspora. She had experienced the paradox between the reality of Africa and the romantic. Harriett said that she, like Eric, wanted her bones to "bleach in Botswana," not in America. She loved Botswana that much. Her goal was to remain in her ancestral homeland. As I mentioned earlier, other persons of the African Diaspora have also had their remains repatriated to and interred in an African country. Clearly this type of action symbolizes an alienation and sepulchral view of the country of their abode. Harriett and I talked about the "double consciousness" of colonized people of color that Frantz Fannon, the philosopher and writer from Martinique, wrote about, and which Du Bois espoused decades ago about African-Americans.[60] This duality of awareness causes Americans of African descent to be divided between their loyalties to America (or the West) and their African genus while coping with the inequities. black Americans must be healthy enough to survive life in the West, smart enough to work around the issues of race, and strong enough to cope with it.

Michelle in her short time in Africa experienced a kaleidoscope of adventures and emotions. Memories both good and bad, enough to last a lifetime, shaped her African-American views about her homeland. She traveled and wandered about in Africa in spite of her inhibitions. She demonstrated great bravery in undertaking the journey. Harriett was challenged intellectually and psychologically. But in the end, Michelle and Harriett would have to resolve the ambiguities about their experiences in Africa by application of their secular standards, ethical and religious values to each experience.

Much of their unbidden experiences could not be separated from those that they expected and dreamed of. For perhaps intrinsic reasons, these experiences were integrated into the journey itself. Michelle imbibed so much of Africa. Her experience at Lake Victoria transcended the intervals of time for her. The "West Winds" of Mariam Makeba, the South African singer and songwriter, blew over her person and was now her inheritance. Michelle had engulfed the ambience of her environment.

• • •

Regardless of the transient fascinations experienced when we travel to different ports of call from time to time, we must come to grips with the fact that life in America is not totally a dystopian experience for Americans of African descent. Many of us live quite well. For Michelle and Harriett, life in America had provided them many opportunities for uplift, many benevolences that aided them in the quality of their lives: education, economic viability, world class health care, employment, a stable government, freedom under the rule of law and respect for human rights, even though historically black lives and black freedoms seldom have mattered as much as white lives and white freedoms.

In a piece of dialogue from a recent television show, *Boss*, one of the actors says, "All the immigrant groups adapted to America except the blacks." I think there is some truth in the statement. But if you think that statement is true, why do you think that is? Perhaps the answer lies in how the blacks got here and how they are regarded and treated. You know, one can get used to a "bad thing," just like you get used to a "good thing." It becomes difficult to wean oneself from both situations. America is not all bad. It is a flawed country certainly, as all countries are. We must take the bad with the good. Americans of African descent are probably the race most disconnected and dispossessed from their ancestral culture and heritage of all people on this earth, save for the few other anomalies that may exist.

While in New York City with Michelle on our weekend excursion, I composed a poem entitled "Africa Beckons Me But America Is My Home," a poem that I think summarizes my sentiments:

> America is my home
> Though Africa beckons me
> My culture wrought
> By passage o'er the sea
> To a land I cannot see
> But America is my
> Home, sweet land of liberty.
>
> Africa beckons me
> The disquiet I know
> If ever I returned to see
> But oh! land of America you are my sanctity
> America, sweet land of liberty of thee I sing
> Why withhold the liberty you promised me?
>
> I wail for Africa unknown to me
> Unless you can cry for me you cannot feel my pain
> Yet I know thee well
> But I cannot dispel what I dream to see
> Africa beckons me
> But America is my home.
>
> Is this a foreign land
> Or my home land?
> If I can once foresee
> The American dream for me
> Perhaps my voyage o'er the sea
> Would cease to be my soliloquy
> 'twill forever be my history and your legacy.

My people may then find some peace
Which will you have it be?
Sweet land of Liberty of thee I sing.

Democracy is laid brick by brick
The mason trowels his mortar joints
Yet I sleep on a bed of thorns
How say you to that
Sweet land of liberty?
What was my original sin?
Did it have to do with the politics of the color of
My skin?
I want to see what I have not seen
To be what I have not been
To rise above the prophecies of hate
To live as though I belong
To feel, what for me, has been unreal
Future possibilities abound
And I know it won't be long
For America is where my fate belongs.

I own, I pay, my ancestors paid
Equity is my cornerstone
My blood, my death, all given
In war and conflict betide
So do not bemoan my entitlement to own

I love thee nonetheless.
Speckled and besmirched,
Trial and tribulation apart.
I know thee well though dispossessed
Africa beckons me but America is my home.

I know 'twill be a longing tale of woe
In the end my plea may not extend.
In spite of wrongs my people are strong.
The self-evident truths that enabled America
In God we Trust, will one day, be triumphant.

• • •

Campbell's *Middle Passages* offers many gems of interest that provide insights into the history of African-American journeys to Africa. I offer some of them for purposes of perspective acquired over the years on the issue of black Americans' emigration to Africa. He cites, "In a nation ruled by descendants of Europe, Africa has long been and remains the touchstone of black difference, the point of departure for any discussion of African-American history, identity, and destiny."[61]

Frederick Douglass is quoted as having said, "Africa was an irrelevancy, a distraction from the struggle for full equality in the United States."[62] Frederick Douglass is further quoted by Campbell as saying, "All this native land talk [. . .] is nonsense, the native land of the American Negro is America. His bones, his muscles, his sinews, are all American. His ancestors for 270 years have lived and labored and died, on American soil, and millions of his posterity have inherited Caucasian blood."[63]

In addition, the author quotes Bill Sutherland, a man who spent many years in Africa as an expatriate, regarding Richard Wright, the noted black writer, saying, "One can't expect a country to solve a problem that is a personal one. If one is seeking a psychological home, then one may automatically project upon that country the home one seeks." Campbell quotes Sutherland as also saying, "Wright had come to Africa seeking his own salvation."[64]

The wise and discerning insight of our forefathers is captured in the following quote from Campbell: "[E]ven in these grim times, the vast majority of free people of color opposed emigration, evincing a determination to stay and fight for their full portion as American citizens." Campbell quotes Richard Allen, a giant in the field of slave liberation and empowerment and founder of the African Methodist Episcopal Church, as saying, "This land which we watered with our tears and our blood is now our mother country."[65] I have been to this church many times and at one time represented the church in a special legal project.

Finally, Campbell tells the story of Keith Richburg, a *Washington Post* reporter who authored the book *Out of America: A black Man Confronts Africa*. Richburg said in summary, "Maybe I would care more if I had never come here [Africa] and never seen what Africa is today. But I have been here, and I have seen—and frankly I want no part of it." Richburg disparages black tourists who come to Africa to reclaim Africa as the motherland. He sees that as balderdash.

Doesn't visiting Africa offer more benefits culturally and ethnically than touring the Louvre in France or the Hermitage in St. Petersburg, Russia, the Uffizi Gallery in Florence, Italy, the British Museum in London, the Galleria dell'Accademia in Rome and the Santa Maria delle Grazie in Milan? All of these I have visited, coming away with an enjoyment of art but with a reinforced sense of white supremacy. Obviously, all of these museums are in majority white countries and are known as the repositories of the world's greatest art. Overcoming the edict of white supremacy is equivalent to wrestling a rabid grizzly bear and coming out alive and well. Good luck.

Notwithstanding the deprivations of Africa, however, visiting Africa balances the perspective and provides the African-American with a sense of where he or she stands in this world, good or bad. Certainly, there is cultural enrichment to be gained by touring the capitals of Europe, but visiting Africa for the African-American, if previously unexposed, has the potential of being, for some, the equivalent to experiencing the Age of Enlightenment in eighteenth-century Europe: perspective is the benefit.

Campbell provides this statistic: "Some twenty-five hundred

African-Americans settled in Africa in the forty years after the Civil War [...], Africa became one of the chief terrains on which African-Americans debated their position and prospects in the United States."⁶⁶ Approximately 3,000 African-Americans live in Ghana today, a country of twenty-five million.⁶⁷ The number of African-Americans living in other African countries or countries with majority black populations is difficult to ascertain. But cumulatively the numbers are small compared with the approximate thirty million Americans of African descent residing in the United States.

According to the Government Accounting Organization (GAO), in 2011 some 445,000 tax returns were filed by American citizens who claimed the foreign earned income exclusion (FEIE), and less than 130,000 claimed that their employer was a corporation. The income, of course, must be earned outside the United States. The greatest increases in foreign employment of US citizens is in Africa and Asia. These are the greatest areas of opportunity and growth.⁶⁸ One can surmise that most of the folks who emigrate are not black. The scant number of African-Americans living in Africa is testament to their explicit acceptance and comfort with living in America, notwithstanding its many faults and the trials they endure.

We know from whence we have come. Is it ever possible to really go back to what could have been or to what should have been? I think not. The fact that African-Americans through the centuries have not returned to Africa in significant numbers speaks for itself about their desire to return to Africa. In the history of America, there has never been a critical mass of African-Americans who sought to migrate to Africa, despite all the hatreds, inequalities, criminal acts, historical efforts and discriminations that characterize life for African-Americans in America.

Campbell provides a Mende proverb that is most appropriate. "You know who people are by the language they cry in." Does this quote aid Michelle in determining her place in the world? Does this tell her about her identity? No! What it does, however, is reaffirm her existing identity as an English-speaking African-American woman. She cried in English, not being fluent enough in any other language to express her disconsolations. But do we literally cry in any language? Yes and no. A cry can be any emotional outpouring or an exclamatory statement. It is the language of the thought behind the emotion regardless of the expression it takes. How Michelle chooses to incorporate her identity into her persona is her own decision. She also has an animus, her deep subconscious self. How in the deep recesses of her being does she see herself?

For most informed Americans of African descent, this can be complicated. She may view herself as a Negro, colored, black or African-American, or an American of African descent, but certainly not African. Her sojourn to Africa reinforced her Americanness as this kind of experience has done with many other African-Americans, and erased many misconceptions she had about Africa, its people, facilities and politics.

Harriett was well past the quest for her identity. She knew who she was. Harriett was looking to incorporate more fully her African genealogy into her African-American persona and anima. Harriett was a mature woman when she arrived in Africa in 1971 for the first time. As an expatriate, hers was a mission to provide help to those who needed it. Despite her African-American identity, Harriett sought to overlay her existing African-American persona with an African persona and in time to replace her African-American identity with that of being African and bring her subconscious along with it. She had the much harder task. She ruefully had to accept rejection by native Africans of her desire to transfigure herself into a native African. Her attempt, one might say, was naïve and an exercise in futility. Although her overtures fell short, the knowledge she gained about Africa, herself, and the culture of Africans was indispensable, and nonetheless transformative in its own sense.

• • •

African culture, including mores, values, religions, rituals, dances, celebrations, gods and languages, chief among them Allah from Islam and Swahili among many other dialects, was kept from African-Americans, forcing them to create a new culture, drawn from the remnants of African culture that could be remembered or smuggled out after capture by slave merchants. That along with strands of Americana that were embraced, Christianity chief among them, formed a pillar of this new culture. Other religions were prohibited from being practiced openly, even at times Christianity. By force and volition, Christianity became essential to the new culture's creation.

Why is Christianity central to the new culture of African-Americans? In my view, it partly has to do with the symbolism of the cross in Christianity. What does the cross symbolize? The cross represents struggle, throes, pain, suffering and tribulation, mental as well as physical death, and the ascendency of the human spirit. We physically die only once, but we die mentally and emotionally many times during our lifetimes. The pangs of hurt and denigration erode the human spirit over time. But we rise again mentally and emotionally; time and time again we "ascend." After physical death we arise: our spirit lives on in those who love us, in the good works we try to do and in those whose lives we have impacted.

What we try to leave behind—the anguish and distress that Americans of African descent, as well as other oppressed people experienced, endured and continue to suffer—enabled the symbolism and the balm of Christianity to be widely accepted. After being slammed down, we rise up and press on, an indomitable resurrection of human spirit. Christianity is a religion of hope, so it is easy to see how its philosophy would easily be incorporated into the psyche of oppressed people, in spite of the fact that Islam was the religion practiced by most Africans before they were enslaved.

This new African-American culture is born in an environment very much antithetical to its existence, devoid of much of what our ancestors created and practiced in Africa, yet is an existential necessity. The creation of Kwanzaa by Mulana Karenga and initially celebrated in America in 1966 is an example of one such strand. Kwanzaa is a celebration of African culture in America by African-Americans observed from December 26 to January 1. It celebrates core principals of African unity, creativity, faith and giving gifts.

• • •

The "last train from Djibouti" is also a metaphor that stands for the proposition that African-Americans are no longer tethered to Africa, if ever we were, except before and immediately after enslavement. Sure, there have been degrees of want regarding Africa, but Americans of African descent have long since realized and internalized that their place is in America. Why abandon the equity we have fought so dearly for over the centuries?

If African leaders were not so intoxicated with power and terminated their tenure in office when the public good is no longer being served, as evidenced by free and fair election results, and eliminated the doggerel of governance for self-enrichment, new modalities of governance would be available to the people. If African leaders, in the words of Christopher Hichens, would stop trousering the public's money and instead applied it to the needs of the people, things would greatly improve. But there is a certain megalomania fed by greediness and the self-interest of elite cliques, a lust for power, avarice and a reckless disregard for the humanity of the people that has characterized some African leaders in some African states. A "let them eat cake" mentality appears to characterize the actions of some past and current African leaders, though this type of conduct is not restricted to Africa.

Realizing that it is difficult to go back even if you wanted to is a stark separation, akin to the breakup of a marriage.

As I move toward the end, let me say that divorce is tough on any level. I know. I have experienced it on several levels personally and professionally. Divorce of any kind, whether from spouse, family, profession, culture or country, is difficult. It can be a wrenching experience. It can be withering and disabling. African-Americans and Africa, though once married and tethered at the hip, are now separated and forever will be estranged geographically and culturally, an attenuated relationship at best. A remarriage is always in the offing if the parties seek to reunite and truly want to do so, if no co-respondent has come between the parties. In this context that co-respondent is America. The tides rise and fall on reunification efforts. But sometimes second marriages work out better than first marriages since experience and perspective are in greater supply.

Harriett's divorce from Eric, announced in open court, was a bittersweet conclusion to a marriage founded on love, embraced within the culture of both partners, yet estranged by the reality of their cultures. It is important that we do not see things through a distorted filter. It is important to attain the right perception as well as perspective. African-Americans, the innocent and injured people, have no grounds for a divorce from Africa but rather need to accept the continent on its own terms—accept its manipulation by world powers, its many deprivations, the ignorance and corruption among some of its leaders. Africa is the composite of all of that, and yet it retains its beauty, its hope, fertility and its essentiality to African people throughout the diaspora. Africa is intrinsic to the existence of black people and the wellspring of all human creation. And it is the bedrock of African people and their descendants. Melanoid people of African descent cannot exist without it, nor should we want to exist without it. Just knowing that Africa is there, that it is biologically and anthropologically the genus of our black existence, is a comfort, or should be, in my opinion.

Black Americans have become "McDonaldized"; that is to say, we have come to expect and measure everything by Western standards. Hence, we are uncomfortable in environments that do not reflect that standard. I suffer from this. But to some like me, Africa is the *elan vital*, the vital force, if not the *sine qua non*, that which is essential, for our existence regardless of how far it deviates from the "McDonald standard."

To others, Africa is a reference point, and to many, unfortunately, Africa is an irrelevancy, as has been shown. The West is the bane of our existence for many of us, save for some exceptions. To be divorced from Africa for African-Americans is equivalent to not having a genealogical or anthropological birthplace. Think how you would feel if someone asked you where you were born, where your home was or where you came from, and you had no response. You would feel like a hollowed-out log, nothing, no center, a vacancy in your soul. A nomad. You would have no connection to anything except the last redoubt that you called home.

Africa should not be seen by Americans of African descent as the Mecca and Medina of cultural rejuvenation and genetic reclamation as some would have it be. Rather, Africa should be viewed by Americans of African descent as a fulcrum, a support. I ask you, what other continent do black people own? Where else in the world do black folks control anything, except for a job for the time being, a house, a car and a business for those who are fortunate enough to have one? Control of one's fate can be tenuous and evanescent. For some, it lasts only as long as the next paycheck or small business loan. For black folks especially, the rope is not very long. Certainly parts of Africa are in shambles, but we own those shambles. We should take pride in what we have. Something is better than nothing. And Africa is a long way from being nothing. If Africa is nothing, why was there such a "scramble" for Africa by the colonializing powers? Africa is not all doom and gloom; there are many bright lights, and I beg to differ with those who say it is.

• • •

While in New York, Michelle and I visited the Statue of Liberty. As I gazed up at the beautiful monument and pondered what it symbolizes for America, I was struck by the mass, height and circumference of the structure. As I walked past with my head up straight, I wondered whether or not my head should be bowed as I passed. I walked upon the land of Ellis Island with its beautiful London plane trees symmetrically planted and neatly trimmed. How many of my ancestors entered America through this port? Or did my ancestors enter through the pesthouses on Sullivan's Island in South Carolina or on Lazaretto Creek in Tybee Island near Savannah, Georgia, or other similar houses along the east coast of the United States?

I say to myself, *If, for one prolonged moment, I could think of America without racism, America would truly be a great country.* Despite the racism, black people have done well in America. Just think how far we could go if racism was less of an issue. So, my heart breaks thinking about what might have been or what could be. Speculation is a luxury for those who can afford it. Dealing with reality is a necessity for all of us, whether we can afford it or not. We cannot avoid it. Reality can break your heart.

As John le Carré's 1963 novel, *The Spy Who Came in from the Cold,* portrays, morality is often the victim of a greater subterfuge. black people have traditionally been too moral and forgiving about things. There is no need to be moral in the pursuit of a "welcoming home"; all that is needed is to be practical.

Americans of African descent have great expectations for America. That belief in a better tomorrow charges our batteries when hope fails. We very much want America to succeed. We have a stake in America succeeding, and we as a people want to succeed with it.

Nevertheless, Americans of African descent must not be captives of prosaic thinking. We live in a global society, so think globally. After years of struggle to find permanent equal justice in the United States of America, at best it will always be problematic: as the saying goes, "Expectations are disappointments waiting to happen."

As we strive to attain a global perspective, one must seek higher ground and discover that your hometown is just one among many; that there are cities greater and more beautiful than the one you live in; that the state where you reside is but one of many states nationally and worldwide; and that there is a world larger than the country of the United States where societies thrive and do some things much better than in the United States.

Home should be our underpinning, our foundation, but not our prison; not just a place where we sleep and eat. Home should simulate the security we find in our deep sleep: the peace and security we feel when we have abandoned our restraints, though not always present. Nonetheless, most of us would agree that the security of our sleep offers, if only for a short while, a respite from a world of woe.

And finally, with regard to the issue of "home," let me share with you a new thought. As African-Americans, we should adopt the view of Siddhartha Pico Raghavan Lyer, the noted essayist and novelist. He is quoted as having said, "I am not rooted in a place, I think, so much as in certain values and affiliations and friendships that I carry everywhere I go. My home is both invisible and portable." As African-Americans we would do well not to be so transfixed on a physical home, but rather we should look for a home that represents our values and where our enduring friendships are.[69] A home where the civilities of society are not discriminatory. A reassessment of what "home" is and means is required from time to time. We must consider breaking with the past. A new paradigm is required.

As Mark Twain wrote, "[T]hrow off the bowlines. Sail away from the safe harbor. Catch the trade winds in your sails. Explore. Dream. Discover." Go where your heart feels content. Make the best deal you can for yourself wherever that might be. Mark Twain also wrote, "May your way be ever open and your travels safe." Go live and settle where your discontent is the least.

If we are alienated in America and if we cannot find suitable accommodations in Africa, for whatever reason, we should make our home where, as Lyer says, our cultures and ideas are accommodated.

And though our predicament is such that the vast majority of us may never leave this country or have the wherewithal even to contemplate it, we should commit ourselves to shake off living a life of proscription and, at least intellectually, if not physically, live a life of freedom. The past can be prologue. Dream big. "Cross the Delaware" to a belvedere of your own choosing, being a more thoughtful person for having gained a worldview.

The train ride from the Port of Djibouti to the Port of Addis Ababa is about done. We just passed Dire Dawa and we are less than 500 kilometers from Addis Ababa. We will be there in a few hours. My exit will then be determined. It has been a fascinating ride on a rickety old train whose track gauge is inconsistent at best. It is a rail line with a rich and enchanting history. I love trains, because they allow you to dream.

ACKNOWLEDGMENTS

In the course of writing a book over a span of years, undoubtedly there are people who make the effort of writing a story, in this case their stories, easier and factual. I am indebted to Dr. Michelle Margaret Palmer Lee for the manuscript she authored in 1994, entitled *Crying All The Way Home*. In the draft dedication she wrote the following: "I had the greatest adventure in undergraduate school. I participated in an exchange program in Africa. Upon my return to the United States, I often shared my experiences with family, friends and colleagues. The response was always the same. People were amazed and touched by my unbelievable stories. But they were true. I've always been told, 'You should write a book about your experiences in Africa.' So, I wrote this manuscript. I did not keep a daily journal, only my memories. I hope you enjoy my memories as much as I do."

Dr. Lee also gave thanks to "Dr. K, whose husband probably saved my life in Africa." So the inspiration that I brought to this task was not hard to come by, nor were the facts of Dr. Lee's journey. Dr. Lee provided a pathway, and I simply tried to bring it to light and place it in flight in a manner and style reflective of the courage she displayed going through her experiences in Uganda. Dr. Lee reviewed several drafts of the manuscript for this book and made many suggestions ensuring the accuracy of the facts described. For that I am truly appreciative.

Dr. Harriett F. Karuhije was gracious enough to spend many hours with me in interviews to share her story. I interviewed Dr. Karuhije over many years while talking causally about her experiences in Botswana. To know Dr. Karuhije is to know of her adventures in Botswana; they are melded together in one persona. Her career as a nurse educator touched the lives of many people both in Africa and in the United States. She remarked that she really wanted to bury and not resurrect her experiences, some of which were painful, that she repressed for many years. She too had been advised to write a book about her adventures. But she was willing to open up to me about the details of some of her life experiences in Africa and in the United States during this epochal time in her life.

Working with two personages, each, at one time or another, advised to write a book about their stories, has caused my task to be a consequential endeavor to capture the essence of their experiences.

I want to thank Dr. Kimairis L. Toogood and Bertrand de Sessan de Margnan, both of Addis Ababa, Ethiopia, for providing me with a valuable resource book about the train and for arranging an interview for me in Addis Ababa with Getachew Tadesse, a retired official of the Addis to Djibouti train in Addis Ababa. Getachew, a native French-speaking Ethiopian, began working for the train service when he was just a teenager and worked there continuously until his retirement. Mr. Tadesse provided me with original French train logs and schedules and other assorted papers pertaining to the train, which Bertrand de Sessan de Margnan arranged to have translated. This interview brought to life the many stories surrounding the colorful history of this train, an essential element in the economic development of Ethiopia.

Justin Wert, PhD, has served as my editor for several years, and together our efforts have resulted in the publication of two books, including this one. Dr. Wert devoted many hours editing the manuscript and providing his insight and perspective on the narrative. Dr. Wert made an all-important contribution to the completion of the manuscript.

NOTES

INTRODUCTION

† Zora Neale Hurston's new book *Barracoon: the Story of the Last black Cargo* (2018), a narrative told to Hurston by the former slave Cudjo Lewis (Oluale Kossola), bears this truth out most painfully concerning all people involved: the Africans taken captive, the African-American author taken captive by the slave narrative's brutal honesty and complexity, the brutality of the Dohemy "Amazons" who cut off some of his fellow Africans heads, and the greedy, heartless, audacious brutality of the white American enslavers.

‡James L. Watson, Asian & African Systems Of Slavery, (Berkeley, California: University Of California Press 1980) 6-7, 9-13.

§Allan G. B. Fisher. "Slavery in the History of black Muslim Africa," 2001. Also see http://www.arabslaveslavetrade.com/ and https://ballandalus.wordpress.com/2013/11/24/trans-saharan-slave-trade-and-racisim-in-the-arab-world/

CHAPTER 1: A BLESSING FROM THE QUAKERS

[1] Haile Selassie I was emperor of Ethiopia from 1930 to 1941. He was Ethiopia's 225th ruler and was credited with modernizing the country. He instituted the Rastafari sect into Ethiopian society in 1948 with the award of land to black people from the West who assisted him in the second war against Italy in 1936. Haile Selassie led the resistance against the Italian invasion in 1936 and reclaimed his country in 1946.

Biography.com Editors, "Haile Selassie 1 Biography," April 2, 2014, https://www.biography.com/people/haile-selassie-i-9325096#strong-l.

Chris Summers, "The Rastafarians' flawed African 'promised land,'" BBC World News, September 12, 2014, https://www.m.bbc.com/news/magazine-28059303.

[2] Swarthmore College was founded in 1864 by John Wharton and his mother along with other Hicksite Quakers. Hicksite Quakers followed the teachings of Elias Hicks, a tolerant and less conservative Quaker. Followers wore plain and simple clothing. Lucretia Mott was an antislavery crusader, Quaker preacher, and advocate for women's rights. Both she and John Wharton and a committee of other Quakers established the college.

Pennsylvania Center for the Book, "Mott," Copyright 2016, The Pennsylvania State University, Penn State University Libraries, https://www.mott.pomona.edu/mott.html.

U.S. News Staff, "Swarthmore College," U.S. News, n. d., http://www.colleges.usnews.rankingsandreviews.com/best-colleges/swarthmore-college-3370

Students of Professor Tatu's Values and Science/Technology Seminar, "Wharton, Joseph," n. d., https://www.sites.lafayette.edu/vast265-sp12/steelopedia/q-z/joseph-wharton/.

CHAPTER 2: TWO POINTS IN THE CIRCLE

[3] Pollin owned the Washington Wizards professional basketball team, formerly known as the Baltimore Bullets. When the Bullets really started flying in DC and with the team having made the decision to move to DC, the decision was made to rename the team the Wizards. Apparently no one wanted to encourage the flying of bullets. Abe Pollin was also the owner of the Washington Mystics, a women's professional basketball team, and the

Washington Capitals, a professional hockey team. In addition to his many credits, Mr. Pollin was also a real estate developer and philanthropist.

CHAPTER 3: THE AWAKENING

[4] Kwame Nkrumah was president of Ghana and prime minister of the Gold Coast its predecessor. He was a proponent of Pan-Africanism which espoused the need for people of African descent to ban together to achieve the most productive result for Africa and the diaspora. He led the liberation of the Gold Coast and Ghana from British colonization. Nkrumah was educated in the United States and in the United Kingdom. He served as prime minister and president from 1957 to 1966.

[5] John Hope Franklin and Alfred A. Moss, Jr., *From Slavery to Freedom, A History of African Americans to Slavery*, 8th ed. (New York: Alfred A. Knopf, 2007), 188-191.

[6] James Monroe sought to enhance the security of the United States by embracing the American Colonization Society, ACS, whose purpose was to send blacks back to Africa because it was felt by many that the races could not live in harmony in the United States. This view was shared by many white people in the late-eighteenth and early-nineteenth centuries.

Jay Sexton, *The Monroe Doctrine, Empire and Nation in Nineteenth-Century America* (New York: Hill and Wang, 2011), 36-38.

[7] African marriages are complex, involving natural law, African traditions of family and property, and culture. Christianity since the end of the colonialization period has had its influence but has not prevailed. North African marriage traditions and those of sub-Saharan Africa are not the same. The role of sex, and especially children and the alliances of families, are intrinsic issues in the institution.

Cormac Burke, "Marriage and The Family in Africa: Position Papers April 1988," St. Josemaria Institute, accessed April 15, 2015, https://www.cormacburke.or.ke.

[8] Beginning in 1914 Marcus Garvey, a Jamaican from Queens Ann Bay, established the Universal Negro Improvement Association, UNIA. He called upon African-Americans to shun the white cultural paradigm and to respect their blackness and African culture. He implored African-Americans to return to Africa and build their own societies.

John Hope Franklin and Alfred A. Moss, Jr., *From Slavery to Freedom, A History of African Americans to Slavery*, 8th ed. (New York: Alfred A. Knopf, 2007), 395-398.

CHAPTER 4: A MOURNFUL INTERLUDE

[9] It was not until 2012 that an association was formed to represent black private investigators. Richard Roundtree portrayed the lead character in the film *Shaft*. A story about a suave black private investigator who operates in New York City, *Shaft* was released in 1971, directed by Gordon Parks and produced by Joel Freeman. The film belonged to a genre of films produced in the '70s known as Blaxploitation films because these films were directed primarily to urban audiences.

National Association for black Private Investigators accessed December 10, 2016, https://www.nabpi.org.

[10] Map of Africa, accessed February 20, 2016, https://www.worldatlas.com/webimage/countrys/af.htm

[11] Official and Spoken Languages of African countries, accessed February 20, 2016, https://www.nationsonline.org/oneworld/african_languages.htm.

[12] Basil Davidson, *The Lost Cities of Africa with Maps and Illustrations* (Boston: Little, Brown, 1987), 7-12.

[13] Dormer architectural features, accessed January 15, 2016, https://www.britannica.com/technology/dormer

http://www.portal.state.pa.us/portal/server.pt/community/traditional_vernacular/2381/pennsylvania_german_tradition/292427.

[14] Swahili is a *lingua franca*, not uncommon in the polylinguistic culture of Africa, and is spoken in several East African countries. In Uganda, Swahili is taught in the schools and is commonly spoken by the non-Baganda people.

Swahili, accessed June 16, 2016, https://www.omniglot.com/writing/swahili.htm.

[15] Other prominent theologians also studied at Crozier Theological Seminary, such as Samuel DeWitt Proctor, a mentor and friend of Dr. King, and the fifth president of North Carolina Agricultural and Technical State University.

CHAPTER 9: BOUND FOR THE PROMISED LAND

[16] "African vs African-American," accessed August 11, 2016, https://www.library.yale.edu/~~fboteng/akata.htm.

[17] Léopold Sédar Senghor, "To New York," in *Selected Poems*, trans. John Reed and Clive Wake (New York: Atheneum, 1969).

[18] W. E. B. Du Bois, "Criteria of Negro Art," accessed August 15, 2017, https://www.webdubois.org.

[19] See, accessed September 21, 2016, https://nationalhumanitiescenter.org/pds/maai3/protest/text10/text10read.htm.

Edward W. Said, *Culture and Imperialism (New York: First Vintage Books, 1994), 50-59.*

[20] See, accessed June 6, 2016, https://m.state.gov/md191417.htm

[21] See, accessed February 18, 2016, https://afritorial.com/tribe-the-baganda-ugandas-royal-kingdom-past-present/; See, accessed February 18, 2016, https://www.buganda.or.ug/.

CHAPTER 11: OH, WHAT A BEAUTIFUL MORNING

[22] Frederick John Dealtry Lugard, "Handbook to British East Africa and Uganda," n. p. 5 June 2007. Web. 29 Apr. 2016.

[23] Prabhat S. "Difference Between Protectorate and Colony." Difference.net, May 19, 2011 <https://www.differencebetween.net/miscellaneous/politics/difference-between-protecorate-and-colony/>.

[24] Timothy Amerit, "Contextualizing a Jurisprudential Cliché that 'Buganda was nothing but a Protected State in the Uganda Protectorate,'" https://www.timothyamerit.blogspot.com/2014/09.

[25] Sandbox Networks, Inc. (US) accessed April 11, 2016, https://www.infoplease.com/country/uganda.html.

[26] Sandbox Networks, Inc., accessed April 11, 2016, https://www.infoplease.com/country/uganda.html.

[27] James Baldwin, "Color," in *Collected Essays: Volume Compilation, Notes and Chronology 1998* (New York: Literary Classics of the United States, 1998), 675.

Kwame Nkrumah, *Class Struggle in Africa* (London: Panaf Books, 1970), 36-37.

28 Nell Irwin Painter, *The History of White People* (New York: W.W. Norton, 2010), 43-58.

29 Helen Bradley Griebel, *The African American Woman's Headwrap: Unwinding the Symbols*, accessed November 5, 2015, https://www.char.txa.cornell.edu/griebel.htm.

"Geles: A Nigerian Woman's Must Have, The History Behind Geles-Culture-Nigeria," accessed November 5, 2015, https://www.nairaland.com/808423/geles-nigerian-womans-must-history.

30 Janet G. Vaillant, *Black, French, and African: A Life of Léopold Sédar Senghor* (Cambridge, MA: Harvard University Press, 1990), 90.

31 Négritude was both an ideology and a literary movement popularized by the black francophone intelligentsia. In essence the concept fostered an appreciation of the common black heritage and identity of all Africans wherever they may be. This concept has influenced such writers as Frantz Fanon, Langston Hughes and Richard Wright all eminently notable writers on the black experience.

Albin Krebs, "Leopold Senghor Dies at 95," The New York Times Obituary, accessed Friday December 21, 2001, https://www.nytimes.com/2001/12/21/world/leopold-senghor-dies-at-95-senegal-s-poet-of-negritude.html.

32 Kanu Ikechukwu Anthony, "Nkrumah and the Quest for African Unity," *American International Journal of Contemporary Research* 3, no. 6 (2013).

CHAPTER 12: HARRIETT'S CHOICE

33 Widener University began as a military college dating back to the years during the Civil War. In 1966 the first group of female nursing students matriculated at what was then Pennsylvania Military College in the nursing program affiliated with the Crozier Foundation College of Nursing. In times

past the Pennsylvania Military College was known as the West Point of the Keystone State. Widener University formally began in 1972.

[34] For a discussion of cultural chauvinism, African tribalism, and ethnocentrism:

See, accessed April 13, 2016, https://www.globalsouthproject.cornell,edu-of-cultural-chauvinsism.html.

See, accessed April 13, 2016, https://www.article.sapub.org/10.5923.j.iljas.20110101.02.html.

CHAPTER 13: *CHUO ELIMU,* SWAHILI FOR "A COLLEGE EDUCATION"

[35] Ferralitic soil accounts for two thirds of the soil found in the country and is useful for urban wastewater removal. This type of soil has also been referred to as lateritic soil, meaning a soil as defined by pedologists, those individuals that study soil science, as a soil that is a red residual soil formed by heavy rains that remove silica and by the enrichment with aluminum and iron oxides especially in damp, muggy and wet weather conditions.

CHAPTER 14: NOTHING NEW UNDER THE SUN

[36] See, accessed January 10, 2016, https://www.open borders.info/Indians-in-Uganda-economic-impact-and-reception/.

[37] James T. Campbell, *Middle Passages: African American Journeys to Africa, 1787-2005* (New York: Penguin, 2006), 18-19.

CHAPTER 15: A RUDE AWAKENING

[38] See, accessed November 19, 2015, http://www.eol.org/pages/24850/details.
Also see, accessed November 19, 2015, https://www.Oregonzoo.org/discover/animals/African-lungfish.

[39] Frances Cress Welsing, *The Isis (Yssis) Papers* (Chicago: Third World, 1991).

Hamil R. Harris, "Celebrated psychiatrist to be memorialized," *The Washington Post*, Web March 20, 2016.

CHAPTER 16: THE BLACK AMERICAN'S BURDEN

[40] See, accessed April 5, 2016, https://www.sahistory.org.za/article/apartheid-and-reactions-it.

[41] https://www.survivalinternational.org/tribes/bushmen

CHAPTER 17: A WILDLIFE ADVENTURE

[42] "Africa Fact," *Lake Victoria Facts*. n. p., n. d. Web. June-July 2016. <https://www.interesting-africa-facts.com/Africa-Landforms/Lake-victoria-Facts.html>.

CHAPTER 18: THE OMAKUMA

[43] Phillip Briggs and Andrew Roberts, *Uganda - Bradt Travel Guides*, 3rd ed. (Bucks, England: Bradt Publications, 1998), 9.

[44] MsAfropolitan, "Polygamy in Africa Has Little to Do with Sex," *MsAfropolitan* (September 26, 2013), accessed July 9, 2017, <https://www.msafropolitan.com/2013/09/polygamy-in-africa-sex.html>.

Admin, "Join Polygamy.com Today," *Polygamy in Africa - Polygamy Articles.* (September 30, 2015) accessed July 13, 2016, https://www.polygamy.com/articles/89746509/polygamy-in-africa, September 30, 2015.

[45] "Join Polygamy.com Today," Polygamy in Africa. (July 23, 2016) accessed July 13, 2016, https://www.polygamy.com/articles/89746509africa.

CHAPTER 19: OREM'S THEORY

[46] Leon De Kock, "Interview with Gayatri Chakravorty Spivak: New Nation Writers Conference in South Africa," *ARIEL: a Review of International English Literature* 23, no. 3 (1992), 29-47. ARIEL: https://www.ariel.synergiespraries.ca/ariel/index.php/ariel/article/viewFile/2505/2458.

[47] Dorothea Orem, a nursing theorist (1914-2007) self-care nursing theory, the Orem model of nursing between 1959 and 2001. Orem's theory defined nursing as "the act of assisting others in the provision and management of self-care to maintain or improve human functioning at home level of effectiveness." Her theory requires individuals to do what they can and to act on their own behalf to maintain their life and health.

Lisa Young, Katerine Edney and Nareida Jaime, "Description of the Model—Dorothea Orem's Self-Care Theory," 14 Nov. 2011, accessed August 4, 2016, <https://www.sites.google.com/site/oremstheory/description-of-the-model>.

[48] Virginia Henderson was also known as the "First Lady of Nursing." Henderson developed Henderson's Needs Theory based upon fourteen components. Essentially Henderson's Need Theory is holistic, covering the wealth of the individual, the physiological, the psychological, the spiritual and the sociological.

Matt Vera, "Virginia Henderson's Nursing Need Theory," *Nurses Labs,* accessed August 6, 2014, https://www.*nurselabs.com/Virginia-hendersons-need-theory?#.*

CHAPTER 20: THE SMOCK AND THE DUFFEL BAG

[49] "mau-mau" dictionary.com Unabridged. Random House, Inc., accessed August 8, 2016, <https://www.dictionary.com/browse/mau-mau>.

[50] Wunyabari O. Maloba, "Mau Mau," *International Encyclopedia of the Social Sciences (September 15, 2018)*, accessed August 7, 2016, <https://www.encyclopedia.com/social-sciences/applied-and-social-sciences-magazines/mau-mau>.

[51] Benjamin Talton, "The Challenge of Decolonialization in Africa," accessed August 8, 2016, https://www.exhibitions.nypl.org/africanage/essay-challenge-of-decolonization-africa.html.

[52] Seymour M. Hersh, "Executive Action," in *The Dark Side of Camelot* (New York: Back Bay Books, 1997), 193-196.

CHAPTER 21: *NEEMA KWA MAHARGE,* SWAHILI FOR "A FAVOR FOR BEANS"

[53] The concept of "dual consciousness" was developed by Frantz Fanon and explained in his book *Black Skins, White Masks* (1952). W. E. B. Du Bois originated a related concept of "double consciousness" prior to Fanon's discussion of dual consciousness. Du Bois's concept of double consciousness is defined in his book *The Souls of Black Folk* (1903). Essentially the concept describes the conflict black people have about living in a white dominated environment.

Frantz Fanon, *Black Skins, White Masks*, trans. Charles L. Markmann (US: Grove Press, 1967).

W. E. B. Du Bois, *The Souls of Black Folk* (Chicago: A.C. McClury, 1903).

CHAPTER 22: A RETURN TO A LEGACY

[54] Denis Cogneau and Alexander Moradi, "British and French Educational Legacies in Africa," Vox CEPR's Policy Portal, Apr.-May 2014. Accessed January 15, 2016, <www.voxeu.org/article/british-and french-educational-legacies-africa>.

[55] International Student, "UK vs. USA Educational System," accessed May 8, 2016, https://www.internationalstudent.com/study-abroad/guide/UK-USA-education-system/.

[56] Remi P. Clignet and Phillip J. Foster, "French and British Colonial Education In Africa," *Comparative Education Review* 8 no. 2 (October 1964).

CHAPTER 23: THE ENCORE

[57] Harriett F. Karuhije and Coralease Ruff, "External Examiners: Quality Assurance in Nursing Education," *Journal of Nursing Education* 40 no. 1 (2001): 5-9.

CHAPTER 25: CAUGHT IN OBETE'S WEB

[58] Norman Tumuhimbise, "Unsowing the Mustard Seed," Norman Tumuhimbise, accessed September 1, 2016, https://www.unsowing7.wordpress.com/ch-1-tracing-the-seed-fron.

CHAPTER 29: DENOUEMENT: THE LAST TRAIN FROM DJIBOUTI

[59] James T. Campbell, *Middle Passages: African American Journeys to Africa, 1787-2005* (New York: Penguin, 2006), 18-19.

[60] Marc Black, "Fanon and DuBosian Double Consciousness," *Human Architecture: Journal of the Sociology of Self-Knowledge* 5, no. 3, (Summer 2007).

[61] James T. Campbell, *Middle Passages: African American Journeys to Africa, 1787-2005* (New York: Penguin, 2006), 64.

[62] Campbell, 67.

[63] Campbell, 13.

[64] Campbell, 331.

[65] Campbell, 60.

[66] Campbell, 103.

[67] Efam Dovi, "African-Americans Resettle in Africa," *African Renewal* (April 2015), accessed September 28, 2015, <https://www.un.org/africarenewal/magazine/april-2015/africa-americans-resettle-africa>.

[68] "Americans Abroad", accessed September 28, 2015, <www.https://www.americansabroad.org/issues/taxation/rebuttal-gao-study-foreign-earned-income-exclusion>.

[69] Angie Brenner, "Heart and Soul," *Wild River Review* 19 (November 2007).

BIBLIOGRAPHY

Admin. "Join Polygamy.com Today, Polygamy in Africa." (September 30, 2015). Accessed July 13, 2016, https://www.polygamy.com/articles/89746509/polygamy-in-africa.

African facts. "Lake Victoria Facts." N. p., n. d. Web. (June-July 2016), https://www.interesting-africa-facts.com/Africa-Landforms/Lake-victoria-Facts.html.

Africa vs African-American. Yale Library. Accessed March 3, 2016, https://www.library.yale.edu/fboteng/skata.htm.

African Lungfish. Accessed June 30, 2017, https:www.Oregonzoo.org/discover/animals/African-lungfish.

African Lungfish. Accessed June 30, 2017, https://www.eol.org/pages/24850/details.

Americans Abroad. Accessed September 28, 2015, https://www.americansabroad.org/issue/taxation/rebuttal-gao-study-foreign-earned-income-exclusion>.

Amerit, Timothy. "Contextualizing a Jurisprudential Cliché that 'Buganda was nothing but a Protected State in the Uganda Protectorate.'" https://www.timothyamerit.blogspot.com/2014/09.

Anthony, Kanu Ikechukwu. "Nkrumah and the Quest for African Unity." *American International Journal of Contemporary Research* 3, no. 6 (2013).

Apartheid and Reactions. Accessed August 5, 2016, https://www.sahistory.org.za/article/aprtheid-and-reactions-it.

Baldwin, James. *Collected Essays: Volume Compilation, Notes and Chronology.* New York: Literary Classics of the United States, 1998.

Biography.com Editors. "Haile Selassie I." *Biography*, April 2, 2014, https://www.biography.com/people/haile-selassie-i-9325096.

Black, Marc. "Fanon and DuBoisian Double Consciousness." *Journal of the Sociology of Self-Knowledge*, no. 3 (Summer 2007).

Brenner, Angie. "Heart and Soul." *Wild River Review* 19 (November 2007).

Briggs, Phillip, and Andrew Roberts. *Bradt Travel Guides.* (2013). 3rd ed. Bucks, England: Bradt Publications, 1998.

Britannica. Dormer Architectural Features. Accessed November 12, 2017, https://www.Britannica.com/technology/dormer.

Burke, Cormac. "Marriage and The Family in Africa: Position Papers April 1988." St. Josemaria Institute. Accessed April 15, 2015, https://www.cormacburke.or.ke.

Campbell, James T. *Middle Passages: African American Journeys to Africa, 1787-2005.* New York: Penguin, 2006.

Cogneau, Denis, and Alexander Moradi. "British and French Educational Legacies in Africa." *Vox CEPR's Policy Portal*, (April-May 2014). Accessed January 15, 2015, https://www.voxeu.org/article/British-and-french-educational-legacies-africa>.

Clignet, Remi P., and Phillip J. Foster. "French and British Colonial Education in Africa." *Comparative Education Review* 8 no. 2 (October 1964).

Cultural Chauvinism, African Tribalism, and Ethnocentrism. Accessed November 25, 2017, https://www.globalsouthproject.cornell.edu-of-cultural-chauvinism.html.

Cultural Chauvinism, African Tribalism, and Ethnocentrism. Accessed November 25, 2017, https://www.article.sapub.org/10.5923.j.iljas.20110101.02.html.

Davidson, Basil. *The African Genius*. Oxford: James Curry, 1996.
The Lost Cities of Africa with Maps and Illustrations. Boston: Little, Brown, 1987.

De Kock, Leon. "Interview with Gayatri Chakravorty Spivak: New Nation Writers Conference in South Africa." *ARIEL: a Review of International English Literature* 23 no. 3 (1992), 29-47, https://www.synergiespraries.ca/ariel/index.php/ariel/article/viewFile/2505/2458.

Denbow, James, and Pehenyo C. Thebe. *Culture and Customs of Botswana*. Westport, CT: Greenwood Press, 2006.

Dictionary.com. "Mau-Mau." Random House, Inc. Accessed August 8, 2016, https://www.dictionary.com/browse/mau-mau>.

Dovi, Efam. "African-Americans Resettle in Africa." African Renewal, (April 2015) Web September 28, 2015, https://www.un.org/africarenewal/magazine/april-2015/africa-americans-resettle-africa>.

DuBois, W.E.B. *The Souls of Black Folk*. Chicago: A.C. McClury, 1903.

Fanon, Frantz. *Black Skins, White Masks*. Translated by Charles L. Markmann. US: Grove Press, 1967.

Franklin, John Hope, and Alfred A. Moss, Jr. *From Slavery to Freedom, A History of African Americans to Slavery.* 8th ed. New York: Alfred A. Knopf, 2007.

Fyfe, Christopher. *Africa: The End of Colonial Rule, Nationalism and Decolonization.* Edited by Toyin Falola. Durham, NC: Carolina Academic Press, 2002.

Garnier, Maurice, and Mark Schafer. "Educational Model and Expansion of Enrollments in Sub-Saharan Africa." *Sociology of Education* 79, no. 2 (2006): 153-175.

Griebel, Helen Bradley. "The African American Woman's Headwrap: Unwinding the Symbols." Accessed May 5, 2016, http://char.txa.cornell.edu/griebel.htm

Harris, Hamil R. "Celebrated Psychiatrist to Be Memorialized." *The Washington Post*, (March 19, 2016) Web March 20, 2016.

Hersh, Seymour M. *The Dark Side of Camelot.* New York: Back Bay Books, 1997.

Indians in Uganda. Accessed March 2, 2016, https://www.openborders.info/Indians-in-Uganda-Economic-impact-and reception/.

International Student. "UK vs. USA Educational System." Accessed May 8, 2016, https://www.international/student.com/study-abroad/guide/UK-USA-education-system/.

Isaacson, Rupert. *The Healing Land: The Bushmen and the Kalahari Desert.* New York: Grove, 2001.

Kalahari Meekats. Accessed March 17, 2016, https://www.kalahari-meekats.com.

Karuhije, Harriett F., and Coralease Ruff. "External Examiners: Quality Assurance in Nursing Education." *Journal of Nursing Education* 40, no. 1 (January 2001): 5-9.

Krebs, Albin. "Leopold Senghor Dies at 95." *The New York Times Obituary*, Friday December 21, 2001. https://www.nytimes.com/2001/12/21/world/leopold-senghor-dies-at-95-senegal-s-poet-of-negritude.html.

Maloba, Wunyabari O., "Mau Mau." *International Encyclopedia of the Social Sciences* (September 15, 2018). Accessed August 7, 2016, https://www.encyclopedia.com/social-sciences/applied-and-social-sciences-magazines/mau-mau.

Map of Africa. *World Atlas.* Accessed September 19, 2016, https://www.worldatlas.com/webimage/countrys/af.htm.

Memmi, Albert. *The Colonizer and the Colonized.* London: Earthscan, 2003.

MsAfropolitan. "Polygamy in Africa Has Little to Do with Sex." *MsAfropolitan*, (September 26, 2013). Accessed July 9, 2017, https://www.msafropolitan.com/2013/09/polygamy-in-africa-sex.html.

National Association for black Private Investigators. Accessed December 10, 2016, https://www.nabpi.org.

Nkrumah, Kwame. *Class Struggle in Africa.* London: Panof Books, 1970.

Official and Spoken Languages of African Countries. *Nations.* Accessed October 12, 2017, https:/www.nationsonline.org/oneworld/african_languages.htm.

Painter, Nell Irwin. *The History of White People.* New York: W.W. Norton, 2010.

Pennsylvania Center for the Book. "Mott." Copyright 2016, The Pennsylvania State University, Penn State University Libraries, https://www.mott.pomona.edu/mott.html.

Said, Edward W. *Culture and Imperialism*. New York: First Vintage Books, 1994.

Sandbox Networks, Inc. Uganda. Accessed April 11, 2016, https://www.infoplease.com/country/uganda.html.

Senghor, Léopold Sédar. *Selected Poems*. Translated by John Reed and Clive Wake. New York: Atheneum, 1969.

Sexton, Jay. *The Monroe Doctrine, Empires and Nation in Nineteenth-Century America*. New York: Hill and Wang, 2011.

Students of Professor Tatu's Values and Science/Technology Seminar. "Wharton, Joseph." https://www.sites.lafayette.edu/vast265-sp12/steelopedia/q-z/joseph-wharton/.

Summers, Chris. "The Rastufarians' flawed African 'promised land.'" *BBC World News*, September 12, 2014, https://www.m.bbc.com/news/magazine-28059303.

Swahili. *Omniglot*. Accessed October 17, 2017, https://www.omniglot.com/writing/swahili.htm.

Talton, Benjamin. "The Challenge of Decolonialization in Africa." Accessed August 8, 2016, https://www.exhibitions.nypl.org/africanage/essay-challenge-of-decolonization-african.html.

Thakore, Prabhat Singh. "Difference Between Protectorate and Colony." Difference.net, January 19, 2011. https://www.diferencebetween.net/miscellaneous/politics/difference-between-protecorate-and-colony/>.

Tumuhimbise, Norman. "Unsowing the Mustard Seed." Accessed September 1, 2016, https://www.unsowing7.wordpress.com/ch-1-tracing-the-seed-fron.

U.S. News Staff. "Swarthmore College." U.S. News. Accessed March 2, 2017, https://www.colleges.usnews.rankingsandreviews.com/best-colleges/Swarthmore-college-3370.

Vaillant, James G. *black, French, and African: A Life of Léopold Sédar Senghor*. Cambridge, MA: Harvard University Press, 1990.

Welsing, Frances Cress. *The Isis (Yssis) Papers*. Chicago: Third World, 1991.

Vera, Matt. "Virginia Henderson's Nursing Need Theory." *Nurses Labs*. Accessed August 6, 2014, https://www.nurselabs.com/Virginia-hendersons-need-theory?#.

Young, Lisa, Katerine Edney, and Nareida Jaime. " Description of the Model– Dorothy Orem's Self-Care Theory." November 14, 2011. Accessed August 4, 2016, https://www.sites-google.com/siteOremstheory/description-of-the-model>.

INDEX

A

Ace 54
Achebe, Chinua 200
African Hall 79, 80, 82, 107
African lungfish 121, 122, 146, 216
Amin, Idi 76, 78, 86, 87, 104, 114, 126, 181, 182, 216, 223

B

Baader-Meinhof 76
Baganda 78, 160
Brown, Vixena 44, 45, 52, 56, 64, 65, 66, 67, 73, 75, 79, 80, 81, 89, 107, 108, 111, 122, 124, 125, 126, 127, 128, 129, 156, 157, 190, 239, 240

C

Campbell, James T. 118, 119, 130, 140, 141, 153, 191, 212, 257, 258, 259
Carré, John le 265
Césaire, Aimé 81
Chester, Pennsylvania 8, 43, 69, 70, 146, 243
circuit court for Montgomery County 12
Connell, Randy 44, 45, 120, 239, 240, 244
Cottingham, Clement 29, 30
Crozier Theological Seminary 274
Cuffee, Paul 25

D

Dire Dawa 6, 18, 247, 267
Douglass, Frederick xii, 257
dukawallas 115

E

Embakasi 75
Entebbe Airport 74, 75, 76, 78
external examiner 211

F

ferralitic soil 108
Ferralitic soil 277
Floyd 51

G

Garvey, Marcus 27, 30, 54, 141, 273
Gordimer, Nadine 200, 201
Great-Aunt Bea 19, 20, 31, 32, 33, 34, 35, 43, 60
Great-Aunt Honey 32, 35, 36, 37, 60

H

Hamites, Lorraine 40
Hansberry 123
Hichens, Christopher 262

I

Isabelle 19, 20, 106, 133, 137, 138, 139, 142, 202

INDEX

J

Johnson, Garrett 48

K

kabaka 85, 159, 160
Kabila, Joseph 84
kafundas 113
Kampala 41, 44, 45, 50, 74, 75, 78, 85, 113, 114, 116, 117, 123, 124, 125, 126, 159, 181, 224, 237
Karenga, Mulana 262
Karuhije, Eric Adyeri 13, 14, 18, 20
Karuhije, Harriett xii, xiii, 3, 7, 12, 13, 14, 15, 16, 18, 19, 20, 21, 22, 24, 26, 27, 42, 43, 44, 53, 54, 69, 70, 72, 73, 74, 86, 98, 99, 100, 101, 102, 103, 104, 105, 106, 111, 130, 131, 132, 133, 134, 136, 137, 138, 139, 140, 142, 143, 144, 145, 158, 161, 164, 165, 166, 167, 168, 169, 170, 200, 214, 269
Kellogg Foundation 203, 207
Kenya 50, 74, 75, 77, 78, 84, 88, 140, 149, 161, 181, 182, 229, 237
Kenyatta, Jomo 96, 182
King, Jr., Martin Luther 43
Kwanzaa 262

L

Lee, Michelle Palmer xii, 3, 6, 7, 8, 9, 10, 11, 13, 15, 16, 17, 18, 19, 20, 21, 22, 23, 24, 25, 26, 27, 29, 30, 31, 32, 33, 35, 36, 37, 38, 39, 40, 41, 43, 44, 45, 46, 47, 48, 49, 50, 52, 53, 54, 55, 56, 57, 58, 60, 61, 63, 64, 65, 66, 67, 68, 69, 73, 74, 75, 76, 77, 78, 79, 80, 81, 82, 83, 88, 89, 90, 91, 92, 93, 94, 96, 98, 99, 107, 108, 110, 112, 113, 114, 115, 116, 117, 120, 121, 122, 123, 124, 125, 126, 127, 128, 130, 133, 146, 149, 152, 153, 155, 156, 157, 158, 159, 161, 162, 163, 179, 180, 181, 183, 184, 186, 187, 188, 189, 190, 191, 192, 193, 213, 216, 217, 218, 220, 221, 222, 223, 224, 231, 233, 234, 237, 238, 239, 241, 245, 246, 248, 249, 250, 251, 252, 253, 254, 259, 264, 268
Locke, Alain 72
Lugard, Frederick John Dealty 85, 159
Lyer, Siddhartha Pico Raghaven 266

M

Makeba, Miriam 151, 254
Makerere University 22, 44, 45, 69, 78, 84, 113, 144, 223, 224, 244, 250
Mary 8, 9, 18, 19, 20, 21, 27, 43, 53, 54, 59, 133, 137, 246
Mary Stuart Hall 79, 80, 81, 107, 120
Muteesa I 85
Mwanga II Mukasa 85

N

Nana 42
Natanyahu, Benjamin 76
Nkrumah, Kwame 23, 89, 95, 96, 140, 141, 167, 183, 198, 272
Nyerere, Julius 78, 87, 96, 183, 223

O

Obote, Milton 78, 86, 87, 115, 181, 223, 224
omakuma 158, 160
Omakuma 155, 158, 159, 160, 278

P

pesthouses 265
Pollin, Abe 15, 271, 272

R

Rwenzori mountains 24

S

Senghor, Léopold Sédar 71, 84, 95, 96
Shelley 9, 33, 34, 36, 112, 238
Simone, Nina 124, 151
Soyinka, Wole 200, 201
Sutherland, Bill 257

T

Toogood, Floyd 269
Twain, Mark 266

U

Uganda 7, 16, 20, 22, 24, 39, 41, 42, 43, 44, 50, 51, 52, 56, 68, 69, 70, 72, 73, 74, 75, 76, 77, 78, 79, 84, 85, 86, 87, 88, 99, 102, 104, 105, 106, 108, 110, 114, 115, 116, 123, 126, 127, 135, 138, 144, 145, 146, 149, 158, 160, 175, 181, 182, 184, 186, 190, 216, 221, 222, 223, 230, 231, 232, 233, 237, 239, 240, 242, 244, 252, 268, 274
Uncle James 35, 36, 37

W

Washington Post 76, 258
Williams, Samuel "Daddy Kake" 27, 28, 36, 51, 228
Woodson, Carter G. 54
Wright, Richard 257, 276

Y

Yitzhak Rabin 76

www.ingramcontent.com/pod-product-compliance
Lightning Source LLC
Chambersburg PA
CBHW030511080526
44586CB00011B/150